D0948364

Process and form in social life

International Library of Anthropology
Routledge & Kegan Paul

Editor: Adam Kuper, University of Leiden

Arbor Scientiae
Arbor Vitae

A catalogue of other Social Science books published by
Routledge & Kegan Paul will be found at the end of this volume.

Process and form in social life

Selected essays of Fredrik Barth:
Volume I

1928

Routledge & Kegan Paul

London, Boston and Henley

First published in 1981
by Routledge & Kegan Paul Ltd
39 Store Street,
London WC1E 7DD,
9 Park Street,
Boston, Mass. 02108, USA and
Broadway House,
Newtown Road,
Henley-on-Thames,
Oxon RG9 1EN
Set in 10 on 12 pt IBM Press Roman by
Academic Typing Service, Gerrards Cross, Bucks
and printed in Great Britain by
Billing & Sons Limited
Guildford, London, Oxford and Worcester
© Fredrik Barth 1981

British Library Cataloguing in Publication Data

Barth, Fredrik

Selected essays of Fredrik Barth. – (International
library of anthropology). Vol. 1: Process and form
in social life
1. Ethnology
I. Series
306   GN325   80-41283

ISBN 9 7100 0720 5

Contents

Introduction

These essays were written during the period 1955–72 (except for chapter 5, Volume I and chapter 7, Volume II, which were especially prepared for this collection), as steps in my own development as an anthropologist. They are partly my response to the thoughts of other anthropologists; but mainly they are my response – aided and encumbered by such thoughts – to various glimpses into the realities of other people's lives and social relations that I have obtained through fieldwork. As I understand my own work, in other words, my intellectual biography would focus mainly on the various fieldwork I have done, and not on the books I have read or the schools where I have studied and taught. The major results of such fieldwork have been presented in a succession of monographs (see Bibliography), which contain my main anthropological contributions, both substantive and analytical. In the lectures and articles republished here, I sought to extract some of the more general positions and understandings at which I had arrived, presenting them together with smaller fragments of data which I judged particularly enlightening for my analytical argument.

Argument, polemical or otherwise, is central to most of the essays; and they inevitably address issues as these appeared to me at a particular time. One might think that they therefore echo old battles long forgotten. If they were to be written today, they would have been designed somewhat differently in response to contemporary debates and arenas. But I regard their essential thrust and content as still current and valid, since I find that the viewpoints they contain are productive for my continuing work and have only been incompletely utilized and accepted by others, and that the views I challenge are such as persist or reappear in only slightly varying forms in the thinking of anthropological colleagues. For these reasons, though the themes and issues that engage me today are partly different (see Bibliography), it is also true to say that I 'stand for' views as argued in these texts.

The essays may be usefully juxtaposed, since they are related as developments of a few fundamental themes and so supplement one another. But I do not imagine that they add up to a complete and unified theory of culture and/or society. On the contrary, they were intended to enter into the wider corpus of social anthropology to influence and modify its development on a few fronts and thereby to contribute to the collective endeavour that is our discipline, rather than erect a personal memorial or a sectarian Grand Theory. In other words, although my work has sometimes been interpreted this way, I have never wished to join or delineate any particular '-ism' in anthropological analysis.

The anthropology which I met in the 1950s was, however, in my judgment seriously crippled by an inattention to fundamental aspects of people's lives. Most particularly, I felt the need to acknowledge the place of the individual, and the discongruity between varying interests and various levels of collectivity. Much of my writing in the ensuing years has consequently focused on the task of developing a perspective on the subjective and goal-pursuing actor. This has entailed taking up the questions of what place considerations of value and utility have in canalizing the behaviour of persons; the variation exhibited in behaviour and the factors generating this variation; and what it is that propels and constrains individual actors and thus shapes their behaviour and their lives. I believe that a conceptual apparatus which can treat these topics *and* integrate them with other major anthropological concepts is an indispensable component in any theoretical system for social anthropology. All the essays collected here relate, in one way or another, to this theme.

There are several alternative vocabularies with which to discuss the circumstances and consequences of these aspects of intentionality, goal-orientation, and rationality. I do not think that social anthropology should adopt any particular one of them and thereby the custom-made epistemology which it entails. We who study the different epistemologies and differing praxis of different cultural traditions should rather engage actively to design our own procedures and positions with respect to such fundamental questions. To do so we need to be aware of the formulations and debates that are current in other disciplines, but not fight shy of assuming the arrogance needed to reshape them according to our own needs. That we have so far done this only little and weakly is no reason not to embrace it as a programme.

My own position on these central issues of epistemology and theory is only occasionally taken up in an explicit way in these essays, but is given a brief presentation in chapter 1. I hold that we must acknowledge that most of the phenomena we study are shaped by human consciousness and purpose. Since social acts are thus not simply 'caused' but 'intended', we must consider these intentions and understandings of actors if we wish to capture the essential contexts of acts. I see little possibility, and no desirability, in defining our object of study so as to eliminate by exclusion this subjectivity of human actors. Where I seem to part ways with most of the transcendental philosophies, and with anthropological colleagues who tend to follow them, is in emphasizing the need to understand behaviour *simultaneously* in two, differently constituted, contexts. One is the semiotic one, where strings of events are shaped by actors so as to embody meanings and transmit messages and thus reflect the rules and constraints of codification. But the same events also enter into the material world of causes and effects, both because acts have consequences and because persons must relate to others who also cause things to happen. This latter context forces actors to consider the instrumentality of acts, in ways which reflect both the constraints of knowledge and value, and the pragmatics of cooperation and competition. Finally, I see a dialectic – albeit between entities on conceptually distinct macro- and micro-levels – between these codes, values, and knowledge on the one hand and human acts on the other. Not only do the former provide premises and constraints for particular acts, but acts also affect codes, values and knowledge by increments and so can change and modify their own preconditions.

Within this comprehensive perspective, most of my discussion in the period covered by these essays has focused on actors' strategies of instrumentality and the aggregate social consequences of such strategies. In quite another connection, Bateson (1972: 490-3) has characterized as a fundamental epistemological fallacy the Western tendency to think and act in terms of the wrong units: in terms of separate individuals rather than systems of interacting persons and objects, or in terms of human groups and populations rather than these in interaction with their environment. Systems theory has taught us (recently) instead to follow the pathways along which information and effects flow, and see these whole circuits or loops as the unit – not the severed chunks which we produce by cutting across these connections of interrelationship. I contend, however, that this fallacy is not limited to Western thought, but is prevalent in many contexts in many other cultures as well. In such cases the logic by which actors operate – predicated by their subjective understanding of the situation and their own interests in it – is often at odds with the aggregate system of interdependencies within which they are acting. In societies with less powerful technologies this is not as ecologically suicidal as it may be in our case, but it is certainly pervasively consequential in shaping society and culture. The focus in the following essays on the strategies of actors provides a methodology for exploring the consequences of such egocentric epistemologies on the part of actors, inherent as I see it in the inescapable directedness of consciousness towards 'something' distinguished from the subject who is exercising the consciousness (Slagstad, 1976; Skjervheim, 1959).

My perspective, and my production over the years, have been shaped by the effort to introduce these considerations in opposition, as an alternative or as a supplement, to conceptual habits that are deeply entrenched in anthropological thinking and keep asserting themselves in various guises and combinations. What I see as most distinctive to my approach is perhaps most vividly expressed in contrast to these other, in many ways more orthodox, perspectives.

The most dominant and most indispensable of them is *structuralism*. I believe it to be fundamental to the conceptualization of any kind of complex reality. But the way it has been adapted to anthropological materials has entailed a predominant focus on 'systems of thought', even when avowedly speaking about the connections of social interaction and people's relationship to their environment. It has also focussed strongly on the macro-level of forms, institutions and customs, ignoring the micro-level of the distribution and interconnections of concrete acts and activities; or else it has confounded the two as if the acts of individuals were a simple homologue or 'expression', of collective macro-structures. As a method, it has tended to achieve clarity – indeed often brilliance – in the depiction of patterns by a high degree of selectivity: by backgrounding and eliminating variation and abstracting the norm, thereby ignoring increasingly more of what seems to me real and vital in people's lives (on the operation of backgrounding in the construction of shared understandings, see Douglas, 1975: 3-4, and elsewhere). In these ways, structuralism has developed in social anthropology in directions which ever reduce our universe of observation. The culturally and humanly rich occasions when people come together in the creative act of shaping collective understandings and cosmologies are reduced to texts, to be distilled into a series of abstract binary oppositions; eating together is depicted in the ciphers of conventional patterns of dishes; and the multiplex phenomena of being and changing identity become principles of recruitment. There are undeniable insights in these abstractions, but they capture only very few sides to life; what is more, I mistrust them for being flawed even within their restricted focus. Thus, I expect there is usually a deeply systematic difference between people's reflective generalizations about macro-features of their world and society, and their conceptualization of their social and physical environment seen as an opportunity situation for action. To search for the reflection of the former in the cases and patterns of social behaviour is therefore unduly simplistic, no matter how sophisticated the analysis of these collective representations may be. There is much perhaps prosaic but truly illuminating groundwork to be done with a far broader perspective and sense of the problem before one can hope to represent the premises of meaning for acts with such rigour and logic – if indeed valid representations of these matters can ever achieve such simplicity.

The following essays try to do parts of this groundwork. In their way, they may also go too far in seeking to achieve a degree of conceptual clarity by oversimplifying and obliterating parts of reality. I feel attracted both to the 'thick description' of Geertz (Geertz, 1973) whereby the layers of meaning and context are elaborately explored and exhibited, and to a methodology of 'watching and wondering' in the gentler tradition of the naturalist (Tinbergen, 1951). But I should not let polemics against a narrow structuralism tempt me to negate my own basic ideal: the analytic virtues of seeking to construct tight and simple models on limited premises. I expect such models to be particularly illuminating, however, if they seek to identify and depict empirical processes rather than perform the arbitrary operations of synthesizing and backgrounding. Thereby they should also avoid the illusory timelessness of these other forms of structuralism, and articulate with the irreversibility of praxis (cf. Bourdieu, 1977) and thus the realities of people's lives. Furthermore, by insisting on *events* and *interaction* as central features of our object of study, we are compelled to confront a far broader and more diverse segment of reality. And finally, the virtue of developing models more rigorously and ruthlessly lies not in believing them to be the only and whole truth, but in the occasion it provides to discover their implications, and what they can and cannot do.

Another deeply entrenched mode of explanation in anthropology is *historical*, whether sweepingly evolutionary or more modestly concerned with particular sequences and developments. I have consistently rejected this as the major focus of my anthropology for three major reasons:

1 It has a depressive effect on the anthropological endeavour to adopt the view that social facts are the results of (previous) critical events rather than being themselves critical: it is more productive to assume until proved wrong that everything influencing the shape of an event must be there asserting itself at the moment of the event. This realization was in my view the greatest achievement of functionalism, and we are ever in danger of losing its benefits under the influence of the linear, causal, and development-oriented modality that dominates our traditional thinking.

2 A method that seeks to explain that which one can know much about (the present) by means of that which one must be content to know less about (the past) is topsy-turvy and ever in danger of producing spurious insight.

3 A historical perspective easily encourages the misrepresentation involved in lightly transforming typological series into developmental sequences.

These considerations need not and should not lead one into a synchronic dogmatism and the rejection of a time perspective. Anyone interested in discovering processes must be alert to sequences over time – though not be prepared to confuse any and every sequence of change in aggregate form with a process, as is frequently done (cf. ch. 5, pp. 77-9). A certain amount of early training in palaeontology and biology made me conscious of how much more productive is the search for the *mechanisms* of change rather than composing descriptions of its phylogenetic course, even in the rigorous sense that such courses are identified from the fossil record (cf. ch. 6). I therefore judge it to be particularly useful to study variation with meticulous attention to co-variation, *both* regionally and through time, as I have done in connection with each of my field studies (cf. for example, Vol. II chs. 1, 2 and 6). But the alternative to a structuralistic indifference to particular events of change is not to mystify change by vesting it with moral or metaphysical properties, as anthropological evolutionists and marxists tend to do. We must struggle to ascertain the dynamics of cultures and societies *in* time as ongoing systems and *through* time as emergent sequences. But this we do best by establishing the facts of the past where possible, and not by conjectural interpretations based on *pre*-established schemas or by pursuing the craft of historiography, no matter how competently. Data from the past are analytically useful when they can surprise us and falsify our hypotheses; otherwise, I see no reason why they should receive privileged interest.

The third dominant mode of thought in anthropology which we need constantly to challenge is *functionalism*. In anthropological theory this viewpoint has mainly flourished through the inappropriate application of considerations of purpose and utility to the macro-level of aggregate systems, rather than the micro-level of decision-making units where it belongs. But it is also nourished by the anthropologist's recurrent experience during fieldwork of the covert fitness and felicity of customs which had initially struck us as arbitrary and senseless.

The essays that follow are concerned to pursue questions of purpose and utility systematically where persons and groups making decisions can be observed, and rigorously avoid them where they provide only inappropriate metaphor or unsupportable teleology. I think we can do better anthropology that way; and it should not be difficult to maintain a broad and meticulous attention to context in the fieldwork situation, as taught by Malinowski, without embracing the holistic and functionalistic axioms by which he justified it. In its vulgar form, a functionalist stance seems to assert that the mere existence of a pattern in a culture other than our own is proof of its functional fit, which again serves as the explanation of its existence. At the same time this image of other, functionally integrated cultures has served anthropologists as a foil against which to condemn our own culture and life situation where we experience a disparity between our own desires and ideals, and the prevailing (aggregate) patterns and circumstances. Surely, these are frustrations which people in all cultures experience, in the disparity between desire and circumstance, what is and what might have been; and only a gross insensitivity to the actual life situation of real people in other cultures could lead one to think otherwise? Nor can I find *a priori* justification, or empirical validation, for a harmony model of culture and society, or culture and environment, either generally or in any particular case. Indeed, even where an approximation of such functional harmony is found, it does not provide in itself any explanation for the existence of the cultural patterns in question unless the *processes* whereby this degree of harmony arises can be rigorously explicated.

The inadequacies of each of the three main viewpoints I have here attacked so summarily arise in each case from the simplicity of one or another aspect of their implicit constituting premises. How could one hope to develop an alternative viewpoint which does not contain analogous flaws of its own? No statement in the following essays is intended to claim that I know of such an alternative; and indeed I have no trust in our ability ever to construct a theoretical framework capable of questioning its own constituting premises. It is in the way that we relate theory to the reality which it seeks to depict that we can hope to create this possibility of falsification and correction of assumptions about that reality. Perhaps it is in my ideals – and hopefully my praxis – on this point that I feel I differ most from a number of my colleagues: I want to work in a discipline in which theory and empirical data are confronted at a diversity of levels.

It is in the very nature of our object of study that difficulties should arise in performing such confrontation with reality with sufficient rigour to achieve anything approaching the operations of testing and 'proof' in the sciences (cf. ch. 1). The anthropologist in studying human behaviour is faced with such a diversity and near infinity of potential data, even for the most modest encounter (cf. e.g. the records of kinesics, as in Birdwhistle, 1970, or the problems of constructing a journal of observations, as in Pittenger *et al.*, 1960). We are consequently ever in danger of having our own selectivity become the main source of patterning in our data. What is more, our methodology of comparison, so fundamental to the theoretical constitution of social anthropology, suffers in comparison with the biological sciences: we do not compare specimens and cadavers, only synthetic descriptions of our objects of study. Above all, the symbolic and social construction of people's realities entail the necessity of comprehending interpersonal events by interpreting them, on many simultaneous levels of meaning and significance, by means of the codes and keys employed in their own culture *as well as* analysing them by canons which we can accept as objectively, materially adequate. Nor can I, as noted above, see any way of escaping these difficulties by a methodology which restricts our data to forms and topics where a greater rigour can be achieved (whether by social survey techniques or New Ethnographies), since these procedures only force more of what may be essentials of human life into the inaccessible void of the unrecorded, and thereby unknowable.

The essential problem of any anthropological endeavour is perhaps most simply described as adopting procedures of thought and observation whereby the anthropologist can transcend his own categories and premises, and thus make discoveries of any degree of profundity, and experience surprises that will affect his preconceptions about cultures, societies and human life.

When the issue is put this way, it becomes apparent that we in fact have a number of procedures at our disposal though these have rarely been used in concert or given proper recognition as the essential underpinnings of a methodology for social anthropology. (What follows assumes the practice of the cluster of techniques summarized under the caption 'participant observation', needed to allow us to be in an adequate observer position at all.) Being essentially ways of relating theoretical constructions and reality, these procedures describe perhaps most succinctly my own ideal of what anthropology should be about.

1 We need to adopt the naturalist's stance of 'watching and wondering'. This involves the construction of extensive and meticulous descriptions, but presented with an economy of words and dimensions. Therefore, it entails model-building – but models constructed for the purpose of more thorough, comprehensive, and economical description. The emphasis on 'watching' entails a recognition of the essential separation of *three* levels: (a) theories, explanations, and other constructions; (b) observations, data; and (c) reality out there. 'Watching' means trying to capture chunks of this reality by transforming them to observations by procedures that entail the least possible selection or construction in terms of whatever theory is at issue, so that falsifying confrontations of theory and observations become possible.

2 We should construct generative models (cf. chapters 2 and 5) rather than attempt to distil representational models from complex data. Thereby, we are led to search for the empirical processes behind observable regularities in the material, and to depict these processes in the operations, or transformation rules which we employ in our generative models. What is more, such models can be used inductively, and the patterns they produce can be confronted with data collected independently of the model's premises. Thereby the procedures for falsification are strengthened drastically.

3 We should capitalize on our unique advantage: that our 'object of study' can help us actively to transcend our categories by teaching us their own. This means recognizing that the actors' categories provide a way to understand reality, *as well as* being part of that reality. In practice, probably most of the productivity of the anthropologist

derives from this source, even though his arrogance as a professional academic, and his defensiveness when his *own* reality is being threatened by the enchanted world of another culture, both militate against such learning.

4 We should expose our scholarship to the demands of practical action so that its incompleteness and unworkableness can be revealed. I see such experiences in applied anthropology as immensely stimulating and challenging episodes in any academic career and have experienced them as such myself. Applied activities raise other and difficult issues, however. The colonial and imperialist involvements of some previous and contemporary colleagues give cause for misgivings. Likewise, our exposure to the insensitive complacency of international organizations, or disillusionment with the independent governments of new nations, may repel. One also becomes less confident of one's own ideological standards when one recognizes the confident idealism with which errors have previously been perpetrated by thoughtful anthropologists. Yet unless we are to commit ourselves to complete social passivity in this world as constituted, there is no alternative to acting while enquiring carefully into whose interests we serve by action, and whether the act to which we become party is in itself defensible, in respect of alternatives. The intricacy and agony of these questions are as inducive to realism in our anthropology as the more external ascertainment of the consequences of practical action.

5 We should focus our observations on real people in real life situations, with a curiosity as to what an investigation into their situation may bring – rather than pursue highly abstracted and demarcated topics of investigation according to predetermined methods. The latter alternative is more suitable for the construction of good grant applications than for the pursuit of innovative scholarship. Both topic and method must be allowed to *develop* in response to the concrete situation of fieldwork and the findings that accumulate.

6 We should espouse the ideal – though not the realism – of cumulative mapping to produce an ethnographic Whole World Catalogue. A discussion of the 'crisis of anthropology' in terms of the disappearance of its subject matter can only arise from an academic practice of conceptual 'backgrounding' to the point of subjective blindness. Reality is entirely different: social anthropology has as its object an immense and still, in many essentials, truly uncharted world. The urgent tasks of anthropology – the recording of swiftly disappearing cultural and social forms which embody the results of millenia of cultural creativity

in countless distinctive traditions – are far more numerous and complex than we can solve with available resources. What is more, the publicized performance of these tasks may in its direct and indirect consequences perhaps also be the most powerful way of resisting the tragic and senseless destruction of ways of life cherished by other people, some of them perhaps happier than ourselves. But on the even broader canvas defined by the life situations of people, there are manifestly more people in the world today than ever, culturally and socially more intricately interdependent than ever before. It seems to me a shocking reflection of the scholasticism of some of our colleagues that this should not be universally recognized to constitute an inexhaustible field for anthropological investigation.

The essays republished below reflect this conception of our object of study and seek to achieve such a relationship between concept and theory and the empirical object. Thus, the theoretical developments they contain are motivated by – or perhaps more correctly, their necessity has seemed to me to have arisen from – the substantive events that I observed. Anyone who has ever attempted serious fieldwork will recognize that events have a sheer mass and diversity far greater than my total published corpus; I have never subscribed to the illusion that it is fruitful to publish materials outside of the areas that have been at least provisionally grasped by a conceptual framework. These essays, much more singlemindedly than my main writings in monograph form, focus primarily on such frameworks: on various ways of conceptualizing which may enable us to build models suitable for fundamentally descriptive purposes: models that enable us to provide coherent, reflective accounts of the interconnections that obtain between wide and varied sets of observations. I see our task in developing theory as an unending struggle to increase the comprehensiveness of material which we can thereby cover, and the elegance and completeness of our coverage.

The various issues and contributions with which I have struggled interweave, reappear and are restated and modified in these various essays. I should like only briefly to point to those which I myself, at the present time, see as the most important:

1 An emphasis on the concrete life situation or opportunity situation of the actor as the essential and significant context for his act. It is not by moving directly to the more rarified levels of norm and pattern, and derivative conceptualizations of deviance or structure, that we can identify the actor's point of view and thus the factors that

impinge directly on - or more correctly, are an inherent part of - his act. First of all, our understanding of what he is doing must be solidly grounded in a knowledge of that particular actor's resources and assets, his alters and significant others, his manifold commitments and interests, and his environmental and communicative options.

2 A persistent effort to develop and clarify our main conceptual vehicle for describing social systems and institutionalized behaviour *viz* the concept of status. This theme seems to me to receive entirely inadequate attention by most colleagues, even though the inadequacies of textbook definitions are widely recognized.

3 The dynamic interconnection between macro- and micro-phenomena (particularly the concepts of *aggregation* and *constraint*), which may provide the most fruitful ways to articulate the central questions of choice, freedom, history and the ontology of society and culture.

4 The relationship between social and cultural phenomena and their environment, particularly their preconditions and consequences in that environment. For this purpose I have sought to utilize an ecological perspective without submerging the anthropological task in it. Consequently, despite my early and fairly comprehensive efforts to introduce ecological thinking into our discipline, I have reservations against some of the major currents and trends in this sub-field, as will be apparent from a reading of the relevant articles.

5 An interest in developing concepts to analyse the process of exchange in interaction - not so as to apply a market model to social life but on the contrary to study the implications of exchange as one of the basic forms of constraints whereby the behaviours of two or more actors are constituted as systems, and thereby to contribute to a general theory of social systems.

6 The relationship between codification and praxis, or how forms of understanding arise from experience, and reciprocally how behaviour and experience are predicated by collective representations. This is only partly articulated in the present collection (see particularly chapter 8) but has been developed further in a separate monograph (Barth, 1975). I believe there is a possibility of integrating much of my previous theoretical work in a broad kind of sociology of knowledge treating this central theme.

There is a temptation in writing an introduction to one's own old articles to repeat, reformulate, and construct ever more cryptic and speculative meta-statements over the same themes. Rather than continue, it would probably be wiser to let the various texts speak for themselves.

Fredrik Barth
Oslo, June 1979

1 Anthropological models and social reality *

In trying to show you the character of social anthropology as an academic discipline, I might try to sketch some substantive and perhaps intriguing findings in the field, or the history of its development, or some of its major intellectual problems today. I have chosen the last of these alternatives, because by showing the general problems we are grappling with I hope to reveal to you, in part no doubt inadvertently, the ways that anthropologists think, and also how our difficulties in part arise from the character of the social reality itself, which we confront and try to understand.

The fundamental questions which social anthropology asks are about the forms, the nature, and the extent of order in human social life, as it can be observed in the different parts of the world. There is no need to prejudge the extent of this order; as members of one society we know how unpredictable social life can be. But concretely, human life varies greatly around the world, and it seems possible to characterize its forms to some extent. We seek means systematically to discover, record and understand these forms.

I wish to emphasize this fundamentally empirical view: we discover and record, we do not comment and evaluate. The fundamental approach is thus that of science and not of moral philosophy. We seek the data not for the insight they may give us in our own 'human' problems of existence, not for answers to ethical dilemmas or the purpose of life. The varieties of human societies is a field of empirical knowledge and inquiry in its own right. It should hardly be necessary to emphasize this, were it not for the prominence of humanist orientation in universities and the utilitarian and 'social problem' justifications used in many social sciences. As well as discovering and recording, we also try to systematize this knowledge about human societies in what may conveniently, if somewhat ambitiously, be called explanatory

---

* The second Royal Society Nuffield Lecture, delivered 26 October 1965.

models – models in the broad sense that they are *representations* of an interrelated set of assumed factors that determine or 'explain' the phenomena we observe.

But there is one circumstance that makes our discipline different from the natural sciences. From our own life, we feel that it is undeniable and true that human behaviour is prominently shaped by consciousness and purpose. Anthropologists are therefore prepared to speak about things like beliefs, obligations, and values, not just immediate, overt behaviour. This also means that an explanatory model for behaviour can be different from the models used in natural science. Human behaviour is 'explained' if we show (a) the utility of its consequences in terms of values held by the actor, and (b) the awareness on the part of the actor of the connection between an act and its specific results. This is what has been called the *subjective* viewpoint, or by Max Weber 'Verstehender Soziologie'. Indeed, most anthropologists seem to feel that unless the actor's point of view can be made understandable in such cognitive and valuational terms, his behaviour cannot be explained. On the other hand, the psychological mechanism behind such 'purposeful action' constitutes a different field of inquiry which does not concern us: our interest is not to refine our understanding of it. Our concern is to understand the different societies and cultures that are based on this mechanism by relating social behaviour to the conceptual and valuational systems of the actors.

This view, however, has methodological implications for how we go about finding the causes or determinants of behaviour. To take a frequently used example: traffic stops at a red light. Can we point to a red stop-light as the 'cause' of auto-drivers stopping their cars, in view of the fact that occasionally a driver will *not* stop at a red light? If one contrary case does not prove us wrong, *how* many cases would it take before this explanatory model was falsified?

There is a sense in which this argument misses the point by not understanding what kind of claims to adequacy we make for our models. To find out if cases of not-stopping challenge our model, we would want to know (a) can they be understood – and dismissed – as cases of inattentiveness? That is, was it the actor's immmediate perception that failed in this situation, though the cognitive rule that red means 'stop' still holds true? Or (b) can these exceptions be dismissed as cases of atypical utilities? The evaluation which makes people stop is compounded of the danger of accidents and the probability of sanctions by the police. If a man has some uniquely urgent reason to travel fast, the utility of arriving quickly might outweigh the risks of not stopping. Only if both these interpretations fail can such an event be truly regarded as a 'contrary case'. Statistics on the overt behaviour of populations do not readily supply a test of the explanation. They certainly do not challenge or confirm statements such as 'red means stop' – and such statements constitute some of our major discoveries in the analysis of exotic societies. One might be tempted to say that a frequent discrepancy between the observed and the predicted behaviour reduces the relevance, but not necessarily the validity, of such models. Yet we do wish to falsify our models by confronting them with empirical facts, and this involves methodological problems to which I shall return shortly.

The empirical bent in anthropology takes a form which is reminiscent of natural history. Indeed, it has sprung directly from that academic tradition. In this anthropology differs from most of the behavioural sciences, which to greater extent have their roots in philosophy and the humanities. Anthropologists tend to seek the strange and the exotic, approaching such matters with the naturalist's curiosity. The effect of such an approach is that one exposes oneself to the greatest possible variety and mass of impressions. The immediate purpose of this is, of course, to collect and cross-check information. But it also colours the anthropologist's theoretical orientation by encouraging eclectic model-building: the anthropologist is concerned about the direct relevance of theories to empirical facts, because of his constant need to order a diversity of such facts. This does not mean that, temperamentally, many social anthropologists may not wish to protect their orthodoxy from uncongenial facts, or to work deductively from a basic theory of society. But the situation that they place themselves in, surrounded by the strangeness of a foreign society, is one that makes this maximally difficult. In this they differ for example from the economist, who works deductively at his desk and seeks to falsify his constructs against a limited range of data. Among us, the term 'armchair anthropologist' has been a standard term of abuse. But perhaps I am merely saying that to the extent social anthropology is a science, it is a very primitive science?

Let me practise this natural history concreteness by taking you briefly to one of the classical loci of British social anthropology, to illustrate the confrontation of anthropological models and social reality. The place is one or another of the communities in the Sudd swamps of the Sudan, inhabited by the Nuer people, made famous through the writings of Professor Evans-Pritchard.

These people live in shifting camps in periodically inundated country. They practise agriculture, though they are more interested in their herds of cattle. In the wet season, the period of floods, they congregate in villages of 50 to 200 persons. Around November they disperse through the country in small cattle camps, until increasing desiccation drives them together around permanent sources of water in large dry-season camps of 100 to 1000 members.

Of the various kinds of order which one may search for in such communities, let us first concentrate our attention on the relations of communities to each other, and to larger territories – what might be called political life. We find a situation where, in disputes and battle, the people who are allied at one moment, over one issue, are opposed to each other the next moment. There are no chiefs or, apparently, stable leaders of any kind. The problem might seem to be one of finding any kind of order at all. It was one of Evans-Pritchard's contributions to show how a political order is maintained in this society without the institution of chiefs and stable authority, through the operation of a framework of kinship relations of a scale quite unmatched in our own society.

Let me first try to depict this order as a system of jural rules governing membership in groups and the institutional relevance of these groups. Nuer men identify themselves as members of tribes and their local segments, down to the level of the local community. This identification refers to residence, and to political duties of a kind which implies or produces a political corporation. The duties are relevant for behaviour in daily life and at ritual occasions, and they are especially dramatically manifested in feud, when groups of warriors wreak collective vengeance.

In all this activity there is a characteristic relativity of groups. Thus if a tribe were divided into two local segments A and B, each with subdivisions 1 and 2, the people of B2 will have primary obligations to each other and unite against the men of B1; but if a man in B1 is harmed by a man in A1 or A2, they will all combine as B's, holding all the A's collectively responsible. There is thus a pattern of situational fusion and fission of groups, depending on the relative positions of the original parties to the dispute within a hierarchy of segments.

Furthermore, each such tribal territory or segment is identified with a clan or lineage within the clan. Clan and lineage membership is ascribed by patrilineal descent – namely, determined by the father's position. The Nuer can thus present an agnatic genealogy that corresponds to the hierarchy of territorial segments: the tribe is identified with a deceased ancestor, each of its primary subdivisions with one of his sons, etc. In that way, the duties between co-members of a community and those between agnatic kinsmen become one. This whole pattern can be represented as a set of 'jural' rules. The rules are jural, although there is no formal system of courts and law enforcement, both in that they are embraced by the Nuer as moral and right, and in that they are sanctioned – compliance is praised and supported, breaches are criticized and punished by public opinion. A jural rule model of the system depicts the regularity of behaviour in terms of group structure: a set of rules regulating the mode of recruitment to groups, and the duties that group membership entails.

Many of the primitive political systems which have been analysed prove to utilize kinship-based criteria of recruitment to political groups. Where the ascription of political rights and obligations is tied to *one* line of descent, either male or female, and genealogies are remembered, this will entail a segmentary form of organization since obligations may in varying situations either be extended to cover distant collaterals or restricted to the near ones. A few basic rules governing localization, line of descent, and the content of the obligations involved will allow us to understand a variety of the basic characteristics of any such specific political form.

Such a representation of the Nuer system, however, does not exhaustively depict the facts which a field worker among the Nuer will discover. For example, the facts of local group composition correspond only imperfectly to the simple model outlined above. Within a camp or a village one will find that some resident men are related to each other in the male line as agnates, others are related through female links and some are connected by marriage only. Only some of the residents in a territory turn out actually to be members of the clan associated with that territory. Social reality turns out to be considerably more complex than the jural rule model – yet it undeniably depicts in idealized form some of the fundamental regularities of the empirical situation.

On the other hand, the anthropologist may choose to construct a different model of these regularities. He can appeal to the Nuer themselves, who characteristically speak about community membership and relations in such agnatic terms: the conceptual categories in which political units and relations are visualized and discussed by the participants

are those of agnatic kinship. Political systems of this type have therefore sometimes been characterized by social anthropologists as systems
where politics is cast in the 'idiom' of kinship. If the actors themselves
conceptualize political sodalities as groups of 'brothers', they use a
concept which implies situational disregard of collateral distance, and
which forces the representation of relations between groups into a
segmentary mould. The characteristics of situational fusion and fission
follow from this, and the anthropologist can thus understand regularities in the political life by analysing the implications of how the actors
conceptualize their political groups – what might be called the relevant
cognitive structures in their culture. The fact that all members of the
community are not brothers, or even agnates, is not as problematical as
it is for the jural rule model: territorial segmentation is implicit in the
basic categories in which political groups are conceptualized. Thus
the detailed discrepancies become rather unimportant and uninterest-
ing: the reality with which such models should be confronted is the
category of discourse, of ritual affirmation, etc. (cf., for example,
Leach,1961).

What have been called 'structural' models of societies have tended to
combine features of these two ways of representation: both as jural
rules and cognitive categories. This has enabled anthropologists to
exhibit the major groups in a society, how they are interrelated in
terms of recruitment, and what is their major institutional field of
relevance.

Nor do such models need to ignore alternative patterns of behaviour
and their implications for the system. Professor Gluckman, in a re-
analysis of the Nuer, has specifically emphasized the effects of the
intermixture in villages of persons from different lineages and clans.
The man living in the territory of a different lineage from his own will
have essentially similar obligations (a) to his distant lineage mates, and
(b) to his local neighbours. This may create dilemmas of cross-cutting
loyalties in the case of feud between groups: as a member of a lineage
he may be on one side, as a member of a village identified with another
lineage he may be on the other side in a conflict. Such a position
both motivates and qualifies the man to act as go-between and peace-
maker in the feud; so the consequence of the dispersal of personnel
outside the territories of their clans is to create both a force and a
mechanism in the service of maintaining peace over larger regions,
and thus paradoxically to maintain the formal pattern which they,
individually, have not followed.

This way of arguing exemplifies in its most explicit form another traditional feature of anthropological thinking: the society-organism analogy as a basis for functionalism, whereby one shows how aspects of form serve a purpose in maintaining the system as a whole. As a way of depicting the prerequisites of system maintenance, this represents a different explanation of form from that of finding the actor's own 'purpose' – a circumstance which has occasioned some confusion in anthropology but which has largely been overcome. Most anthropologists, however, have chosen not to pursue this view of society further and have not adopted a Darwinian perspective.

Structuralist models thus enable us to depict the gross morphology of societies, and have made it possible to describe and compare a great diversity of forms. But with an anthropologist's field experience, it is difficult for long to avoid raising, in some form, the question of why specific actors behave the way they do. The structural kind of model emphasizes cognitive categories and the positive and negative sanctions of jural rules. But living in our Nuer village, we cannot but be impressed by the 'case stories' around us: why did our neighbour choose to live with his mother's or his wife's kin? Some cases are easily explained. Among the Nuer there are a number of small lineages and clans that have no land of their own and must live interspersed among others. There are also individuals and lines that have been adopted from defeated neighbouring tribes. But many others, though members of clans which have aristocratic rank in their home territories, yet choose to live elsewhere as foreigners. Why?

To answer such questions, we must go back to the basic view of behaviour and utility which served as our initial point of departure. The simplest structural argument would be that there are jural rules, implying sanctions, which support the established patterns; so most actors acknowledge these and act accordingly, while some deviate from the rules in random fashion. Alternatively, we may find that the rules are themselves inconsistent and thus produce variability in behaviour. But rather, we may look more closely at all cases of behaviour and ask what it is that makes people act the way they do: what goods are people after, and how do cognitive categories, rules and sanctions – as well as the local ecology – constrain their possible courses of action in pursuit of such goods? Though he does not utilize it in constructing his basic model of Nuer society, Evans-Pritchard, the fieldworker, does not fail to recognize such factors. He notes that there are variations in population density through Nuer country, and that it therefore may be more advantageous for a man to live as a foreigner in an area of ample land, water and grazing than as a member of the dominant clan in an overpopulated area. He also refers to some men's desire for autonomy: collateral lines are arranged in order of seniority, and members of junior lines may sometimes achieve greater autonomy away from their collaterals than close to them.

To depict such facts and discover and interrelate such explanatory factors systematically, however, we need to build models of a different kind. Regularities in behaviour can be represented as relative frequencies, i.e. as a kind of order that emerges from the independent activities of multiple actors; and our task then becomes one of showing how this order is generated. The model most readily available for this is one of utilities, and can be represented as one of choice under constraints. Such a model, incidentally, can also generate a *range* of behaviour, if assets and opportunities are distributed unequally between the members in the system – a condition that can be readily observed and depicted in any society.[1]

Among Pathans in Pakistan's former North-West Frontier Province, I have myself studied a political system from this point of view (Barth, 1959a), in an attempt to analyse politics in a descent system with jural rules not unlike those of the Nuer, but where political relations of alliance and patron-client types are also recognized. Empirically, what happens is that lineages very largely fail to fuse and be mobilized as political units. Instead a two-party system develops, composed of small lineage splinters permanently pitted against each other, while the rest of the population aligns as clients of leaders in each of these two parties.

Among these Pathans, lineage membership and the right to utilize resources are transmitted, as among the Nuer, in male line, and the obligation to avenge harm caused to agnates is upheld. As among the Nuer, only a fraction of the population in a community has such lineage membership, but the rest are not adopted or assimilated or spoken of as brothers – they attach themselves as clients to patrons who have lineage status.

Now in the case of conflicts, it is easier to mobilize clients than equals in defence of one's own interests: over the former one has economic and political sanctions that provide effective authority, whereas the latter are rivals in many fields. Furthermore, lineage members can aggrandize themselves by conquering land – and this again gives more clients and even greater independence of collaterals. Such land can be conquered only at someone else's expense; and there is a clear tactical advantage in attacking *close* agnates – thereby mobilizing the smallest possible opposed group, since only those more closely related to the victims than yourself will rise in defence of the owner's, and their own, prior rights to the lands in question. This means that lineages tend to break up in opposed splinters or fractions. When such splinters seek allies for support against their close collateral rivals, they can find them in similar, distantly related splinters of other lineage segments, by promising mutual support against their respective rivals. In this situation, then, A1 and B1 tend to form a stable coalition against A2 and B2. The stronger coalition will be victorious in a confrontation – which means that there will be a consistent pressure towards the systematization of larger and larger coalitions, culminating in the formation of a two-party system of two large, dispersed political blocs.

This system can be simulated as a game of strategy and coalition-forming by utilizing the Theory of Games (Neumann and Morgenstern, 1947). Thereby, a more rigorous model can be constructed, based on the notion of value and utility and showing the tactical constraints on choice which generate such a political form (Barth, 1959b). We can thus see that a kind of order, in the sense of regular patterns of behaviour, emerges that cannot be adequately depicted in terms of rules with jural sanctions, nor as the direct expression of a cognitive pattern. A jural rule model would show us the structure of lineages with reference to land rights, but would not explain political alignments. The jural rules governing political relations merely state that a client may join any patron he likes, and a patron may join any coalition he likes – rules that very imperfectly depict the regularities that may be observed. Nor does the cognitive structure of a two-party system and the participants' awareness of the processes of balance between the parties explain the regularity of political opposition that divides each lineage. The games model thus allows us to depict some further aspects of political order which the previous models could not readily encompass.

The lineage-politics problems I have sketched above are of course only one limited aspect of the social order among the Nuer, as among other peoples. Anthropologists are equally concerned to study economic or ritual behaviour. But such institutional categories as politics or ritual are perhaps best regarded as conveniences of communication and provisional description: through studying such fields of behaviour, we seek to arrive at an understanding of a more comprehensive order which can be represented as a *social* system: a complex system of social positions and interrelations in terms of which behavioural regularities in many institutional fields may be understood and their congruence and interdependence discovered.

In the previous Nuffield lecture, Professor Solow discussed the problems of micro- and macro-analysis in economics, and pointed out the difficulties experienced in that discipline in connecting the analyses of determinants of individual behaviour with those of aggregate behaviour. Any study of human behaviour will be concerned with this question; yet you may have noted that I have not treated this as a particularly troubling problem from the social anthropologist's point of view. Indeed, I would say that it is one of the strengths of anthropological analysis that we are more consistently concerned and able to interrelate the individual and the aggregate level than most of the behavioural sciences, though this is probably achieved at the cost of some elegance in our analyses of both.

In part, the greater unity of the micro- and macro-level is achieved by our emphasis on understanding the actor's subjective point of view as our own point of departure. This leads us to try to characterize the aggregate system, not by operationally sophisticated and well measured indices, but by the shared cognitive categories and gross values of the participants in the system. Whether as an interest in a native informant's description of 'custom', a careful attention to native words and concepts, or an increasingly sophisticated participation in discussions of the *Realpolitik* of a local area, the anthropologist seeks to form a picture of the macro-system in categories related to those which the participants hold, though without accepting their account of the system as empirically correct. Also it should be recognized that most anthropologists work among groups or are interested in problems for which we are provided no aggregate data by statisticians. We must accumulate them ourselves through our observations and from informants, and will thus tend to accumulate them in categories that are those of the individual actor's cognitive schema and our own intended analysis, producing thereby also an inadvertent congruence between the micro- and macro-levels.

A common feature of anthropological models is that they presume the relative stability and maintenance of form and are concerned with explaining persistence rather than change. This is not to deny the facts of change, but springs rather from a realization of the precarious nature of any semblance of order and continuity in so volatile a matter as interpersonal behaviour in a human population. The explanation of relative stability and order is sought in the permanence of determining or limiting factors. The underlying viewpoint has been expressed in the axiom that 'there are no privileged moments' (cf. Gellner, 1958) – that patterns of social form are not related in a uniquely illuminating or derivative way to specific events in the past, and thus adequately understood by a historical explanation. Though the axiom in this general form is probably untrue, it has proved very fruitful in directing investigation towards verifiable constraints in the present rather than reconstructed events in the past, deduced often from the very facts which they are called upon to explain. Naturally, this viewpoint is equally adequate as a basis for dynamic models as for social statics – an assertion which is regarded as more debatable among humanists than I expect it will be among a group of scientists. Some attempt has been made to express this viewpoint by means of a distinction between 'historical' and 'structural' time; mostly it is merely implicit in the kinds of explanations that are sought and the models that are built.

In the manner of a naturalist, then, the anthropologist builds a model, or a number of loosely connected, partial models, of the society he observes around him as an ongoing system. But what are the observations whereby the adequacy or inadequacy of these models are tested, or documented, by the investigator?

Anthropologists are here faced with a great methodological problem: the distance between our concrete sensory impressions of events 'out there' in a society, and the kind of data one can use to falsify anthropological models. The question at issue is, fundamentally, the nature of the 'social reality' with which we can hope to confront our models: what kind of order do we have reason to think that we will find? According to the anthropological view there are, in each society and culture, 'natural' categories of events – consisting of *social statuses* and *meanings* – which are unique for each system and must be discovered; and the extent of order in social life becomes apparent only when observation and description takes place with reference to such categories. In other words, we look for entities of the same epistemological order as 'element' in chemistry or 'species' in zoology, but are prepared to find unique and unexpected systems of these in each new society we study. To discover these systems, we need to understand the place of social events in the context of the society and culture in which we observe them – by analogy, we might say that we need to be able to 'translate' the meanings of events in a foreign culture before their significance can be recorded.

We thus need to process our direct impressions so as to transform and categorize them in a way that makes them into data. This processing can be discussed under three headings:

1 The simplest of our requirements is that of aggregating from single items to patterns of expectations or obligations in a social system or frequencies of behavioural forms. Field experience has made it quite clear that such patterns or regularities are not adequately summarized in what an informant will tell us about his own society. Rather, we try to arrive at a knowledge of these aggregate patterns by combining many repeated, or otherwise mutually confirming observations including (a) actions of people in concrete situations, (b) spontaneous verbal assertions by participants, (c) ritual establishment or confirmation of relations between persons, and (d) elicited verbal explanations and generalizations by informants. On this level, the anthropologist can check, verify and falsify in a thoroughly scientific way, based on a sound methodology.

2 But when an anthropologist makes the simple assertion: 'There is a relationship of dominance and authority of headmen over villagers' – what actual items of observation could document or falsify this statement? Say that we observe a villager A hand over a spear to villager B – what can it be taken to indicate about dominance and authority between A and B, namely what is the *meaning* of this transfer in this culture? Is it:

(i) A case of exercise of common rights, on the principle what is mine is also yours, i.e. A is equal to B?

(ii) A case of alms-giving or other assistance, or perhaps ceremonial investiture of a warrior novice, involving a prestation from a superior to an inferior, i.e. A is higher than B?

(iii) A case of tax or tribute-paying, or perhaps ceremonial submission, i.e. A is lower than B?

Many cultures, like our own, impute any and all of these three meanings to such a concrete transfer – besides sale, gift, or loan, each with other social implications or 'meanings'. In an unknown culture, however, there is no way of predicting which one or several of these obtain, or which other meanings may also be implied in the act.

As a participant inside a culture and a society, one knows the code and the alternative meanings the act may have. One also knows the contents of the relationship between a headman and a villager, and one probably even knows that A is a common villager and B a headman. One can therefore judge by context which alternative meaning holds in this case, and understand that A is expressing his submission under B by giving tribute. But as observers who wish to demonstrate or falsify the presumed inequality between A, who is a relatively undistinguished villager, and B, who has been identified at another occasion as a headman, how does this event help us? We have to *translate* to give the act its appropriate meaning in the culture, and this seems to require previous knowledge both of the 'code' and of the social relations.

3 Still one open question remains: were A and B acting in their capacities as commoner and village headman? These are small and intimate local groups where we observe the same people in what we must distinguish as different capacities: we see the village headman at home being a father and a mother's brother to various people, we meet him in the fields being a cultivator on his own land.

We also see the same equipment, a spear, used as a kitchen utensil to cut meat, or as a weapon, or as an object of wealth for barter and payment, or as a sign of rank. How do we break the code so we no longer talk about naïve categories like spears and men, but about headmen, fathers, signs of rank, items of tribute? Our anthropological models are not about people and spears, and cannot be falsified by even the most exhaustive statistics on the gross activities of people or the uses of spears. Indeed, we can legitimately doubt that such statistics would reveal very marked regularities at all – certainly most of the order in social life characterizes other units than these. Events involving men and spears need to be translated in terms of what they mean, in a social system and a cultural idiom, before they become *data* to the anthropologist.

But once we have performed this translation, have we not 'cooked' our evidence so that it must fit our models – is the operation of translation one that is independent enough of our models so that it can produce data that can falsify these models?

Though some of my colleagues might argue otherwise, I would say that we have no theoretically founded methodology whereby we can break into this closed circle and start translating. Some linguistically oriented anthropologists in the United States are trying to develop such a methodology (cf., for example, Frake, 1962); the British tradition is much weaker in its theory on this point. Its practice, on the other hand, has been both rigorous and successful, involving a nearly total submersion in the foreign culture through the technique of participant observation. The purpose of this technique is to create an optimal learning situation, and this involves control of the native language, continual presence in the community, discontinuation of contact with members of one's own society, and participation in as wide a range of activities in the native community as possible. This is a situation that makes one maximally sensitive to the reactions and controls of members in the foreign society. Not only does it increase one's awareness of what is going on in that society; it also enhances its importance to oneself, as the only source of human companionship and contact. It is in this situation, by an imaginative leap into the unknown, that one breaks into the closed circle of the foreign culture and obtains the 'bridge-heads' from which one can begin to work.

It is not too clear what are the clues which we use to obtain this initial minimal understanding. I have had the experience of trying to analyse and edit the rich, but unprocessed, field notes of a colleague who died during fieldwork, and have experienced this frustrating feeling of having so much information but no understanding, somehow lacking some part of the key to the significance of the recorded events. I was finally able to go to the area in question, and see the people spring to life. Even after that, I am not quite sure what had been missing and what it was that I observed that suddenly gave meaning to my colleague's record. But part of it was the setting, the landscape – not in the poetic sense, but as a place to live. I knew of course that the notes dealt with a herding people in a mountain desert – but my colleague, living in it, had taken the details of this setting for granted; and to understand the significance of acts I needed to know, or see, what the feasible alternatives to any particular act were, which aspects of the form of behaviour were connected with the pure necessities of the demanding task of living in this environment, and which were arbitrary, reflecting the prejudices of the culture and the spirit of the actor.

Some methodology can also be based on the fairly readily observable and objective difference in a social relation between parties who initiate a sequence of interaction and those who cannot do so, or those who can terminate such a sequence of interaction and those who must always respond. Such criteria come closer than anything else to providing an observationally based, culture-free definition of 'authority' (cf. Chapple and Coon, 1942).

But mostly, I think the clues we use are those that reveal attitudes and values by emotional display. We have assumed provisionally, and so far without being disproved, that basic reflexes such as laughing, crying,

screaming, trembling, etc., are released by the same basic attitudes and
emotional states in all *Homo sapiens*. By observing such emotional
display, therefore, we can obtain clues about the significance or meaning of cultural idioms. Thus Bateson (1958) tells how he constructed
a provisional interpretation of a transvestite ceremony among a people
in New Guinea on the basis of second-hand information, and how his
understanding of its meaning was suddenly transformed when he saw,
during the first complete ceremony he attended, how the males dressed
as women were treated as figures of fun and laughed at during the performance, while the females personified arrogant male warriors and
were proud and aggressive.

By these means, the anthropologist in the field catches hold of clues
as to the meanings of acts, and progressively builds up a participant's
map of social conventions, of the different social situations, and what is
regarded as suitable for persons in different positions in the different
situations. He thereby learns to differentiate the roles and statuses of
the social system, and to interpret activities in the contexts that are
culturally appropriate, and that define their meaning. Fortunately, all
idioms do not, like the example of the transfer of the spear discussed
above, stand for radically opposed meanings in different situations;
some turn out to be very unequivocal and can be used as signposts
wherever they appear. By aggregating very many diverse facts and,
through the successes and embarrassments of participation, having
them related and systematized, the fieldworker progressively improves
and expands his understanding of the social life around him. Participation also gives opportunities for what has sometimes been called social
dramatization: the technique whereby the investigator positively seeks
to create the situations where he can act out certain behaviour and see
whether his activities are understandable and acceptable to others. This
technique seems very closely equivalent to the experiment as a means
of testing or falsifying hypotheses about the cultural meanings of acts,
on the level of the individual datum, once a minimal threshold of
understanding has been passed.

As a result of fieldwork pursued in this way, the anthropologist gets
to know the significance of acts as a participant, which means that he
can translate into technical equivalents with some of the authority of a
'native speaker'. He can then couch his observations in categories and
concepts that give the greatest degree of regularity and order to his
data, because they are categories which relate directly to the actor's
own consciousness and purpose, and he can show the consistency of

meaning and valuational attitudes exemplified in the various idioms
and forms of behaviour, thereby simplifying the descriptions and
'making sense of' whole syndromes of activities.

In other words, it is as fieldworker rather than as analyst that the
anthropologist produces data in this 'translated' form. The operation of
translation is thus to a considerable degree independent of the analytical and explanatory models constructed by anthropologists.

Therefore, there should be no objection to using these data to falsify the models,
and to the extent that a model successfully depicts or explains a great
number of data of this processed, translated kind it compels belief in
its validity. The fact that the production of such data makes great
demands on the skill of the anthropologist is perhaps regrettable but
does not mean that the discipline is unscientific – every scientist knows
the importance in his own work of skill in the laboratory or in the field.
The critical requirement is that the constructs and models of the discipline are confronted with reality in the form of independently ascertained empirical data; and this operation, as I hope I have shown you,
lies at the heart of any anthropological investigation.

Perhaps this cross-cultural translation is the most striking contribution of the anthropologist. Professor Firth, when recently invited to
visit Scandinavia, offered to give a lecture on his Polynesian material
with the title 'Twins, birds and vegetables' – a puzzle even to the most
hardened anthropologist, but no mere flight of whimsy in terms of
the classifications, dichotomies and identities of Polynesian culture.
It is the anthropologist's strength that he is able to show how even the
superficially most bizarre features of a foreign culture have significance
that connects them to more mundane aspects of life and relates them to
the more familiar quirks of our own culture. It will always be a central
part of his work to find the cognitive twist that unlocks and makes
sense of the codes of an exotic culture.

The results of social anthropological research are generally given the
form of a *monograph*, which combines the presentation of a considerable
amount of descriptive material with more general theoretical analysis
and discussion. I think it is correct to say that these monographs are
often surprisingly readable, even to the non-professional. This read-
ability derives very prominently from the way in which the strange and
exotic are described in their bizarre detail and then, by the ascription
of an English equivalence or significance, transformed into meaningful and thus sensible activity. The cross-cultural translation thus also
serves us as a surprisingly effective literary technique of presentation.

What is more, the monograph has a classic unity of time and place: it is typically a synchronic study of a small, delimited community. It thus provides a picture of unity and integration. Even where our actual analysis fails to show the interdependence, this image of the culture and society as a 'whole' remains – a unity of perhaps spurious, but none the less convincing, character.

By these means, we try to collect and systematize observations that enable us to depict the reality that confronts us: the regularities of life in human communities. We regard this reality as the resultant of the behaviour of many actors, separately shaping their own acts according to their subjective view of the opportunities offered by their world and their society. But what we observe is overt behaviour and the objective consequences of this behaviour – whether sought or unsought by the actors.

Social anthropologists construct models which seek to take this into account. We feel we cannot adequately represent, much less understand, the forms of regularity except with reference to their underlying determinants, and this entails the need to map out the culture, the actor's own categories and meanings, to depict the social system.

I have tried to sketch for you the three most common kinds of model which social anthropologists make use of, whereby they depict the social order:

1 A system of jural rules, consisting of the basic ideas about interpersonal obligations and rights which are embodied in a culture. Some anthropologists would go further and claim a reality of its own for this, the 'moral community'.

2 A system of cognitive categories, especially those whereby the members of a society conceptualize and order their own social statuses and social groups.

3 An interactional system – a model that depicts the constraints on individual behaviour that arises from the behaviour of others in a social system. Such models assume some form of 'economizing' or competition or strategy on the part of actors whereby they mutually modify their behaviour in respect to the objects that are valued in their culture.

By relying mainly on the first of these forms of representation, one will tend to construct rather static models of each society as a set of rules, and one can show a remarkable consistency and integration between various features of order. Less interest centres on actual behaviour in deviance from these rules, and the timelessness of a synchronic study tends to lead to an assertion of stability for such systems. In its naive and original form, the explanation of social order was simply sought in the 'customs' of the exotic culture.

Dissatisfaction with the built-in assertion of stability has led either to a recognition that the jural rules which a culture stipulates need not be consistent, so dilemmas arise which lead to variant behaviour, or alternatively to the abstraction of order as a system of cultural categories, as a mental artifact of the actors. Such cognitive systems have *structure*, in a variety of forms, and can be depicted as stable. But, though used as a guide for behaviour, these mental patterns may not be realizable in overt mass behaviour – so these models can also be used to explain the facts of instability and degree of disorder that seem to characterize social reality. Final explanations for these models are to be found in the basic cognitive processes of the mind.

Finally, the third type of model seems to me to give the greatest scope for empirical investigation of the nature and degree of order, through attention to relative frequencies of behaviour, the determinants of this order and the social processes whereby they act. Having always been faced with the enormous task of simultaneously translating from strange and exotic cultures to give observed behaviour any meaning at all, it is only recently that social anthropologists seriously have begun exploring such more complex and sophisticated models. But it already seems clear that they enable us to analyse natural or ecological constraints in a common framework with social constraints and thus encompass a large variety of determinants in a single, analytically coherent model, and also provide a possibility for understanding not only the degree of disorder, but also *change* by means of simple cumulative feedback mechanisms in such models. Building on the skills and concepts we have accumulated so far, there is thus a reasonable hope that we are about to experience a further rapid increase in the empirical and analytical adequacy of social anthropology.

2   Models of social organization I*

Introduction

These essays are an attempt to consolidate and use generative models in social anthropology. Drawing on concepts and viewpoints which are current in anthropological literature, I delimit and construct a few simple models of this type, discuss the way they can be utilized and their relation to empirical processes in society, and illustrate their utility as applied to a few examples. The essays are essentially the text of three lectures presented under the heading 'The explanation of social forms' at the London School of Economics in the winter of 1963.

Form in social life is constituted by a series of regularities in a large body of individual items of behaviour. Much effort in social anthropology has been concentrated on the necessary step of constructing models or patterns descriptive of such forms, whereby structural features of the society are exhibited. The kind of models which I discuss here are of a different kind. They are not designed to be homologous with observed social regularities; instead they are designed so that they, by specified operations, can *generate* such regularities or forms. They should be constituted of a limited number of clearly abstracted parts, the magnitude or constellation of which can be varied, so that one model can be made to produce a number of different forms. Thus by a series of logical operations, forms can be generated; these forms may be compared to empirical forms of social systems, and where there is correspondence in formal features between the two, the empirical form may then be characterized as a particular constellation of the variables in the model.

In these respects the models which I discuss are similar to those already in use in certain fields of anthropology, notably the componential models of kinship systems (Goodenough, 1956) and Leach's

* First published by the Royal Anthropological Institute of Great Britain and Ireland, 1966.

topological models (Leach, 1961). Where I believe I differ from these, but follow the example of various other disciplines (Theory of Games, evolutionary genetics, etc.) is in adding a further, very important limitation: the logical operations whereby forms are generated should mirror actual, empirical processes which can be identified in the reality which is being analysed. This limitation is necessary to make the operations significant (cf. Neumann and Morgenstern 1944); and it makes the model-building activity subservient to the objectives of an empirical science.

Very briefly, I hold that such models can have three important uses:
1 They provide a kind of understanding and explanation which a model of form, however meticulous and adequate, can never give. To study form it may be sufficient to describe it. To explain form one · needs to discover and describe the processes that generate the form.
2 They provide the means to describe and study change in social forms as changes in the basic variables that generate the forms.
3 Finally, they facilitate comparative analysis as a methodological equivalent of experiment. Models descriptive of form merely permit one to lay out typological series and point to differences and similarities, or to specify the logically unrestricting transformations whereby one form may be converted into another. The adequacy of a generative model, on the other hand, is tested by its success or failure in generating the observed forms; it contains implicit hypotheses about 'possible' and 'impossible' systems which may be falsified by comparative data.

The level of complexity and sophistication reached in these essays is very low. However, I believe that the study of social anthropology cannot today be advanced much by sophistication and refinement of its current total stock of concepts and ideas. Rather, we should make a careful selection among them, and among concepts available in related fields, to isolate a minimal set which is logically necessary and empirically defensible. The implications of any such set should then be explored and exhausted before further complexity is added. The following is presented as a first sketch of one such set of concepts, and a preliminary exploration of some of its implications.

The analytical importance of transaction

The validity and utility of the following discussion depends on a particular view of the constitution of social phenomena. Though this view is neither unorthodox nor susceptible to serious challenge, it is important to establish it explicitly. For this purpose, one of Radcliffe-Brown's last and perhaps most authoritative statements may be cited:

> the concrete reality with which the social anthropologist is concerned in observation, description, comparison and classification, is not any sort of entity, but a process, the process of social life. The unit of investigation is the social life of some particular region of the earth during a certain period of time. The process itself consists of an immense multitude of actions and interrelations of human beings, acting as individuals or in combinations or groups. Amidst the diversity of the particular events there are discoverable regularities, so that it is possible to give statements or descriptions of certain *general features* of the social life of a selected region. A statement of such significant general features of the process of social life constitutes a description of what may be called a *form of social life*. My conception of social anthropology is as the comparative theoretical study of forms of social life amongst primitive peoples. (Radcliffe-Brown, 1952: 3–4)

The 'general features', the regularities in social life, thus have to do with the repetitive nature of acts, which we observe in our investigation of a social system. Our first descriptive characterization of our findings, then, must be one involving *frequencies*. No matter how crude our techniques for registration and counting are, our claim must be that we have discovered some non-random frequency distribution in actions. The patterns we report may most realistically be viewed as frequency distributions around a mode. My argument in the following pages follows from this, and is briefly summed up in the simple statement that our theoretical models should be designed to explain how the observable frequency patterns, or regularities, are generated.

The most simple and general model available to us is one of an aggregate of people exercising *choice* while influenced by certain constraints and incentives. In such situations, statistical regularities are produced, yet there is no absolute compulsion or mechanical necessity connecting the determining factors with the resultant patterns; the connection depends on human dispositions to evaluate and anticipate. Nor can the behaviour of any one particular person be firmly predicted – such human conditions as inattentiveness, stupidity or contrariness will, for the anthropologist's purposes, be unpredictably distributed in the population. This is also how we subjectively seem to experience our own social situation. Indeed, once one admits that what we empirically observe is not 'customs', but 'cases' of human behaviour, it seems to me that we cannot escape the concept of choice in our analysis: our central problem becomes what are the constraints and incentives that canalize choices.

The structuralist's view has been, as I have understood it, that these constraints on choices are moral: society is a moral system. This view leads to a type of analysis where regularities in the pattern of behaviour are related to a set of moral constraints and incentives which stipulate the critical features of that regularity. Thus for example the regularities summarized in a status position are specified as a series of rights and obligations which summarize *all* the regular aspects of behaviour which are associated with that status.

By this transformation, one form, in the sense of a set of regular patterns of behaviour, is translated into another, virtually congruent form, made up of moral injunctions, which are made logically prior to behaviour. The model does not depict any intervening social process between the moral injunction and the pattern. There is indeed no science of social life in this procedure, no explanation of how actual forms, much less frequency distributions in behaviour come about, beyond the axiomatic: what people do is influenced by moral injunctions.

If a concept of process is to be analytically useful, it must refer to something that governs and affects activity, something that restricts and canalizes the possible course of events. These restrictions should go beyond what can be contained in static or general kinds of limitations. Just as the description of a game of cricket is more than a description of its binding rules, so a description of a process of interaction should contain more than a listing of reciprocal obligations. The study of process must be a study of necessary or probable interdependencies which govern the *course* of events. We have recently seen how the variety of forms of domestic unit in a society can be understood by a view of family development cycles (Goody, 1958). The general lesson we may learn is that by a simple analysis of a process we can understand the variety of complex forms which it produces.

This is the kind of understanding and explanation of form which should be sought. Explanation is not achieved by a description of the patterns of regularity, no matter how meticulous and adequate, nor by replacing this description by other abstractions congruent with it, but by exhibiting what *makes* the pattern, i.e. certain processes. To study social forms, it is certainly necessary but hardly sufficient to be able to describe them. To give an explanation of social forms, it is sufficient to describe the processes that generate the form.

In the following I wish to explore the extent to which patterns of social form can be explained if we assume that they are the cumulative result of a number of separate choices and decisions made by people acting *vis-à-vis* one another. In other words, that the patterns are generated through processes of interaction and in their form reflect the constraints and incentives under which people act. I hold that this transformation from constraints and incentives to frequentative patterns of behaviour in a population is complex but has a structure of its own, and that by an understanding of it we shall be able to explain numerous features of social form. Indeed, as I interpret the above citation from Radcliffe-Brown, the processes which effect that transformation are our main field of study as social anthropologists.

As the object of systematic investigation, these processes have been sorely neglected. Even the work which has been heralded as a prototype of processual analysis – that of the development cycle in domestic groups – focuses on processes which arise not from social facts, but from the extraneous biological fact of creeping senescence.

The consequences of having overlooked generative problems are perhaps most strikingly revealed in our most-used concept of status. Introduced into the field in a pair with role, the two concepts together equip us to analyse the fundamental social process whereby binding rights and obligations are made relevant in particular social situations. Instead anthropologists chose to concentrate on the static concept of status, and the analytic possibilities of the paired concepts have only recently been explored by Goffman (1959). Goffman argues that agreement on a definition of the situation must be established and maintained to distinguish which of the participants' many statuses should form the basis for their interaction. The process of maintaining this agreement is one of skewed communication: *over*-communicating that which confirms the relevant status positions and relationships, and *under*-communicating that which is discrepant. The effect is to generate stereotyped forms of behaviour in these situations – behaviour which is not specified in the rights and obligations comprising the status, but which emerges as regular features of the *role* – because of these situationally determined requirements of over- and under-communication which he aptly calls 'impression management'.

We may distinguish two types of problems to which such views may be applied. One concerns the way in which a person completes/

consummates a successful role performance by selecting from his total repertoire those gestures and idioms which will serve his needs for 'impression management'. This is where Goffman concentrates his discussion. The other type of problem, with which we are mainly concerned in the present connection, is that of institutionalization: how a multiplicity of individual decisions under the influence of canalizing factors can have the cumulative effect of producing clear patterns and conventions. Goffman's arguments are also applicable here. The same problems of impression management arise for all incumbents of a status. The punishments and rewards of varying degrees of success will make a majority modify their performance in the direction of the optimum; and the more a certain type of behaviour is statistically associated with a status, the more it will be reinforced through serving as an idiom of identification. We may thus construct a model whereby complex and comprehensive patterns of behaviour (roles) may be generated from simpler specifications of rights (statuses), according to a set of rules (the requirements of impression management). The role thus generated should represent the optimum around which empirical behaviour may be seen to cluster.

Such viewpoints serve as a necessary part of a model for the whole transformation from factors affecting choices to empirical regularities in social life; and I shall return to them in connection with the treatment of some illustrative material. However, to generate gross forms we need to start on a more elementary level. The limitations which define each social situation are compounded of the rights and obligations of the set of statuses which is relevant in that situation: we need to understand the nature of the interconnection between the statuses which are combined in such sets[1] so as to be able to construct rules governing the combinability of statuses in a generative model. One basis for such rules may be found in the *transactional* nature of most interpersonal relations, in the reciprocity which we impose on ourselves and others. In any social relationship we are involved in a flow and counterflow of prestations, of appropriate and valued goods and services. Our own and our counterpart's ideas of appropriateness and value affect our relationship in two major ways. Firstly, they determine which statuses may serve as complementary positions in a situation, i.e. be combined in a set: only those involving commensurate prestations are relevant counterparts in a social relationship. Secondly, they affect the course of interaction in a relationship: the flow of prestations is not random over time, for each party's behaviour is modified by the presence and behaviour of the other in a progresssional sequence.

The general notion of reciprocity is of course old and familiar in anthropology; indeed, it seems to be fundamental to our view of social relationships. Though its meaning is not frequently made explicit, I should think few will quarrel with one of Leach's formulations: 'In any such system of reciprocities one must assume that, overall, both parties ... are satisfied with their bargain, and therefore that the exchange account "balances".' (Leach, 1952: 51.) Yet the analytical status of 'reciprocity' in social theory is far from clear, but is capable of being developed in several ways (see esp. Homans, 1958; Stanner, 1959). In the present context, it lies at the heart of an analytic concept of transaction: one may call transactions those sequences of interaction which are systematically governed by reciprocity.

Each and every case of interaction does not have these characteristics. It is possible to define a relationship of incorporation as an analytical opposition to a transactional relationship - one where a value optimum, probably for a restricted range of values, is sought for the *sum* of partners, and not for a single party. Such partnerships can engage as units in transactions *vis-à-vis* other persons or groups; internally, their interactions will not be systematically governed by reciprocity. Yet there are limits in most cases to the losses, or inequalities of gains, which people are willing to bear through such incorporation, and these restrictions on the constitution of relationships of incorporation will be developed and utilized below (pp. 63-75). Finally, we have all of us seen cases of what we have interpreted as altruism - a kind of fundamental negation of the transactional relationship. But transactions we have also seen, and a clear concept of transaction, leads us to a recognition of a very fundamental social process: the process which results where parties in the course of their interactions systematically try to assure that the value gained for them is greater or equal to the value lost.

Put this way, one may see that transactions have a structure which permits analysis by means of a strategic model, as a game of strategy. They consist of a sequence of reciprocal prestations, which represent successive moves in the game. There must be a ledger kept of value gained and lost; and each successive action or move affects that ledger, changes the strategic situation, and thus canalizes subsequent choices. Many possible courses of action are ruled out because they are patently unsatisfactory, i.e. an actor must expect that value lost be greater than value gained. In such a model the incentives and constraints on choice are effective through the way they determine what can be gained and lost; and each actor's social adjustment to the other party in the transaction is depicted in terms of alter's possible moves, and how they in turn affect ego's value gains. The structure depicted in this model is a successional one over time - in other words, it is a model of process. The importance of process and the analysis of choice has been given increased recognition in anthropological writings, particularly through Firth's important formulation of the distinction between structure and organization (Firth, 1954). I have elsewhere used some of the formal apparatus of the Theory of Games to analyse political choice (Barth, 1959b). The particular formalism of the Theory of Games is not as important for anthropological purposes as is the theory's fundamental character as a generative model. It can serve as a prototype for a processual model of interaction; and in concentrating on *transaction* as the analytic isolate in the field of social organization, I am emulating what I regard as the most crucial aspect of the theory for our purposes. What is useful in this view of transactions is that it gives us a logically consistent model of an observable social process. It is a model whereby one may *generate* forms according to the rules of strategy, given the parameters of value; and these forms generated by the model may then be compared to the empirical patterns which one has observed. The logical analysis can be rigorously separated from the cumulative presentation of data; and the adequacy of such a model can in each case be judged by the degree of fit between the patterns which are logically generated and the patterns which are observed. We are not committed by any prejudged 'view of society' - the adequacy of the transactional model for any and every particular relationship is continually on trial. And since the model claims to depict actual empirical processes, all its parts and its operations - its exchanges, its value parameters, etc. - may be questioned and checked.

A measure of the analytic importance of such a concept of transaction is the fact that it is implicit in our whole idea of *values*. It is meaningless to say that something has value unless people in real life seek it, prefer it to something of less value, in other words maximize value. This can only be true if they usually act strategically with respect to it, that is, make it the object of transactions between themselves and others.

I should emphasize that this does not imply a claim for explanatory adequacy for *all* aspects of *all* behaviour. No doubt man has a psychological constitution which affects the way he behaves. But as a social anthropologist I am concerned with exploring the effects of social determinants on human behaviour, and these vary with reference to such factors as value and strategy. Furthermore, in real life, men also enjoy and consume value, and act with indifference to it. What I am suggesting is that transactions are of particular analytical importance because (a) where systems of evaluation (values) are maintained, transactions must be a predominant form of interaction; (b) in them the relative evaluations in a culture are revealed; and (c) they are a basic social process by means of which we can explain how a variety of social forms are generated from a much simpler set and distribution of basic values.

The first two of these themes will be explored further in the next chapter; the third I shall now seek to illustrate. The major elements of the generative model called for in such an illustration have been presented. Transactional behaviour takes place with reference to a set of values which serve as generalized incentives and constraints on choice; it also takes place with reference to a pre-established matrix of statuses, seen as a distribution of values on positions in the form of minimal clusters of jurally binding rights. From this point, through the formation of status sets, and the implications and restrictions of transactional relations and impression management within these sets, I propose to generate gross forms of social behaviour which correspond to empirically observable patterns. The generative sequence will in this case be linear. In the second chapter I shall take up the question of feedback and change of values and statuses. The material which I use for this illustration comes from a study in progress of winter herring fisheries.[2] The analysis of a fishing vessel at sea offers certain advantages as an illustration: the social system is small and clearly separable, the activity is highly stereotyped, and each person occupies a single status of overwhelmingly predominant relevance to the interaction that takes place on board.

First, one needs to specify some features of the ecologic situation: that combination of relevant environment and technique which sets the scene for behaviour. The herring arrives on the coast of Norway in large and smaller shoals towards late winter; time and specific locality are unpredictable, as are the various periods when the herring, having arrived on the spawning grounds, rises up towards the surface where it may be caught. Of the possible techniques for catching we are concerned with the use of purse seine. This requires a large vessel of 100–140 feet, two small boats of 25–35 feet from which the seine is cast, and a small motorboat from which the precise occurrence of the herring is located and the casting of the net directed. The purse seine containing trapped herring is then slowly hauled in, and the fish loaded into the mother vessel. If the operation is successful, a catch worth £5,000 can be made. On the other hand, a precious hour may be wasted hauling in an empty net, and there is always a risk of total loss of net, valued at *c.* £6,000.

The statuses involved in these operations are defined by contract: a *skipper* with right of command on the vessel, including the direction of the course and the decision to lower the net-casting boats, a *netboss* who, once the boats have been lowered, has the right to command and direct the casting and drawing from his small motor launch, and finally two groups each of six *fishermen* who perform the manual work. Another five to seven men are engaged in various duties on the main vessel and need not concern us here.

The three types of statuses described make up a set in terms of division of labour and authority. The various rights are distributed in such a way as to make possible a series of transactions over complementary prestations. These basic transactional relations have the following characteristics, which spring from the minimal status set:

the *fishermen*: provide labour for those with a right to exercise authority; there is no contractual limitation on hours of work, or the types of tasks to which they can be put, and their subordination is in this sense absolute. In return for the season's work each receives one share of the gross catch;

the *skipper*: makes decisions and takes full responsibility for the vessel and crew; he seeks out the places where the herring may be, and brings the means of catching to the scene of operations, in return for 2 to 3 times the share of a fisherman;

the *netboss*: brings the expertise of 'feeling' the herring and the promise of securing and increasing the gross catch. He directs and takes responsibility for the whole casting operation. In return, his share of the catch is 2 to 5 times that of a fisherman.

The next step in the transformation from this simple complementary distribution of rights to the patterns of behaviour it generates, is the strategic analysis of transactions. What effective limitations on each party's choice are implicit in this structure?

Firstly, as defined by their rights, the relation between fisherman and skipper is one of comprehensive subordination and command. But two considerations militate against unbridled exercise of imperative authority on the part of the skipper. The work prestations required from the fishermen are highly varied and frequently demand alertness, rapidity, and high co-ordination, i.e. they require 'co-operation' from all. This means that the skipper must convert the contractually imposed submission to a voluntary and spontaneous one, by exercising authority only to the extent that this is approved and accepted, and the prestations demanded are proportionate to the rewards. Secondly, the contract is for a single season (*c*. 2 months) and the quality of the crew for the next season will vary in accordance with the skipper's reputation. Since the quality of the crew is an important factor in determining success measured in catch, and thereby the skipper's profits, the relation between skipper and crew is converted into a continual bargaining relation.

As for the skipper and the netboss, their relation is complementary in that they divide authority and responsibility. The netboss relieves the skipper of the chancy decision of when and where to cast, thereby protecting the impression of infallibility which is so important to the skipper's performance. On the other hand, he is a challenge to the authority of the skipper by being in supreme command during casting.

I shall concentrate on the preliminary, and temporally quite predominant, phase of searching for herring with the whole crew concentrated on the main vessel. This situation has technical/ecological characteristics which in an important way affect the strategy of the actors – most importantly the dramatic unity of time and place. Having transformed his relationship of command over the fishermen into a voluntary relationship of leadership and acceptance, the skipper can no longer maintain the maritime convention of the bridge as a sacred and off-bounds area for the fishermen. Indeed, most of the fishermen congregate there, being idle but continuously alert in anticipation of finding the herring at any moment, without prewarning. They search the horizon, use the binoculars, listen to the radio, and watch the echo and asdic, if either is functioning; they converse quietly with each other, and savour the anticipation and thrill of stalking the herring as a wild, valuable and elusive prey. All parties on the bridge, then, interact with reference to their status on board; there is a constant flow of prestations in the sense that messages are exchanged, rights are exercised, and performances evaluated – yet there is no consummation of transactions. The strategic analysis of this behaviour in terms of a model of transactions might seem problematical, since the nature of the bargaining situation between the parties is so problematical. The model would seem to be more relevant e.g. to the analysis of a business exchange, where stipulated amounts of valued goods pass between the parties and there is a ledger of flow and counterflow until the transaction is completed, as shown by a balance in the value ledger.

The bridge differs from this, but is like much of social life, not in that continual evaluations and a ledger are absent – for there is plentiful evidence here and elsewhere that such ledgers are kept – but in that there is no transfer of tangible value. The whole interaction depends on and maintains relations of trust; the prestations on the bridge are in a sense *token* prestations. This must be so because in contrast to the business transaction, the transaction between fisherman, skipper and netboss is not about stipulated amounts of value, but about the *chances* of catch in return for willingness, effort, and competence. What is being offered and evaluated in this phase is expertise, qualities of leadership, and reliability, as revealed by actions and reactions; i.e. promises that will eventually lead to consummated transactions, through the further phases of the fishing operations.

It is because of this that the third and final stage of the transformation – that involving Goffman's 'impression management' – is of such importance for this example. The bargaining on the bridge is about token prestation, i.e. impressions, and thus involves very marked features of over- and under-communication. Consequently, this final step is crucial for generating the marked patterns of highly stereotyped behaviour which were observed on the bridge.

These patterns may be briefly summarized and explained as follows: the *skipper* exhibits behaviour suggesting confidence, knowledge, and experience. He gives very few clues as to what he is thinking, communicates little, in contrast to the others on the bridge, and never elicits comments, evaluations, or advice from any other person. The most important aspects of the role seem to be the emphasis on careful rationality and finality of decision. Through this pattern he can assert leadership without referring to positional authority; he claims rationality without making the basis and logic of his decision available for critical scrutiny. The only positional privilege he utilizes is the ban on a subordinate initiating an argument.

The *netboss* acts out a very different role: he is spontaneous, argues and jokes, and gives off evidence of inspired guesswork, flair, and subtle sensing. He is recognized, and lives up to his reputation, as being unafraid of the consequences of his actions; he can brag about gambling and drinking bouts. All these dispositions and talents are regarded as qualifications for his skill in sensing the herring and daring to cast at the critical momentary optimum. At the same time his joking behaviour is a constant denial of any claim to authority on the bridge in challenge of the skipper and is in this respect in marked contrast to the institutionalized pattern of gross and continual cursing and assertion of authority on his part during the net-casting operation. Finally, the latent character of his functions, and his separation from the skipper, are emphasized by his relatively more frequent absence from the bridge than the other crew members. This last point would also lead one to expect, in terms of the generative model, a greater variability in the role of netbosses than that of skippers.

The *fishermen*, finally, exhibit a remarkable pattern of persistence and involvement by being largely present on the bridge during all idle hours – in one case during 72 hours of search a number of them were continually wakeful and present, apart from hurried meals. This pattern can only be explained in terms of *their* transactional obligation, involving prestations of willingness or eagerness and constant readiness to work, as well as their interest in observing, evaluating, and controlling the dispositions of the skipper.

The regularities of behaviour generated by this model could also be, perhaps more conventionally, described as specifications of the three statuses; the various features could be enumerated and with some degree of legitimacy identified as expectations on the part of participants in the activities, and so in a sense as obligations incumbent on those occupying the statuses. This alternative way of looking at the material seems to me less satisfactory on two important counts.

Firstly, it requires a more complex and detailed listing of arbitrary, unconnected determinants of observed behaviour, each with a differing degree of validity and force. This results from the absence of explanatory hypotheses, which would have made possible an ordering of some facts as derivative of others, and the absence of a generative sequence, which can be designed to produce any combination of frequentative patterns. Secondly, it is developmentally misleading. I would claim that we can observe the generative primacy of some factors, and the social processes of institutionalization; particularly, we can see how simple contracts about a few basic rights come first, and role stereotypes emerge afterwards.

Thus in the development of the netboss, there is evidence that his scope was more limited, and his role-play less marked a generation ago, at a technological stage when the visible signs of herring were gulls swooping and whales blowing around an area of sea, and the underwater shoal of herring was felt by means of a lead weight on a string, against which the packed herring struck. At that time, being netboss was a specialized talent and skill in one or several crew members, and lacked the *prima donna* character depicted above. With increased capital investment, echo and asdic equipment, the present netboss role emerged as a kind of logical opposite to the skipper – two roles which could formerly be combined. On the other hand, very recent technological developments have now made it possible to cast and haul the purse seine directly from a specially equipped main vessel, with all phases of the catch directed from the bridge; and it will be possible to follow the doubtless major shifts in role patterns that will result from this change in the strategic situation.

A generative model thus seems truer to life, and much more comprehensive in the variety of facts which it systematizes and relates. Nor is its particular appeal limited to the quasi-industrial situation on board a fishing vessel. Bateson experimented with such models in his analysis of male bravado among the Iatmul (Bateson, 1958) and I think one may readily see how even in the particular form exemplified here the analysis may be used to explain the form of much of the behaviour which we more or less meticulously describe in our ethnographies, from the vision quest among the Plateau Indians to the role of the leopard-skin chief among the Nuer.

Let me pursue one more pattern of behaviour which is generated from the particular factors which I have outlined about the herring fishing crew on the bridge. This concerns the decision-making process, where strong biases on choice are generated which result in marked patterns of movement for the fishing fleet as a whole.

The decision on where to search for herring is of course the first, and in that sense most vital, decision affecting the chances of making a catch. It may be taken on the basis of various kinds of relevant information: disregarding the modifying conditions of sea and wind, these are: radio reports and forecasts on herring from two marine biology research vessels; radio telephone conversations between, or calls for assistance in net-hauling from, other fishing vessels; the vessel's own asdic; and finally, binoculars, whereby one may follow the movements of other close vessels, who presumably have information other than what one has oneself. There are two points to remember about this information: all of it is public on the bridge; and taken together, it is still very incomplete and fragmentary as the basis for a rational decision.

The skipper's dilemma is continual: the vessel has to go or be some-where always, so the decision can never be ignored or postponed. Success or failure depends on it: by being where the herring appears, one has a good chance of full catch, whereas with the size and be-haviour of shoals as they have been over the last years, latecomers to the casting grounds get nothing.

The pattern of movement of vessels on the fishing banks is so ex-treme that it cannot fail to strike an observer immediately: the several hundred vessels of the fleet constantly tend to congregate in small areas of the immense, and potentially bountiful, expanse of sea; most attention is concentrated on discovering the movements of *other ves-sels*, and most time is spent chasing other vessels to such unplanned and fruitless rendezvous.

The foregoing sketch of different effective constraints and incentives on choice explain how such a pattern is generated. It is for the skipper to take the decision of choosing the vessel's course; but he does so in the context of important transactionally determined constraints. There can be no doubt that a vessel's chance of finding herring is greater if it strikes out on its own than if it follows other vessels. Thus the purely technical and economic considerations should favour such a course. But if a skipper, without special information to justify the move, decides to go elsewhere than where other vessels go, he demands more trust in his transaction with the crew. They are asked to respect his judgement, as opposed to that of the other skippers; they are thus asked to make greater prestations of submission than they would other-wise have had to. The skipper also risks more by not joining the cluster: if a few vessels among many make a catch, the crew and the netboss can claim that it might have been them, had the skipper only given them the chance. If the vessel on the other hand follows the rest, they are no worse off than most, and the onus of failure does not fall on the skipper.

Secondly, the absence of a catch matters less, so long as other ves-sels *also* fail – the measure of a skipper's competence and success is not absolute, but relative to the catch of other vessels. The factor affecting the skipper's ability to recruit a good crew next season is his position in the catch statistics, not the gross amount.

These patterns are self-confirming: good skippers with good and stable crews will have greater freedom of choice because greater pre-stations of trust can be demanded; the same boats and skippers will consistently top the lists of resultant catch, and they will be regarded as élite boats, who most often find the herring and whom it is an advantage to follow. Being first, they will tend to get best results, and so on. Thus from the same fairly simple factors of the technical and ecologic situation, and a basic distribution of rights on elementary statuses, a variety of behaviour patterns may be explained. On the vessels, by analysing the implications of these factors on transactions and impression management, a series of markedly stereotyped, detailed roles may be generated. Similarly, between the vessels of the total fleet grotesquely unadaptive patterns of movement and congregation can be shown to result. To the extent that these patterns fit observed regularities of behaviour, these latter may be said to be explained by the processes depicted in the model; to the extent they do not fit, the models may be redesigned in an attempt to discover and depict other relevant processes.

I have elaborated this illustration so as to exhibit the kinds of steps which are necessary and possible in an analysis based on a concept of transaction as social process. The crucial points I have wished to emphasize are:

Where we construct a model of an actual social process, it becomes possible to describe complex empirical forms in terms of relatively few specifications of variables in this model.

Such a description of process *explains* forms in a way which cannot be achieved by a meticulous enumeration and comparison of the formal features of a body of data.

The concept of transaction, by helping us to isolate a basic social process, is a simple but powerful tool when applied systematically. It depicts the strategic limitations imposed on persons who engage in social activity with a view to obtaining something of value; simultaneously it shows the compounded effects which multiple independent actors, each seeking to pursue the transactionally optimal course of behaviour, have on each other, and thereby the gross frequentative patterns of behaviour which will tend to emerge in such situations. As I have tried to indicate by occasional references, I do not claim any great originality for any of the concepts or ideas I have used here – I will, however, argue that the analytic power of this particular combination of concepts, consistently pursued, is very great and has been overlooked in anthropology. In the next two essays, I seek to explore further implications and possibilities inherent in these viewpoints.

3   Models of social organization II

Processes of integration in culture

It has become common in anthropology to claim integration of culture
as axiomatic, and frequently to build it into definitions of culture in
such a way as to make it incapable of empirical investigation (e.g.
'the subject of our enquiry is *standardized behaviour patterns*; their
integrated totality is culture', Nadel, 1951: 29). I propose in the
following to regard the integration of culture as questionable and a
matter of degree, and to pose empirical questions as to how these
varying degrees of integration are produced and maintained. By integration I shall simply mean the extent to which phenomena constitute
a system, show determinacy and consistency in relation to each other.

The empirical welter of 'standardized behaviour patterns' clearly
exhibits various logically independent kinds of consistency or integration. For our purposes importance attaches to the nature and degree of
integration between *values*, since these have been represented as the
determinants from which social forms (or 'standardized behaviour
patterns') may be generated. The parts of culture between which I
seek integrating processes are therefore values. The view that a culture
is, on a certain level of analysis, constituted of a basic set of values
seems to be generally accepted. Indeed, this can be made a crucial
level of analysis, as suggested by Bateson's sophisticated discussion of
codification and evaluation as aspects of the same central phenomena
(Ruesch and Bateson, 1951: 176). As I shall be concerned with the
aspects of comparability rather than differentiation, I shall concentrate on evaluation. I shall not attempt to introduce or adopt any
special rigour in the terminology – though its absence in anthropological discussion is at times confusing – but will use the terms more
or less idiomatically as they seem to be used in the current literature.
Speaking of values, I shall be concerned with people's principles and
scales of evaluation, as well as with such abstracted amounts or ratings
of preference which appear to be relatively stable over time.

The problem as I see it is to understand how any degree of systematization and consistency is established and maintained between the different values that coexist in a culture. I hold that these values are empirical facts which may be discovered – they are not an analyst's constructs, but views held by the actors themselves. They are views about significance, worthwhileness, preferences in/for things and actions. I have represented them as being initial to items and sequences of behaviour – they are the criteria by reference to which alternative actions are evaluated, and on the basis of which choice is exercised. Yet there are no grounds for claiming them to be objectively correct, natural or true; they are canons of judgement which people impose on things and actions. If each such view or canon is arbitrary and manmade, what are the processes whereby they are systematically related to each other, become interconnected and integrated?

The integration of culture is frequently represented as one of logical or psychological consistency. This would imply a process of contemplation or introspection through which disparate values are compared and revised in the direction of consistency. There can be little doubt that some such processes do take place in the human mind; but they are only to a slight degree available for observation by a social anthropologist; nor do they seem to explain the patent *in*consistencies in various respects which characterize the views or values of many people.

Alternatively, the 'functional' view of cultural integration has been explored by anthropologists. It seems to lead by logical inevitability to a Malinowskian theory of need fulfilment, and to be highly problematical.

Instead, I feel we should look closely for the social activities which may effect comparison and revision of the values held by people; and for this purpose I wish to pursue the implications of transaction as a process. I will argue that in the transaction we can observe and study a basic process which creates consistency between the different standards of evaluation in a culture.

This effect is implicit in the basic features of a transaction. It is constituted by a basic flow of prestations between two or more actors; in its most elementary form 'A' offers prestations 'x' and 'B' reciprocates with prestations 'y', thus $A^x \rightleftarrows_y B$. Furthermore, according to the definition (pp. 38-9) each party consistently tries to assure that the value gained is greater than the value lost. This defines two thresholds: for A, $x \leqq y$, for B, $x \geqq y$.

The offer or performance of such a transaction has two aspects which concern us here. Firstly, prestations 'x' and 'y' are made transitive to each other, in the sense that they must be compared and made commensurate and interchangeable both by 'A' and 'B'. This means that the values of 'x' and 'y' must be compared. If their significance and worthwhileness cannot be judged by the same canons, some over-arching value principle between those disparate canons must be constructed. This constitutes a step in creating consistency of values.

Secondly, through offering, perhaps bargaining over, and consummating a transaction, 'A' and 'B' (and those who may constitute their audience) are in a position to compare their respective judgements of value. This leads us initially to the question of how agreement over a transaction can be reached between the parties. There would seem to be three kinds of bases on which parties may agree on an exchange. Either they have different views which lead to differing evaluations of the prestations, so that both can profit. Secondly, one party may hold faulty information, or otherwise be disappointed in his expectations, i.e. he may be cheated by the other. Thirdly, and in institutionalized transactions most characteristically, the parties may differ with respect to their particular circumstances, i.e. the two have situationally or temporally specific and differing 'needs'. I feel it is necessary to distinguish a person's continually shifting profile of preferences and appetites from a profile of stable judgements of value to which people also seem to subscribe. These more stable values, by which different situations and longer-range strategies may be compared, are more basic to an explanation of social form. Indeed, the situationally unstable indices of preference may be derivable from the stable values, and the employment of a concept of 'needs' avoided, if one analyses each actor's situation more fully. Thus a certain prestation, in goods or services, may be for 'A' – but not for 'B' – a necessary condition for another, more worthwhile or valued state. The total value gained by 'A' is thus augmented in the situation, and both 'A' and 'B' can obtain a net gain from the transaction. Whatever the basis for the transaction may be, through it the parties receive information indicative of each other's principles and scales of evaluation. Through repeated transactions I would argue that these aspects are reinforced, and that the values applying to those prestations which flow between parties become systematized and shared. They become systematized because when, and only when, we are faced with the repeated necessity of choice, are we forced to resolve dilemmas and make some kind of comparison between, and evaluation of, the alternatives with which we are presented. They become shared, or institutionalized, because in groping for a solution to the dilemmas, we prefer to use other people's experience as our guide rather than risk the errors implied in a trial-and-error procedure. Thus we adopt their principles of evaluation, and collectively grope towards a consistency of values.

This argument does not explain how over-arching, more general principles of evaluation are constructed, i.e. it cannot predict the particular form which valuational consistency will take. But it does make a step towards understanding which areas of a culture will exhibit greater consistency, and towards isolating the social process which is operative in effecting cultural integration.

As a process generating consistency in values, social transactions would seem to be more effective and compelling than any contemplative need for logical or conceptual consistency in the minds of primitive philosophers. Indeed, one might claim that it is no coincidence that Socrates formed his contemplations as a dialogue – a quasi-transaction, a bargaining over messages – or that our own philosophical colleagues come together in seminars and debates to explore which views are 'better'. On this background, one may also rephrase and readily accept Parsons' perceptive point that the accumulation of a single body of logically consistent science only began when scientific viewpoints became the object of transactions between specialists, and accumulated gains in merit could be converted into university chairs (Parsons, 1952: 343). Similar arguments may be applied to classical cases of value inconsistencies like the American Negro dilemma, where the effects both of an increased variety of cross-racial transactions and of public debate in precipitating a crisis have been demonstrated (e.g. Myrdal, 1958).

In constructing this model of the process whereby the integration of values is effected, I have started out with as few assumptions as possible: I have envisaged an hypothetical, initial situation of an unordered set of arbitrary, disparate values. They were regarded as arbitrary because they are man-made. They were regarded as disparate because there is no evidence that in real life they need be derived deductively from an initial set of assumptions, themselves consistent, but rather that they are separately designed to compare the relative worthwhileness of specific objects and actions. The logical effects of processes of social transactions on such a minimally integrated set of values would seem to be clear. Values become progressively systematized as they are used to mediate the comparisons of prestations in transactions: over-arching canons or principles of evaluation are necessary for persons engaged in such transactions. Secondly, values become progressively shared by being made known through transactions: the principles of evaluation, and their uses, become public and serve as guides in the choices of others. The process of transaction thus simultaneously generates trends towards integration and institutionalization. Finally, in an on-going system, where patterns of behaviour are generated from a set of shared values, the resolution of individual dilemmas of choice by the construction of over-arching principles of evaluation will have a feedback effect on the shared values. The shared values will be modified and 'corrected' in the direction of greater consistency and integration, and other patterns of choice and behaviour will in turn be generated.

This view of a feedback effect absolves us from the difficulties inherent in the provisional, linear form of the model used in the first chapter, where social forms were generated from values. These problems are faced in their most comprehensive form in Arensberg's suggestive discussion of the logical and empirical priorities of social arrangements, culture patterns, values, and actions (Arensberg, 1957, particularly pp. 102-5). Clearly, every instance of transaction takes place in a matrix of values and statuses, the latter being a basic social arrangement, a distribution of values; and the constraints and incentives on choices are determined by such basic frameworks. But not only do the cumulated resultant choices produce patterns which again affect and modify choice; as I have sought to develop in the argument above, instances of transaction affect in turn both the canons and distribution of values, and in part compel the 'correction' of these values. Thus actions can have a feedback effect which make them logically on a par, and in a certain sense developmentally prior to, values and social arrangements.

Before I take up this thread of the argument, and relate it more specifically to the analysis of anthropological material, there is one further feedback effect which should be emphasized. Through transactions, evaluations are not only 'corrected' with reference to consistency and sharing; they will also be modified in the direction of consistency in terms of natural and external criteria, i.e. they become less arbitrary. This will result because through being offered in transactions, prestations are also made subject to the cost-demand-price mechanisms of the market. Regardless of our initial evaluations – if something becomes dirt cheap, we may start treating it as dirt; in other words, we tend to revise our evaluations. I am not suggesting an identity of value and market price, but merely an effect of market price on value. Availability, production costs, and alternative sources will affect the value which can be ascribed to one's prestations in a transaction. Only by being hedged in by taboos, i.e. through comprehensive controls on production and exchange, can entirely arbitrary evaluations of goods be maintained in the face of such pressures.

I understand this view of transactions and values to provide the basis for Stanner's important analysis of cargo cults (Stanner, 1958), and much of the preceding groundwork of discussion is implicit in the way he develops it. Through his analysis, cargo cults provide a test case for major aspects of this view of transactions. Briefly, he argues that the cults are human offers of mystical transactions with the spirits over a precious good. Further, that the native valuation of cargo is 'factitious' – not because it is man-made, but because it is inordinate. Finally, he suggests that the scale of destruction during the cargo movement may be equated with the scale of loss which would be endured if cargo were present, and thus expresses the 'value which the Melanesians might try to give to cargo were it theirs, though they would soon discover that to do so would make for chaos in their transactional life' (ibid., p. 3). Thus, because the transaction fails to be consummated in a cargo cult, the evaluation of cargo need not be adjusted. Cargo and other prestations are in fact not made commensurate and exchangeable, and the factitious evaluation of cargo can persist; the cult is not integrated with other parts of the culture. Thus this test case would seem to vindicate the view of transactions as the process whereby the integration of values is effected.

A positive case of how transactions affect and modify values might be brought in, whereby the types of interconnections which I am discussing are made concrete. This case illustrates both the developmental primacy of action over institutionalized value, and the effects which the social fact of pattern of choice by others will have on an individual's choice. The material I use, on men's house feasting and political leadership among Swat Pathans, has been published elsewhere (Barth, 1959a) in a fuller context.

In the traditional pattern of organization in Swat, chiefs maintain positions of leadership through hospitality in their men's houses, expending wealth in rice, etc., in return for political prestations of submission from followers, who consume the rice. The followers thus obtained are used to protect and preferably expand the landed estate of the chief, from which the wealth in rice derives, in a circle of conversion. The values and strategic circumstances underlying this institutional complex have been described: a high value on autonomy, might, wealth, and hospitality in a situation of anarchic rivalry between chiefs, who compete for clients, will generate this and a number of other characteristic patterns of choice.

In a situation without alternative market outlets for rice, there was indeed no alternative course whereby any separate one or several of these values could be effectively maximized. Since the initial pacification of the lower Swat valley in 1895, and particularly since the emergence of a centralized native state in the rest of the valley, and the construction of a road network in the nineteen-twenties, a real alternative has been present, involving the transport and sale of rice in the grain markets of Peshawar, one hundred miles distant. This offer of a new kind of transaction of perishable for imperishable wealth presents the individual chief with a dilemma of choice, demanding over-arching principles of evaluation of hospitality, might and wealth relative to each other. Simultaneously, the native ruler offers some degree of security of title to land for a chief in return for a reduction in his autonomy.

A few chiefs started acting in deviation from the old pattern as early as the late nineteen-thirties; they gained greatly in wealth but lost their political following by discontinuing their men's house feasting; they lost their autonomy through having to rely on the ruler and his power for the protection of their estate; however, he tended to use them in delegated positions of administrative prominence, so few suffered a visible loss in might.

During my fieldwork in 1954, evaluations of the gains and losses implied by the 'new' pattern were highly varying and discrepant; but its increased frequency was having a marked feedback effect. The cumulative advantages of commercialization as measured in wealth were becoming increasingly marked, and wealth itself progressively more highly valued. Secondly, strategic factors were changing; those pursuing the traditional pattern felt increasingly under pressure. The use of force was controlled and punished with increasing rigour by the ruler, so the effectiveness of a large following for expansive and even defensive purposes was declining. Thirdly, the autonomous influential chiefs, not the wealthy ones, constituted a challenge to the ruler. As their numbers decrease the pressure on them can be increased. As a result, the evaluation of hospitality by clients declines: the costs of receiving hospitality, implied by the recipient's political commitment, are increasingly onerous. A brief revisit to Swat in 1960 revealed a predominant change in the main valley, with men's houses serving mainly as places for the demonstration of wealth towards co-members of the wealthy élite, and clientship disappearing as a vital relationship. Thus changes in the opportunities for conversion of value from one form to another compel changes in the principles of evaluation, once new choices begin to be made; while changing frequencies of choice are accompanied by changes in the strategic situation which may accelerate (or in other cases inhibit) further change.

To explore the empirical correlates of differing frequencies of transaction on value integration, one may turn to the literature on market spheres (Firth, 1939; Bohannan and Dalton, 1962). In the study of primitive economics one is familiar with sectors or spheres of exchange, separated by boundaries which inhibit exchange transactions in various ways. The goods and services within a sphere may be freely exchanged for each other, but the conversion of valuables in one sphere into those of another are made infrequent, difficult, or impossible through various restrictions on such transactions. This failure of transactions to take place across the boundaries should correlate with a low degree of comparability of goods between spheres; value integration should prove to be greater within than between spheres.

We may adopt this view not only on what we conventionally regard as 'economic' exchanges, but look at all the prestations that circulate in a society in terms of what are their appropriate reciprocals, and thus observe the resultant patterns by which value in its different forms flows. Just as yams and *kula* objects in the Trobriands belong in different market spheres and thus flow in different circuits, so one might say in our society that political prestations, though they imply reciprocity, belong to a different sphere from that of sex, or from that in which money circulates, and cannot legitimately be reciprocated for in such forms of value. Nor are they readily made commensurate to one another: the value of a wife's fidelity in a suit for damages, or the price of a noble title, are magnitudes about which little agreement seems to prevail. Thus the goods that are valued in a culture are not thereby *ipso facto* made comparable and commensurate to one another. Only in so far as they are used as reciprocal prestations in transaction are the evaluations connected and integrated.

This may seem to imply a chicken-and-egg kind of argument: do transactions fail to take place where values do not make goods comparable, or is it the failure of transactions which explains the lack of consistency in values? I should like to argue for the latter, committing myself to a view of transactions as a significant integrative process in culture, and suggest that attention to the role of entrepreneurs can give insight into the process.

The relevant characteristics of an entrepreneur are that he is involved in the management of an undertaking, he is an innovator, and he seeks profit (cf. Belshaw, 1955; Barth, 1963). Since he is recognized as seeking profit, we are assured that he will systematically try to maximize value – i.e., all his relations as an entrepreneur will be transactional. The combination of management and innovation implies that he is involved in multiple transactions and that he initiates new activities. This must mean that he engages himself and others in interchanges of some goods and services which were previously unconnected as reciprocals in transactions. In other words, innovation for an entrepreneur must involve the initiation of transactions which make commensurable some forms of value which were previously not directly connected. Entrepreneurial activity thus tends to make a bridge between what before was separated.

The entrepreneur seeks profit. The big potentialities for profit lie where the disparity of evaluation between two or more kinds of goods are greatest, and where this disparity has been maintained because there are no bridging transactions. Such disparities can persist where the goods in question belong to different spheres, and are separated by barriers to the conversion of values – barriers of cost imposed on such conversions through available modes of trade and production, or sanctions of shame or punishment. The successful entrepreneur bridges this barrier by designing a new type of transaction, one which circumvents or otherwise reduces the costs of the conversion and thus makes it possible to exploit the disparity of value to make profit. Such a bridge will effect a new pattern of flow of value, and through market mechanisms should lead to a progressive adjustment and 'correction' of evaluations. An element of consistency in evaluations which was previously absent will be established through this process, and the side effects of entrepreneurial activity should thus be to increase integration. Cultural integration will result progressively from repeated transactions effecting a flow of value between points specifically sought out by entrepreneurs because of the absence of value consistency.

The way in which entrepreneurs make available and spread new styles in design, or fashions in clothes, is a straightforward example of this process. The cases in which the entrepreneur through his activity brings out real value dilemmas and forces a revaluation and decision on a population, are more complex and far-reaching in their consequences, and therefore also more interesting. The current development of modern trawling in Northern Norway may serve as an example. In a region of periodic hidden unemployment and occasional labour for low wage, entrepreneurs have been mobilizing labour for the new style of highly capitalized fishing by offering a new kind of transaction: quasi-industrial employment on an essentially all-year basis for a moderate wage.

The offer was immediately accepted as attractive by local farmer-fishermen, and there are waiting lists of potential crews for new vessels. Yet labour relations on the trawlers are unsatisfactory and there have been cases of whole crews leaving the vessel on its arrival in harbour – only to be replaced by a new crew from the waiting list. The new contract in fact brings out value dilemmas previously undiscovered because they were not the object of transaction and choice: what is a fair wage for fishing, what are monetary equivalents of differences in expertise, what is the value of free time, of autonomy, of a regular home life? These are magnitudes which people conceptualize and compare only when they need to treat them as quantities on a balance sheet of gains and losses in a transaction. Nobody sits down and speculates on the relative value of being regularly with his wife and of increasing his material standard of living until this is a real dilemma of imminent choice; and when this happens people's initial judgement of relative value may be wrong, in the sense of not satisfying them in the long run. Their initial evaluations are adjusted and changed through a period of bargaining, trial and conflict over the terms of the transaction, and the institutionalization of its form is accompanied by the development of new, and more consistent, evaluations encompassing and integrating a larger field of the culture.

The process whereby this institutionalization takes place is badly in need of study. I would suggest that one important characteristic, which significantly determines its direction, is a tendency generated by the strategic situation of bargaining whereby entrepreneurs are able to present 'package deals' which greatly reduce the field of choice for a population.

To indicate more fully the kinds of questions that might be taken up in such analysis, I should like to present an example from Lappish culture in Northern Norway, using the entrepreneurial concept in its most extended sense, to analyse a political enterprise which affects and changes the basic values and very cultural identity of a population.

I base this directly on the material and highly original analysis presented by Eidheim (in Barth, ed. 1969).

In inner Finnmark in North Norway there lives a Lappish-speaking population, culturally diverse but categorically distinguished from Norwegians. They have tended to be economically impoverished and politically unorganized; through centuries of contact they have accepted cultural loans and accumulated a host of discrepant values. Shame over membership of an underprivileged minority is mingled with strong personal attachment to ethnic identity; a high evaluation of comfort, prosperity and 'the new times' coexists with fear and rejection of urban ways and commitment to traditional values.

In this setting, there emerged after the war a labour politician whose platform was to bring the welfare state to the area. As an enterprise, this gave him profits in the form of political power, social recognition, and economic sustenance; to obtain these, his task was to organize the population and obtain their votes in local elections. The 'welfare state' platform was well suited for this: schools, subsidies and loans for development, and other benefits, all highly valued by the local population, could be provided by the state once requests in the proper bureaucratic form were forthcoming. A picture of Finnmark as the underprivileged periphery of a nation state served as the entrepreneur's charter, both in relation to voters and to the centre.

But this charter threatened Lappish identity and other values equally held in the population. A contrary current can be noticed which became particularly pronounced in the very community where the same politician was active. Pan-Lappish meetings were held, respect for the Lappish language was demanded. A liberal politician, head of the school board and with an expertise on bilingualism in elementary schools (cultivated through studies of education in Wales, and on American Indian reservations), emerged as a rival political entrepreneur, basing his activity on a charter of respect for ethnic identity, pride in own culture, as well as material welfare.

Through the nineteen-fifties there followed a period of strategy and counter-strategy between these two rival entrepreneurs, each defining and manipulating 'the Lappish question' for his own ends, each offering his clientele a 'package deal' in transaction: one promising modern life and welfare state benefits in return for undivided political support and the rejection of Lappish language and culture; the other offering protected Lappish identity, perhaps in an intellectualized and romanticized form, without serious loss of prosperity but implying the threat of loss of autonomy through a *de facto* reservation status.

These actions do not merely represent a progressive organization for political purposes of a previously unorganized population. The entrepreneur who wishes to make himself the leader of such a movement must find some *drive* behind the movement – and this he finds in values never before satisfied on any scale, in offering transactions to clients whereby they can realize conversions of value which never before were possible for them. The competing entrepreneurs seek out inconsistencies in values, the potential from which they can draw political benefit lies precisely in the irreconciled values. There they make themselves interpreters and mediators of basic cultural dilemmas: they force a showdown through their rival offers of transactions, and the choice presented to the clients is not the whole gamut of possible combinations and adjustments of disparate evaluations, but whole 'package deal' alternatives. The result of this entrepreneurial activity must be a choice in the form of a reconciliation to one or another alternative and a concomitant settling of value preferences. This resolution has not yet taken place, and the present moment is one of crisis in Lappish identity, when the main direction of culture change seems to be at stake. The inconsistencies that have been building up over generations of technical, economic and educational innovation have been brought out by the activity of the political entrepreneurs, who have made them critical through presenting them as alternative offers in transaction. It is this offer which compels the creative work of making over-arching principles of evaluation which will make disparate values commensurate and lead to an integration where there previously was none.

The separation of 'social' and 'cultural' kinds of abstractions has been problematical in anthropology, and the conceptual autonomy which is often ascribed to these abstractions lies at the bottom of much current theoretical difficulty. As has been clearly seen by Stanner (Stanner, 1959, especially pp. 122–7), the isolation of the natural triad of person-object-person, as in the analysis of transactions, resolves this self-made intellectual dilemma. In this chapter I have tried to show how a concept of transaction gives us a model not only for a social process, but also for a process whereby integration is effected between the different values of a culture.

In the fact of a flow of prestations we observe what may be analysed both as social relationship and as valuational consistency; and a developmental viewpoint, utilizing the concept of the entrepreneur, makes it possible for us to identify and observe empirical processes of change in relationships and values. With this model we can attempt to measure the effects of this process on culture. We need not build an assertion of integration into our definition of culture, because we have a model for at least part of the process which generates such integration. Through it, cultural integration or disintegration should become amenable to analysis.

At the same time, these viewpoints relieve us of what might appear to have been an idealist position implicit in the argument of the first chapter. The initial model for generating social forms had an apparent linearity, from ideas and values which through a complex transformation in terms of choice, strategy, and role-playing generates frequentative patterns of behaviour. It thus gave primacy to values over action, and for the purposes of analysis of any particular case of behaviour I think rightly so, since all behaviour takes place in a matrix of values and social relations. But the analysis of the cumulative effects of transactions has enabled us to isolate a feedback process, whereby values, though initial to each item of behaviour, become modified and changed through their results. Thus the relative priority of values or actions is reduced to a question of convenience in terms of what type of paradigm one wishes to generate: the model depicts an interrelation of the two which should be equally relevant to cultural and social analysis.

4 Models of social organization III

The problem of comparison

The purpose of comparison in social anthropology cannot merely be to name and classify, in a tradition of butterfly-collecting (Leach, 1961). Our purpose must be to further explanation by comparison, both negatively, by using different examples to falsify hypotheses, and positively, by mobilizing a mass of detail, consistent with a hypothesis, to compel belief.

Used in such fashion, comparison is a methodological equivalent of experiment, its utility being that it permits us to observe concomitant variations (cf. Nadel, 1951, 1952). There have been various suggestions as to how such natural experiments can best be brought under control: through intensive regional comparisons (Schapera, 1953) and by limiting the span of variation in forms in other ways (Eggan, 1954). Despite such controls, however, the procedure of comparison has consisted of a morphological matching of forms so as to locate differences, and a concentration of attention on the correlation of these morphological differences. The control does not lead to any procedure which differs from that utilized on cross-cultural area files; it still leaves the field open for ad hoc hypotheses to explain concomitance, and the control represented by limited variation remains a hit-and-miss attempt in terms of the significance, and nature of interconnection, of the variables.

I wish to show how analysis by means of generative models to some extent reduces these weaknesses and improves the methodology of comparison. The basic argument for studying process has been formulated by Boas: 'If anthropology desires to establish the laws governing the growth of culture it must not confine itself to comparing the results of growth alone, but whenever such is feasible, it must compare the processes of growth' (Boas, 1940: 280). Social forms, as I have tried to show, may be regarded as the results of processes – they are frequency distributions of behaviour which may be explained as the outcome of social processes acting on a limited number of determinants.

Comparisons based on such a view seek to exploit the natural experiments where these determinants are varied, through comparing the processes whereby they ultimately result in different social forms. The differences between comparisons based on models of form and those based on models of process are as follows: a model of form is a pattern which describes major features of the empirical units under study. Several such patterns may be laid out side by side, and the comparison consists of noting differences, and discovering possible consistencies in the correlation of various aspects of these differences. Such a discovery may either be used to falsify previous hypotheses about the interconnectedness between these aspects, or to suggest new hypotheses about such connections.

A model of process, on the other hand, consists of a set of factors which by specified operations generates forms. Through changes in one or several of these factors, different forms may be generated by the model. Comparison then becomes a crucial test of the validity of the model: one sees which forms the model may be made to generate from changes in the determining factors, or variables; one looks for empirical examples of such forms; and one ascertains whether that set of factors, and the processes deriving from them, may in fact be observed in the examples. The value of the comparison is thereby increased in a number of ways. The clear separation between logical operations on the model, and the observation of process and form in the examples, makes the 'control' of comparison more rigorous: it is open to logical check and is concentrated on that which is most important to the hypothesis. The hypothesis itself, as it finds expression in the model, is more readily falsified: it depicts processes as necessary interconnections of elements in terms of time, or succession, and frequency; it implies limitations on variation and the impossibility of certain forms, in contrast to the continuous variations allowed for in most typologies. Finally, it compels belief more strongly since it encompasses a wide variety of data and is consistent only with certain definite constellations of possible findings.

As an exercise in comparative analysis utilizing generative models, I shall discuss descent groups and the problem of unilineal descent, treating material from the Middle East largely published elsewhere (Barth, 1953a, 1959a, 1961). To mark the point of departure adopted for this analysis, I might emphasize my disagreement with the treatment of the topic in much literature on lineage systems. Lineages, it is often held, are characteristic of systems where political relations are cast in the idiom of kinship. One may describe a pattern of kinship organization and a pattern of political organization, and no necessary interconnections are postulated other than the supposed fit between them - a fit with respect to mutual consistency as structures. For comparative work, all one can do on the basis of such a viewpoint is to develop a typology of lineage systems, based on political and kinship characters, and classify cases according to this typology.

The empirical situation in the Middle East, however, presents the following picture. Among different tribal peoples, corporate unilineal descent groups are often, but not always, prominent features of the sociological landscape. Yet there is no particularly striking fit between the structure of the kinship system and the political system, nor clear differences in kinship system that correlate with the presence or absence of corporate lineages in politics. What cannot fail to strike an observer, however, is the fact that in some areas, unilineal descent groups are constantly being beaten down by external physical force, only to spring up again like weeds in a garden; while in other areas, once they crumble, they seem to disappear without a trace. The obvious explanation for such a pattern of differential occurrence and vitality must be that the things we call unilineal descent groups *grow*, as a result of processes under specific circumstances. To understand and explain this social form, then, we do not want a typology of its variants: we want to specify those processes and circumstances. This is a kind of problem which requires comparative analysis, and which promises to lead to an explanation of the absence, or presence in a restricted variety, of such descent groups.

To perform the analysis, I need to relate the concept of descent to that of incorporation, briefly alluded to above (p. 38). The discussion by Radcliffe-Brown (1935) of the distinction between rights over persons imposing a duty on that person (*jus in personam*) and rights as against the world (*jus in rem*, and over things) led to the isolation of a basic social principle, that of corporation around a shared estate. Between shareholders in an estate there must emerge a relationship of jointness, or incorporation, since for certain purposes their interests are identical and inseparable. Their activities *vis-à-vis* each other with respect to the rights they share can never have a transactional form; their strategy must be directed towards maximizing the sum of their assets. Yet there remains the problem of economizing: resources and labour which are invested in such a joint endeavour are thereby deflected from other joint endeavours in which a person also participates, and from developing his possible private and truly exclusive assets. I shall assume that in a relationship of incorporation, though it differs from one of transaction, evaluations of gains and losses through membership are still made, and that an offer of incorporation is not accepted, and a corporate group is not mobilized by a member, if that person's losses through membership are greater than his gains.

Now on to descent. Descent is clearly a principle for the allocation of rights of the kind defined as *in rem* or over things. Furthermore, the rights in question, though they are exclusive as against the world, are not held exclusively by single persons; they are rights held simultaneously by a delimited number of persons. A definition of terms for the principles of allocation of rights on the basis of birth or genealogical position, exhausting these distinctions, will differentiate:

Rights held:	consecutively	simultaneously
in rem	inheritance	*descent*
in personam	succession	equivalence

Descent is then the allocation on the basis of genealogical position of rights held by a restricted group as against the world. It has in other words the characteristics which should generate the kind of social form known as a corporation, and relations between descent group members should follow from the restrictions specified for a relationship of incorporation.

In specifying the form of descent we find in a society, we should not attempt to elaborate a list of all the empirical data on observed relations between mother and father and children. We know that rights *in personam* are irrelevant to the form of descent. We also know that when persons hold simultaneous rights as against the world to an estate, a number of processes of interaction are initiated which we may subsume under the term incorporation and need not enumerate each time. The economical procedure is to feed into our model of these processes only that minimum of specifications which is necessary to *generate* the empirical form we have observed. These specifications of the form of descent would seem to be two: to which relatives are the descent rights ascribed, and what are these rights. When I arrive at the treatment of comparative material, I shall restrict myself to these two variables, or indeed to only one of these, since the descent line in the Middle East is uniformly agnatic.

First, however, there is one further point to clarify. My argument for the logical manipulation of models is reminiscent of Leach, particularly in his Malinowski lecture (Leach, 1961). There, he abstracts the relationships 'q' for filiation with the father, 'p' for filiation with the mother, and manipulates the mathematical function $Z = p/q$ to produce varieties of form. The distinction between this use of models, and the use which I am proposing here, lies in the kinds of restrictions I feel must be imposed on the logical operations one is permitted to make on the model. I require my model to depict empirical situations and the operations on them to depict empirical processes (cf. p. 33). It is not sufficient to subject oneself to the discipline of mathematical rules; put naively, how do we know that the 'Z' we have constructed can be varied from 0 to infinity, or that the 'p' we have abstracted is subject to continuous variation from 0 to 1? The only way we can hope to avoid logical solecisms is by taking care that the manipulations whereby we transform or generate mirror empirical social processes. Otherwise, we have no assurance, in our movement between abstraction and observation, that our perfectly valid concepts satisfy the requirements implicit in various mathematical operations. To use a gross illustration: a person's preferences may be ordered on a scale from say 1 to 10, and such preference scales may be used quite validly to compare preference profiles in different populations or for different types of goods. But the numbers of such preference ratings cannot be added together – they are cardinal numbers and do not stand for the kinds of quantities on which the mathematical operation of addition can be performed. Indeed, quite apart from that, it seems that our preferences are a kind of phenomenon which can never be treated by simple addition, that compound or aggregate preference can only be represented by far more complex mathematical operations. I would argue that the validity of a comparative analysis utilizing generative models depends on a very careful methodology on this point. Specifically, the validity of the operations performed on the model must be demonstrated, and this can only be done by showing in what way they represent or depict processes which are empirically verifiable.

I shall now attempt to sketch a comparative analysis of some political forms among tribal peoples of the Iranian-speaking family, with special reference to patrilineal descent groups and the circumstances under which such groups emerge as significant corporate bodies. I shall try to generate the different forms of groups, and major characteristics of their activities, from relatively few specifications about descent and other basic structural principles, using the simple rules governing transaction and incorporation. Thus, I shall for example disregard people's notions about the whole set of behaviour appropriate between Father and Sons – these are predominantly *in personam* rights and thus not directly relevant to the present issue. Specifically, we need to consider in each case – given that the descent line is uniformly agnatic – first, what are the rights *in rem* which are allocated by descent. Secondly, what other structural principles have relevance to the same kinds of rights – i.e. what other basic means and patterns are there for the distribution of these values. Finally then, what groups and activity patterns are generated from this through the processes of people living and acting together, as mirrored in the operations of incorporation and transaction. To avoid misunderstandings at the start, may I set the ethnographic record straight by emphasizing that in the areas I discuss, rights or obligations in blood feuds are *not* a part of descent rights, but are regarded as a right or obligation to revenge which devolves on the heirs as an inseparable part of the inheritance; while political allegiance, though to a variable extent implicit in descent, is everywhere a potential matter of free contract for men, as individuals or in groups.

The first variant I wish to analyse is that exemplified by some autonomous Kurdish tribes in the south-eastern mountain areas of Iraq. They are organized in politically corporate units composed of the male members of patrilineal descent groups. Tribesmen are placed by a genealogical charter in a segmentary system of groups and subgroups, and these are mobilized intermittently in a pattern of situational fusion and fission. In other words, they exemplify a simple lineage type of political form, comparable to that, say, of the Tiv (Bohannan and Bohannan, 1953).

Rights to agricultural land, and to grazing, are ascribed by patrilineal descent, and the land around a hamlet or village is held as a joint estate by the descent segment occupying that village. Thus individual plots are held on temporary tenure by the users, and between descent group members there is adjustment to changing need through the reallocation of land. Sons are not dependent on their fathers for the gift or inheritance of plots, but will receive a share of the estate when, because of marriage, the need arises. There are very few persons in the community who are not lineage members, thus there are no other significant transactions about access to land and use of land: the predominant pattern of ascription is by descent.

These rights ascribed by descent are very essential rights to territory and to the main productive resource, so one would expect descent to be basic to political organization. It is possible to generate the whole lineage form of organization from these crucial features of descent. The essential point is the nature of the joint interest, and the pattern of incorporation that follows from it. Co-members of a descent group, tilling separately, share potential rights to all land belonging to that descent group and thus share an interest in preventing the encroachment by anyone else on that right. They will therefore fuse as a body against an external threat, yet split into opposed segments over issues of internal rivalry, thereby producing the usual lineage paradigm. And this will be the predominant pattern since it is the most economical. Persons could only obtain land through other transactions by offering prestations in return, and these would constitute additional costs, making the transaction less profitable than is the exercise of descent rights. Likewise, a different pattern of political incorporation through contractual alliance would only provide the same kind of support against external threat at the cost of counter-prestation of some sort, whereas from lineage fellows such support is a matter of self-interest and requires no compensation.

The processes of growth and segmentation by which such a system maintains itself through time is also self-evident. Patrilocality and fighting, loss, and reallotment provide the mechanisms whereby the balance is maintained between numbers, strength, and area within a territorially ordered patrilineal descent system. The resilience of the system in the face of external pressure - Ottoman, Persian, English, and currently Arab nationalist attempts at imposing external administration - is truly remarkable.

Yet by only a slight variation in the basic elements, a radically different form may result. Given descent rights to the same kind of value, namely agricultural land, held as a joint estate with temporary allocation, patrilineal descent groups do not emerge at all as corporate political units under the following two connected circumstances: (i) if there is no adjustment to need, i.e. agricultural land is allocated without regard to number of men, only according to the genealogical charter, and (ii) if many persons in the community do not obtain rights to land by descent. This is the situation among Swat Pathans, described more fully elsewhere (Barth, 1959a, b). Here, I should like to argue purely from this simple model, exploring the logical ramifications of these changes of variables and comparing them to the Kurdish lineage system above, as well as controlling them as against the empirical facts of Swat Pathan organization.

Firstly, the fact that many persons in the community fail to obtain rights to land through descent means that there are persons eager to obtain access to land by other means. There can thus be transactions about access to land, in return for prestations of comparable value. The prestation which the landless are most apt to be able and willing to provide is that of labour; throughout the areas discussed this is also the expected reciprocal. In contrast to the Kurdish situation described above, where such tenancy relations are rare, they are the rule in Swat; and around each landowner, who may or may not do any tilling himself, there forms an aggregate of clients who perform all the work of cultivating in return for a fraction of the crop.

The joint interests of landowner and sharecropping client are great, and one would expect a political relation of incorporation to spring from it. The relative strength of this joint interest as compared to that between fellow descent-group members will be a significant factor in determining the form of descent organization, while its importance to the tenants as compared to their joint interests as an under-privileged proletariat will determine the role of class in politics. One would expect, from first principles, that the joint interest in wresting crops from the land would take precedence over that of being residual heirs to each others' share of the landed estate. Likewise, in all tribal areas of the Middle East it takes precedence for tenants over working-class identification. The result is the formation of solidarities crossing descent group lines, uniting members with non-members more strongly than with co-members. For the record, it should be noted that these ties of incorporation are also supported by feast-giving in Swat.

In the further alignment of this minimal, compounded political unit, however, descent remains potentially relevant: will the pattern of incorporation be based on the joint interests of the landowner with his descent group fellows, or is it based on the alternative of contractual alliance? Again, we must look at the balance of gains and losses which a person may obtain by entering into these alternative alignments, and assume that the actors will choose the one most advantageous to them.

The joint interest which ties a landowner to his fellow descent-group members is not, as in the Kurdish case, one which arises through a continual readjustment of holdings according to the needs of the descent group as a collectivity. Instead, each male holds a fixed share by virtue of his genealogical position, and this share is passed on to sons as an inheritance to be divided by them, or it passes to collateral agnatic heirs in lieu of sons. *Descent* rights as opposed to rights of inheritance and succession are limited, strictly speaking, to two aspects: reciprocal rights as residual heirs, and the right to participate in the periodic councils on which a temporary allotment is made of fields, proportionate to the fixed shares held by members. These rights are divisive rather than joint in their implications. Conflicts over allotment can be serious, and the procedure for allotment of fields results in collaterals being neighbours, with all the consequent implications of competition for irrigation water, labour, etc., without the counterbalancing active joint interests as against the world. The result is a negative charge on the relation between collateral agnates; and contractual alliances with less closely related landowners, directed primarily against such close collaterals, are therefore more advantageous for the actors. Within a framework of territorial councils composed of descent group members, the actual political bodies that emerge are dispersed political blocs, compounded of descent group splinters and their clients.

There are also developmental or demographic aspects underlying such a social form: the process whereby a population is replaced and maintained effects a basic distribution of personnel in statuses, on which such social processes as alliance-forming, tenancy contracts, etc., act. This developmental view reveals an interconnection between the two features singled out here as significant determinants – the lack of adjustment to need in the allocation of land rights, and the large number of persons who do not obtain any rights to land. Imagine an initial situation of equal land rights for all men of a territory. If they are held in the Kurdish pattern, with internal adjustment to need, differential growth and other chance circumstances will have no major cumulative effects on the distribution of these rights. When held on the Swat Pathan pattern, on the other hand, prolific lines and segments will have less land per member than will less prolific lines; and any process such as conquest and eviction which may lead to loss of rights at any point will have the effect of stripping succeeding generations of such rights. The result will be an increasingly uneven distribution of rights in the population, including both persons with such small shares as to make them insufficient as a basis for subsistence, and persons entirely without land rights. There is no evidence for any such 'initial' equality in Swat; but the process of sloughing-off which the model depicts, whereby the landless population is swelled by the descendants of defunct landowning lineages, can be observed empirically. Thus the demographic situation today may be seen as consistent with, and a product of, the particular form of these rights among Swat Pathans.

The comparison shows that the apparently minor ways in which the character of descent rights among Swat Pathans differ from those of the Kurdish example, are still sufficient to generate over time a different distribution of value on persons, and to define a different optimal strategy for politically active individuals. By performing the same operations on models with these two sets of specifications, very different social forms are generated in the two cases – forms which are entirely consistent with the gross features of the empirical societies in question.

A third form may be produced by varying the ecologic circumstances, from a major dependence on agriculture to one of pastoralism. Among nomadic pastoralists, though land and territory may be ascribed by the same formal descent rules as among agriculturalists, land is a different kind of resource and the way in which rights over it are exercised will differ. I shall explore some ramifications of this difference with special reference to the case of the Basseri tribe of South Persia (Barth, 1961).

Among pastoralists, the herd may be regarded as a crucial implement for exploiting resources in land. The Basseri regard such herds as private property; there is no 'collective insurance' of redistribution within descent groups after losses of stock, and no joint ownership of animals. A son, when he marries, will receive a part of his father's herd as an anticipated inheritance, and thereby lose any further rights to the estate of his father.

Land, on the other hand, in the form of rights to grazing, is allocated by patrilineal descent and held as joint estates by large groups conceived by the members as unilineal descent groups. But there is a significant technical difference between agriculture and grazing with respect to how land is utilized: for grazing, the estate need not be subdivided and plots allocated – all owners may exercise their rights simultaneously. That which constitutes the most crucial joint action by descent group members in Swat – the allocation of fields to shareholders in the joint estate – is absent and unnecessary among the Basseri. Consequently, also, the issue which differentiates the Kurdish and the Swat situation, that of adjustment to differential growth and need between descent segments, does not arise in the present case. There is no control on the number or proportions of animals grazed by different owners, and size of production is regulated by success in herding and husbandry, not by descent right distribution.

With unallocated rights to land within the descent group, there can be no possibility of transactions over access to land. All herd owners in a community must share rights of access, if one lacks these rights he cannot obtain them from any party other than the whole group of owners, which considering the disparity of numbers could only take the form of incorporation, not exchange.[1] In significant respects, therefore, the determinants of this system are more like those of the Kurdish example than those of Swat, and one might expect patrilineal descent groups to emerge as important corporate units. However, we need to investigate more closely the nature of the joint interests of descent groups with respect to the kinds of joint decision and action they need to take, to depict the strategic optima of choice and thereby perform the right transformation from the determinants to the frequentative patterns of behaviour.

In the Basseri case, the joint interests which we need to consider are more varied than for the Kurdish agriculturalists. Firstly, there is the interest in protecting the shared rights to grazing and territory as against outsiders. For defence against encroachment by others, and for basic security of life and property, those who share territorial rights are drawn together by self-interest to form a community. But among nomads, a community can only be maintained by achieving repeated, active agreement within it on concerted movement and migration. And the policy of movement and migration is one that significantly affects success in herd management – i.e. it is a matter of primary importance to the management of private capital and the achievement of personal wealth and prosperity. The optimum from the point of view of protecting descent rights, and for security, is residential incorporation in large groups; from the point of view of herd management, optimal opportunities are achieved by dispersal and independence of movement. Residentially compact groups – and thereby the groups which exercise rights jointly, and constitute the most significant corporation – will emerge as a compromise between these conflicting considerations and be of intermediate size. Their composition will depend on the factors whereby agreed decisions on migration policy can be achieved: through similarity of interests and judgement and/or through influence of one over others.

Unless one introduces the size and composition of herds as a variable, there is no significant way of differentiating persons by the first factor. The second one, of a variegated distribution of interests, is a more interesting factor for generating regularities in community composition. Membership in the inclusive descent group is shared by all, and thus will not differentiate. Minimal segment nuclei of father and sons, forming around a joint herd, will as noted be divided upon the marriage of a son and thereby dissolve as far as any joint interest in capital or other wealth is concerned. The joint interest which must be brought in to make the model match up with the ethnographic facts is one in *women* as a kind of value in which clusters of men share interests: father or in lieu of him brothers on the one hand, husbands and sons on the other. Particularly during the betrothal period, a father-in-law will exert great influence over a son-in-law, but also after marriage their joint interests persist. Thereby a community of interest will arise, and a network of mutual influence assert itself, inside a bilateral kin group, and the effective pattern of incorporation among Basseri is thus notably structured by bilateral kinship, reinforced by the involuting effect of cousin and other close kin marriage.

Crucial rights, though they are allocated by descent, and held jointly, need not result in the emergence of lineage groups as corporations. Among the Basseri, such lineages are, so to speak, nipped in the bud by the dissolution of the joint herds of father and sons, and the establishment through marriage of a new and discordant joint 'estate' in the form of shared interests in a woman between a man and his affines. Migratory communities form around these interests, and the larger descent group that holds joint rights to territory becomes ineffective in maintaining its exclusiveness, because it is split in non-homologous parts with a low capacity for joint action. Despite clear descent rights, and growth points for the emergence of lineages, contrary processes of incorporation are initiated by other factors, and the patterns of choice and behaviour that result have a form which is significantly different from that generated in the previous two examples.

Some of the basis for the preceding analysis has been an implicit assertion that the important differences in social forms which are exhibited are not correlated with comprehensive and profound differences in cultural values. I would argue here, as in the previous chapters, that we have been altogether too ready in social anthropology to produce special explanations for everything, in the form of appeals to the culturally unique and specific background for every variation or characteristic we observe. Instead, I hold that it must be the object of our analysis to reduce this appeal to uniqueness to a minimum, and rather see *how few* specified differences are necessary and sufficient to explain, or generate, the gross differences in social form which we observe. Fortunately I can conclude this comparative exercise with a fourth case which may serve as a crucial experiment and vindicate the procedure. In this empirical case cultural factors *are* practically held constant, and only the rules for allocation of rights to agricultural land are varied. The case is from the foothills area of Iraq Kurdistan, based on my own fieldwork there (Barth, 1953, 1954). In this area, people like the Kurdish tribesmen of my first example come under the sway of an administration which does not recognize collective rights to agricultural land, and through land settlement and registration of titles has succeeded in removing the collective tribal estate.

Some of these villages are inhabited by Kurds who have recently settled there from areas characterized by lineage organizations; in other villages one may observe the changes as land settlement and administration slowly encroach on formerly tribal areas. The people in these cases are hardly different from their neighbours or their fathers in basic culture: it is the land tenure system and little else that has been radically changed. Inheritance rules, respect for father, standards of virility and honour remain the same. Yet the political corporations which they form *are* radically different. Villages very rarely fuse for joint action; and factions within villages are composed of bilateral kindred, not of descent segments. Indeed, these internal factions have a form resembling the migratory units of the Basseri – the internal effects of having uniform and unallotted descent rights are similar to having no descent rights at all. Thus, as one would predict from the model, the Kurds who are without joint rights in land are more like the distant and in many other ways dissimilar Basseri in the form of their political corporations, and unlike their otherwise similar neighbours and cousins who hold such joint rights.

Back then to a more general discussion of descent. Despite a strong and apparently widespread common tradition of patrilineal ideology in the Iranian area, one finds among tribal peoples there great differences in descent group structure, and differences in the relative importance of descent in politics. These differences do not correlate in their magnitude with the general degree of cultural difference, as measured by the overt criteria of dress and language, or estimates of historical genetic distance derived from such criteria. Rather, the form of descent groups and political corporations may be shown to vary according to the clear and definable – and perhaps superficially seemingly insignificant – differences with regard to the specific character of descent rights. A hypothesis that these rights, as factors affecting the choices people make, are the major determinants of descent group structure, would seem to be vindicated.

The comparative analysis of these cases has proceeded not by a direct comparison of forms, but from the view that there are *determinants* of form, and that valid comparison presupposes an understanding of the processes whereby forms are generated from such determinants. Thus the comparison has become an exercise in the use of generative models on the complex and intractable material which anthropologists try to handle. To the extent that the exercise has succeeded, the comparison has attained the form of a kind of 'controlled experiment' where the factors deemed crucial have been varied, and the resultant forms compared. This procedure requires several steps, which in this brief and incomplete exposition have been partly interleaved, but are none the less logically distinct: (i) the formulation of an hypothesis about empirical determinants and processes which affect form: (ii) the construction of a generative model with variables depicting these determinants (here: the specific content of descent rights, and the other principles of allocation which affect these same rights), and operations depicting the processes (here: transaction, incorporation, growth); (iii) finally, the comparison of the forms generated by the model, and those of the empirical cases.

The purpose of the comparison must be to explain differences – explain in the sense of locating the determining factors, and showing how variations in these factors can have those specific, ramifying effects which characterize the forms. Admittedly, it is very difficult to maintain any great rigour in these comparisons. Because of the complexity of the material, even when grossly simplified, each new case introduced in the comparison compels one to introduce new factors as variables. Properly, one should then return to the previous cases, expand the model to include the new variable, and repeat the analysis. A careful attention to this rule conflicts with an ideal of simplicity. Yet despite such laxness, which may prove necessary considering our material, a conscious use of generative models in comparison would seem to represent a step forward in methodology. It makes explicit those hypotheses which we all entertain about determinate interconnections; it makes it possible to encompass a greater variety of data in single, structured hypotheses; it isolates more clearly the logical operations from the empirical observations and thus facilitates the falsification of hypotheses. Perhaps most importantly, a use of generative models directs our attention to the observation of the processes whereby form comes about, rather than a narrow concentration on form alone, and may lead to a greater sophistication in the way we depict these processes.

5 'Models' reconsidered

In republishing the preceding three essays fifteen years after their conception, it may be useful to add a fourth chapter. My purposes are several:

1 I have been surprised and discontented with how, in the variety of issues raised, my concept of 'transactions' seems to have caught the main attention of most readers, sometimes to the apparent exclusion of other themes. I should like to re-emphasize these other themes, which I presented in the essays, in the hope belatedly of strengthening their impact.

2 The essays have lately received a certain amount of explicit attention and criticism (mainly Paine, 1974; Skvoretz and Conviser, 1974; Kapferer (ed.), 1976; Evens, 1977). I should like to clarify some misinterpretations made by one or several of these doubtless sympathetic readers, and therefore liable to be made also by others; I should also like to defend certain points which they have attacked.

3 Finally, I feel a need to elaborate a few passages in what was no doubt too spare a text; though I shall refrain from rewriting the essays in the form I might have given them today, I can explicate some matters that were previously left implicit.

Generative models

If I envisaged these essays as a plea for a paradigm shift in social anthropology, the banner I would have chosen must contain as key terms 'generative' or 'process' and not 'transaction'. So much anthropological description and analysis before and since has had the form 'these things are so because here is the structure which they exhibit'. the essays in Models of social organization, and most other work I have done, have aimed at a basically other way of thinking about anthropological materials: that our representations of regularities should take the form of showing the relevant conditions, factors or mechanisms which *affect* the states of the world which we observe. Such models have variously been called simulation or generative models. The kinds of insight into social and cultural phenomena which they provide are of a different character from most forms of structuralism (cf. Leach, 1968, esp. 14:488); and my claim was that they provide 'explanations' of a different order. So I want to show that our data can be arranged in models of this kind: models which depict how some facts affect the form of others, how some features of reality may be understood as the results, or epiphenomena, of other equally empirical circumstances and features – i.e. how some forms are 'generated'.

When applied to broad fields of human life and activities, I understand this to be a very exciting, and ambitious, undertaking. Yet when the direction of this ambition is sensed by sceptics, it has sometimes been escalated as a prelude to criticism and rejection. I have never pretended to depict how forms are generated from scratch. To depict how certain forms are generated is to provide a model which specifies a set of preconditions, and a set of rules of transformation which give one or more outcomes. Sometimes, these outcomes may be connected with the specified preconditions, in which case the model also has an added dynamic property: the outcomes may reproduce their own preconditions, or they may change them in determinate ways. If so, we are able not only to give an explanation of form, but also an explanation of *marginal changes* in form. These may even be extrapolated to raise further questions about connections, and about change; but they cannot be expected to provide the story of creation. In the logical, stepwise presentation of a model, on the other hand, one may have to start from scratch, as I did in some passages of the preceding essays. This must not be misread as an attempt 'to get from an essentially presocial individual to a genuine or objectivated sociocultural phenomenon' as one critic (Evens, 1977: 589) has chided me for trying and failing to do. It must be important, and elementary, for us to recognize that all the acts we observe take place 'with reference to a set of values . . . (and) a pre-established matrix of statuses. . . .' (above, p. 40).

Process

The concept of 'transaction' was deployed, among others in the preceding essays, in an analysis designed to embody and exemplify this generative way of thinking about social and cultural regularities and was not intended to become the central focus of a substantive social theory.

Far more essential to my analytical focus on generative models is the general concept of 'process'. We are accustomed to a very loose use of this concept in anthropological writing, as if it were a suitable term for any and every kind of sequence in time. I wished to argue that much analytical power can be gained by using it in a strict sense, for a generalizable set of linked events which keep recurring, the necessary interconnections of which, and the consequences of which, can be clearly described. 'Growth' is a clear and simple conceptualization of one such process, analytically more powerful the more precisely its mechanisms - i.e. the nature of the necessary linkages between its constituent events - can be specified. In the physical world, 'evaporation' may serve us as an example. Note that it is not coterminous with 'desiccation', which is a description of changes in the state of the world consequent to the process of evaporation in combination with a certain number of other factors. A process of evaporation is equally at work in such states of the world as 'flooding', 'waterlogging' or 'salinization'. Perhaps most excitingly, as a component process in the natural cycle of water on earth, 'evaporation', with 'condensation' provides the invisible pieces of a larger puzzle and becomes powerfully explanatory in a model that seeks to represent the whole system.

'Transaction' was introduced as an attempt to conceptualize one such process in social life: I tried to define its basic, constituting linkages between component events, and explore its consequences under varying circumstances. But it does not provide a paradigm for 'society'.

Two further points should be stressed regarding processes. (i) A major advantage of conceptualizing in such terms lies in the greater naturalism it can give to our models. In social life, we observe not only the outcomes of culture and society at work but also much of their workings since events take place *between* actors, available to observation. Consequently we have no need to resign ourselves to a 'black box' construction. We can make direct observations of processes, and synthetic statements about their regular features. These we can utilize in our model building: a process can be schematized in the model as a logical operation or a transformation rule which depicts the empirical linkages between events. The generative properties of the model are thus designed to reproduce empirical processes; thereby not only the outcomes, but also the operations, are susceptible to empirical falsification in terms of how they match up with empirical observations of the processes they mirror. For this to be realized, of course, a first requirement is that model and reality must not be muddled. Real people perform social acts, they do not 'generate social action' (*pace* Evens, 1977:586). The recurring test is whether the logical operations we perform on our models after they are constructed, and the outcomes they generate, are revealing of major patterns in the empirical co-occurrence of events, and the distributions and forms, which we observe.

(ii) Functionalist imputations can be avoided without eliminating all teleological explanation. The imagery that outcomes are 'generated' emphatically does not imply that outcomes are those intended by the actors, or that they are particularly beneficial for some person, group or category and therefore justified. Purposes figure in these models, for they are models of how men act, and human acts entail purposes; but the whole model cannot be designed in terms of pervasive purposes, for the anthropologist's model seeks to generate outcomes that depict what actually occurs as observable events in the lives and interactions of people, and not simply provide deductions from moral or other valuational premises which those people embrace. The introduction of awareness and purpose as components of some transformation rules, when this seems empirically substantiated, resolves the problem and allows unlimited scope for investigating the place of purpose and consciousness in social life. Others of the processes depicted in the anthropologists' model will need to be of an entirely different ontological status, to capture other aspects of the reality within which people live.

Event vs. aggregate

This is a third, and essential, theoretical component of the argument of 'Models': that the relationship between phenomena on the two levels of acts vs. aggregates is far more problematic than structural-functionalists in their theory, and also most others in their practice, have been prepared to recognize. Yet, with only the most basic awareness of this dichotomy and willingness to handle it, highly fruitful concrete analyses thereby become possible.

This form of distinction is far more productive than the individual vs. group mold into which my thought has been forced by critics (see esp. Paine, 1974:16ff., Evens 1977:581ff.)[1] Much closer to my analytical intentions would be to speak in terms of the paired concepts of act vs. social system, or for a number of purposes, micro vs. macro. In my view, such dichotomies must be seen to refer not to different

kinds, and certainly not to different degrees, of reality; rather, we may
regard them as different faces of reality.

I understand the constituent events of social life to be characteristically micro, performed by actors (individuals and corporate groups).
These events or acts are conditioned by, and in turn together constitute, the aggregate level. Processes provide the key conceptualizations
for depicting how aggregation comes about, and explaining aggregate
form. The aggregate has markedly emergent properties, and these must
be acknowledged and described in their own terms, but without inappropriate reification of their structures. The fact that actors themselves often harbour such reifications must enter into our models at
the appropriate points, and not be regarded as a *carte blanche* for us
to do the same. Most importantly, we must make no facile assumptions
that there is a congruity between those factors which predicate acts –
especially the forms of consciousness and purpose which constrain and
propel actors – and the major aggregate consequences of acts. Thus, in
the examples exercised above I argue that the interactional events
aboard the herring vessels which generate an aggregate distribution
of the fleet are not predicated by the main features of this distribution.
The self-interested labour and political support rendered by clients in
Swat have the aggregate consequence of securing the unequal power
and privilege of the chiefs. And the 'lineage' pattern of fusion and
fission among tribal Kurds does not arise from their undeniable awareness that such indeed *is* the aggregate pattern, but rather from their
response to the rule of reallocating equal per capita shares of a joint
estate.

It is essential that the dichotomization of these two levels must not
lead to their separation for distinctive analytical treatment. Regarded
separately, they may invite study by the incommensurate methods of
phenomenology or hermeneutics, vs. hypothetical-deductive logic, as
concluded by Evens (1977:593). This precludes an effective analysis
of their interdependence. Paine on the other hand in his critique
seems to refer to this dichotomy under the captions alpha and omega
(Paine, 1974:17, 19), and is regretful that I do not seek to unite them
in a 'gamma' form of integration where the difference between the
two levels is overcome. Both these misinterpretations and modifications
of my position remove an essential dynamism from my 'Models', and
thereby return us to the impasse that troubles much contemporary
anthropological thinking (cf. Bloch, 1977, and below p. 82): where
to locate endogenous sources of change in a system. I see no basis for

a nostalgic or utopian view that social systems should properly submerge the individual harmoniously in the body politic. On the contrary, I should always expect aggregate outcomes, and emergent properties on the macro level, to be at odds with individual and collective intentions, and so to elicit dissatisfaction and innovative action from individual actors and parties – i.e. events which entail change. This source of change can only be depicted where the two levels are distinguished, but contained within a single framework of analysis.

Saying vs. doing

This is the fourth and final theoretical intention which I see as fundamental to the preceding essays: to unite in one analytical model what has variously been separated as culture vs. society, meaning vs. instrumentality, saying vs. doing. Most clearly in the last pair of concepts, we recognize two fundamentally different ways in which acts are connected: as symbols or constituents of symbols of a communicative code, and as physical events in a material world. In the same way as argued above concerning event and aggregate, the two must be distinguished and each described in appropriate terms. But they must be united in any model which seeks to represent the determinants of human acts, for it is a fallacy to conclude that saying and doing can be distinguished as different acts, or even different aspects of acts, even though their various consequences can be so grouped and distinguished. With regard to 'saying' in a literal sense, the physical effects of the noise involved may be so limited that it can be disregarded, though people who pronounce spells think differently. But with regard to 'doing', we must recognize that not only do human acts have the material consequences that can be observed – they are also 'understood' by actor and spectator, and so must always carry essential meanings. In other words, the *same* acts and aspects of acts are *simultaneously* instrumental and communicative, and their form cannot be explained by the analysis of only one of these contexts.

A piece of mine, published elsewhere, on the ritual life of a group of nomads, constitutes my first attempt to make this particular point explicit (Barth, 1961: 135-53); but it does not seem to have been read in these terms (Douglas, 1970:x-xii). In a later publication (Barth, 1975) I have sought to focus more comprehensively on these problems. The argument of 'Models', particularly in its second essay, is that an immensely important 'dialectic' arises from this fundamental joining of the communicative and the instrumental in the single act. Very simply, it can be said in this way: actors can and must act in terms of their own awareness and consciousness, i.e. their 'meanings', and this must entail the shaping of the act in terms of its symbolic context. But acts have material consequences, and things do not always go the way one thought or expected they would. When actors discover that this is the case it may be necessary for them to think again, tentatively even think differently. Though outcomes must be interpreted by the actor, the unexpected in them cannot always be interpreted away by him.

To picture social life as a perpetual conversation (e.g. Bloch, 1977: 278ff.) may be a great step forward (or back to Malinowski) from the chorus of harmony suggested by the structural-functionalists, but it falls so far short of reality as to be still entirely inadequate. One's actions are not only statements, to be confirmed/disconfirmed socially by being/not being meaningful and understood: they are also operations on an environment, exposed to the pragmatic confirmation/ falsification of being materially effective or not. In 'Models' I was concerned to acknowledge the role of *both* these tribunals. We need to see how people's discourse sustains an 'as-if' social construction of reality, which in turn affects their experience, learning, and the course of their lives. But we must also acknowledge that acts have material consequences quite regardless of whether people are aware of the connection, and that these consequences similarly affect and determine people's lives. Nor should we imagine that these two tribunals are unconnected, and can be treated as, on the one hand, a fantasy world of meanings and on the other an unacknowledged world of material causes. We must pursue our anthropology in such a way as to discover just *how* the two are linked: how the act mediates between them by being simultaneously of both, and how this may generate new experience and new forms of insight among actors, and a dynamic tradition of knowledge on the aggregate level. I have sought to develop these perspectives further in more recent work (Barth, 1975). I see this coexistence, confrontation, and occasionally collision of the subjective and the objective in the act as a major wellspring of cultural and social change.

Analytical schema

We may now review briefly how these themes inform the argument of 'Models', and provide an analytical schema for it and most other essays in this collection.

1 We must conceive of our object of investigation as containing a very wide variety of phenomena: motivated and aware actors, groups, codes of communication, values, environment, institutions. To cut out only a sector of this doubtless entails blinding oneself to significant determinants, while to assume an overall integration of 'culture' and 'society' is unwarranted. We must be prepared to exercise versatility in modes of conceptualization of the form and extent of interconnection: through causality, process, aggregation, emergence, feedback etc.

2 We should approach the object at the observationally most favourable point, which is generally where units capable of action (persons or corporate groups) are revealing their understanding and affecting each other and their external environment by acting and interacting. The grounds for choosing this initial focus are methodological rather than ontological: we start where our own necessary presuppositions about this complex system of interconnections are simplest, fewest, and most directly falsifiable.

3 To discover the meanings of these acts we must place them in the contexts of the social encounters where they occur. To do this we need to identify the prevailing definitions of the situation - i.e. what are the manifest capacities in which the actors engage each other (statuses), what are the rules of context (codes), what are the tasks (material effects sought)? A role analysis is required, since observable patterns are role transformations of these underlying features: for example, actors commit each other to the rights and duties of statuses, but not to the particulars of role solution even where these are standardized.

4 Next we establish the intentionality of the participant actors by learning what choices the actors know they are making, or are understood by others to be making, in shaping their acts. This we best do within those definitions of situations which are made by actors themselves. The anthropological method here constitutes a procedure - *not a theory* - whereby we enter reality as socially constructed by others. It is only once we are there that we can hope to make it analytically commensurate and available to other such worlds by means of generalized concepts (cf. Kapferer, 1976:4 for an acknowledgement of some features of this solution to our problem). By this procedure we are provided by the actors themselves with the essential help to transcend our own categories. A necessary context for the intentions, purposes and choices of any actor is his concrete opportunity situation: his own understanding of his environment and options, and the pragmatic

constraints under which he is acting. The most powerful methodology for understanding this context is provided by the study of (limited) variation: between persons pursuing slightly different goals, between persons with different assets, between actors operating under differing social and ecological circumstances in closely adjoining communities, etc.

5 We must then proceed with the main model-building operation. On the one hand we want to establish how some acts are linked in sequences, and what the outcomes of these sequences are. On the other hand we want to establish what the aggregate result of many such sequences and outcomes are. This means alternating between (but not confusing) logical operations on models, and empirical observations of processes and patterns. The close attention to variation noted under point 4 is equally essential at this phase: it allows us to discover co-variation (cf. Nadel, 1951, esp. pp. 229 ff.) and thus establish or falsify concrete hypotheses about connections. The processes we identify as event sequences must be given rigorous definitions as transformation rules in our models. My attempts to give precision to concepts such as transaction, incorporation, game of strategy, production, etc. are meant to serve this purpose. The outcomes of such operations on the model are compared again with empirical patterns, and their aggregate with empirical features of the society. What I here briefly refer to in a metalanguage we must recognize and expect to be a very complex operation. Even the simplest aggregation rarely takes the form of addition, as is somehow often assumed. The properties generated by aggregation are emergent, and rarely recognizably similar to the intent of any participant. To argue that an analytic search for such aggregate consequences is to make 'the group essentially an instrument of the individual' (Evens, 1977:582) is fatally to underestimate its productivity.

6 The preceding steps have brought us half circle to a macro-level of systems. It remains to complete the circle back to the micro-levels: to look how these macro-outcomes may (marginally) affect those factors and conditions that were specified at steps 3 and 4. This will variously involve (i) the actors' assets; (ii) their environment – both the physical environment and the options entailed in the acts and distribution of assets of others; (iii) changes in the institutional features of the society, in the nature of changed forms of consciousness, changed values, and changed conventions. These marginal changes as generated within the model may in turn be confronted with, and illuminate, life histories and recorded historical changes in the society.

Transaction and incorporation

In my judgment these concepts derive their analytical power from the way in which they embody the general, theoretical features I have emphasized under the preceding headings. They aim *not* to classify the component elements of social systems, i.e. relationships, but to identify two fundamental and elementary *processes* in social life. Transaction is explicitly referred to as exhibiting a structure of successional character (p. 37). It aggregates the acts of the minimum of two separate social actors; and among its emergent properties, I would still maintain, is an increased sharing of valuational judgments between participating actors. By this I am not propounding that transactions lead to shared moral ideas, and similar views of what constitutes The Good Life – only that the value which people place on those goods which they make transactions over will become more congruent. Incorporation is an even simpler – i.e. less specified – model of a process whereby several parties aggregate as a unit. What emerges from this process is a collective with the properties of a single actor for certain purposes, reflecting the common interests of members and their coordinating capabilities. My use of the two terms in these essays was no doubt broad and imprecise; but the formulations most ignored by critics are in my judgment the most useful. We should think of them not as a partial (much less an exhaustive) typology of relationships, but rather as specifiable processes which, under certain circumstances which we want to identify and explore, can dominate the shape people give to their acts, and thus also the emergent properties of social aggregates.

The issues of 'maximizing' and of 'values' will be taken up in the following sections; let me first here discuss briefly the basic unit of description and analysis. Though clearly stated to be *status*, I have often been misinterpreted to be speaking of the *individual*, with a consequent loss of analytic power and consistency. This focus on status, however, entails a number of problems and potentials which were only sketchily indicated, if at all in the text, though they have in part been explicated elsewhere (cf. chapters 7 and 8).

The original text of 'Models' clearly argues that the units or elements which are joined in corporate groups are not whole individuals, but only certain capacities of individuals, *viz.* a component status. Likewise, the units that interlink in transactions are corporate groups, or 'individuals' only in their capacities as encumbents of one or a few statuses. In this perspective we can regard all social systems as patterns

of linkage and aggregation of such statuses variously in relationships
(minimally two statuses in conjunction, often a great number in a set)
corporate groups (units through the common set of members, their co-
ordination and representation), persons (the total repertoire of statuses
held by an individual at any one time) and careers (statuses linked as
an unfolding series in time). This way of conceptualizing all societies
doubtless poses some problems (cf. chapter 7); but it should absolve
us from any suspicion of naive physicalism (Evens, 1977, esp. 580-2).
'Models' clearly indicates how the definition of situations in encounters, whereby 'individuals' are disaggregated and only certain of their
capacities are made relevant, is a precondition for the actors themselves
to achieve comprehensibility and ordered interaction.

To this focus on status in 'Models' is linked the, in part implicit,
argument that since a status can be regarded as a bundle of rights and
duties which is made relevant in intermittent encounters, then the
encumbent of any such status, or the collective which forms a corporate group - i.e. each social 'actor' - is faced with an inescapable task of
'management'. Each status-encumbent and each corporation may be
seen as a 'management unit' for the assets represented by these rights,
and the liabilities entailed in the duties. This premise is only partly
made clear in 'Models' (cf. Salisbury, 1976:41 ff. for a criticism based
on this), though in part explicated elsewhere (e.g. chapters 6 and 10).
Essentially I see it as an inescapable existential problem or task of social
actors to husband their assets as a continuing fund (with which minimally to secure the capability to meet the demands associated with
the status). They may ignore it at their risk, they may fail in it and lose
the assets and even the status, they may act in ways which are not optimal in terms of some particular definition of rationality; but by standards of connection and awareness that define the status (and its
rights and duties) in their culture, the way in which they attend to
this husbandry will necessarily have consequences for them and others.
Transaction describes the process that results if actors consistently try
to order the flow of prestations between them by the self-interested
premises of a reciprocity which protects this fund (cf. 'Models': 37-8).
That this concept of transaction does not claim to describe, or determine, all behaviour should have been clear from the original text, and
will be stressed again below. Here, let us first pursue the issues relating
to the interlinking of statuses through behaviour a little further.

One is that which has generally been discussed under the rubric
of role dilemmas. A person may find himself in a situation where

obligations in one relationship require behaviour which is disruptive
(e.g. disqualifying or repudiating) for another relationship. This does
not only arise as between the different statuses combined in one person
(e.g. Vol. II, chapter 4) but may also arise within a single status set
(e.g. between skipper-netboss-fishermen, pp. 40–6 above). Indeed,
the distinction between the two types of cases is not altogether clear
and may sometimes be an artifact of how status categories are constructed by the actors themselves (cf. chapter 7, p. 124). The essential
point is that behaviour will often be profoundly shaped by considerations arising from social factors outside the relationship which is relevant at the moment, e.g. from the construction of the social person, not
just his activated status.

Conversely, the rights and assets, i.e. the 'fund' associated with a
status can, within the pattern of some social organizations, be utilized
by the person in his behaviour in other relations, or be supplemented
from the funds of such other relations. In other words, 'the individual',
specified as a social person, emerges as a management unit for some or
many coordinating purposes: some rights arising from one capacity of
the person are transferable to other capacities of the person; some kinds
of assets are husbanded and allocated as between many component
statuses. The options or impediments to such transfers are particularly
significant for the linking of statuses in careers. Another emergent on
this level of aggregation of statuses has been represented as Economic
Man, where the assets of property and own time as labour exhibit
a high degree of such transferability. These perspectives on how the
social person is constituted were not given central attention in my
discussion in 'Models', though I judged them to provide a promising
alternative in the prevailing Parsonian conception of the individual as
a 'level of integration'. But they provided the basis for an argument
of how certain constraints and patterns of manipulation arise which
impede the processes of incorporation and thus the formation of corporate groups, as explored above (pp. 62 ff.). It is most unfortunate
to confound these effects with the effects of transactional processes,
as has clearly been done (Evens, 1977:593; Paine, 1976:64).

These issues would all seem to provide fertile analytical questions,
particularly if they are pursued in a framework that seeks to explore
how various patterns of constraints and opportunities on the micro-
level aggregate into consequences (and hence, also, constraints) on
the macro-level.

Power and choice

Attention to differentials of power is an essential component of any
analysis of choice that proceeds from the strategic perspective adopted
in 'Models'. Yet much critical commentary (cf. Paine, 1974:6 ff., and
Kapferer (ed.), 1976: 5 ff.; Asad, 1972) has fostered the imputation that
I fail to acknowledge the existence or importance of power. However
muddled these criticisms may be in my view, my own position clearly
needs restating.

Firstly, I see it as essential to locate all behaviour in its situational
context, and so (*contra* Kapferer (ed.), 1976:14) give great attention to
extra-individual factors. But these factors I understand to be brought
into play *through* social action (ibid:15), i.e. I see events on the micro-
level as arising in a complexly structured context. We thus need to
represent an initial situation before particular acts and sequences take
place, and the feedback effects of their outcomes on those initial
features that can be identified. I fail to see that this is achieved by
introducing a homogenized and abstract concept of power into the
discussion, as Paine attempts. With it we might be in a position to give
actors, or individuals, their respective scores on a scale of power as an
initial condition for their interaction. But my judgment is that the
transformation from status to role and the explication of the strategies
of interacting parties require a far more detailed specification of power
for what and in which circumstances. This I have systematically tried
to provide – within the bounds of the schematism of examples – by
characterizing *statuses* and *tasks* (cf. also chapter 7). The roleplay
and strategies of skipper, netboss and fisherman in chapter 2, or the
interactions and evaluations of Swat landowners and tenants in chapters
3 and 4, cannot be illuminated except by a close attention to power in
the sense of the *concrete* strengths and weaknesses of their respective
positions. How was this in fact done? In my view, it was done by
specifying the rights and duties that define statuses, the assets of
different actors, the resources to which others desire access, the ways
these are applied to tasks. This was done without the explanation
that we are speaking of power differentials. It could be said, but it
would not be illuminating to say, that the skipper 'has' power because
he hires and fires netboss and fishermen. For some purposes this is
decisive, for others not at all. They need access to a ship, he needs
various categories of specialized labour. Who holds the advantage of
power on any particular issue cannot be read from this, or from a

carefully averaged index of respective power, but depends greatly on the particular circumstances of that issue. This is precisely what much of the interaction on the bridge is about, as I try to show; and the outcomes of individual and collective acts will be decisive for the subsequent distribution of collective and individual assets, many of them entailing 'power' of various kinds, both during and at the end of the winter herring season.

On the theoretical level, it is equally essential that one should not draw the entirely erroneous conclusion propounded by Paine (1976: 7 ff.) that choice depends on equality and that a clear disadvantage of power precludes choice for the weaker party. There are few encounters where we interact with an equal in any more rigorous sense of the term. But there must be even fewer situations where man is not faced with a range of identifiable, alternative acts for which he might opt. It is analytically impermissible to eliminate a major part of this range from our consideration by arguing that the acts in question would be self-defeating, unpleasant, or suicidal to the actor, and then select as example some particularly tragic human situation where only one, or perhaps no, option remains as even moderately acceptable – thereby claiming to have demonstrated that sometimes man 'has no choice'. Yet this seems the thrust of the argument Paine advances in connection with the position of a slave (ibid., p. 8) in a passage where this issue is confounded with several others. His conclusion would follow only if 'choice' were defined as the situation of being faced with a plurality of attractive alternatives. My own short definition of the term would rather be the situation where, after the act, others can tell you, or you can tell yourself: 'That was stupid'. I fear that many a slave has regretted some particular act in precisely those terms. No matter what rhetoric sometimes tells us, choice is not synonymous with freedom, and men and women rarely make choices under circumstances chosen by themselves. What is more, the unfortunate circumstance of a gross disadvantage of power does not mean that strategy is unavailing – indeed it may be all the more essential to the actor and all the more pervasive in shaping his behaviour. This is indicated, for instance, by how profoundly life in prisons and other coercive institutions has been illuminated by analyses focusing on 'The strategies of the weak' (e.g. Mathiesen, 1965).

An entirely different matter is the evident fact that persons can only enter into transactions over such goods and services as they in fact command, i.e. which they have to offer or to withhold. There are life situations where these are few, and there are relationships where only a small fraction of what flows between the parties can be manipulated. But even then, much of the attention of actors seems to focus precisely within this small area of maneuver, and to create elaborate interaction on that basis. Therefore, the social life which we observe may be pervasively affected by transactional processes even where these do not generate the major constraints that determine the system.

A final issue should be mentioned here, though we shall return to parts of it later: even if the model of choice underlying the argument does not fail to acknowledge power, may it not err in assuming actors to be perpetually and pervasively aware in their decisions and acts?

I have emphasized the central role of values and intentionality in shaping human behaviour; but this does not assume perfectly aware and deliberate actors, only that awareness and intention are formative of what such behaviour does show of regular pattern. It is enough that we posit that people intermittently deliberate over their desires, acts, and achievements, and have the ability sometimes to recollect experience and devise plans. Otherwise we can acknowledge that behaviour is often automatic, habitual, impulsive, passionate or random: apart from the regularities which occasionally emerge from rather special psychological or psychotic causes, it seems reasonable to trace the main causes of stability and pattern to mental processes which we group as consciousness.

Or to put the issue differently: we know from ourselves, and from conversation with others, that many acts have subjective purpose and intent. Yet how could we, unless we arrest an actor at the moment of his act and question him on his state of consciousness, know whether a particular goal or purpose was prominent in his mind? And need we know this in every case to be able to analyse it in such terms? Sometimes indeed we may hear him deliberate, and may deliberate with him, and thereby learn some of his reasons to act as he does. But without such evidence, his acts may yet (i) be so interpreted, even to the most Machiavellian extent, by others – and thereby carry these social meanings; (ii) be tacitly, covertly, or unconsciously strongly motivated in him; and (iii) have important and beneficial consequences for the actor in terms of his own values.

If we acknowledge at all the existence of consciousness and intentionality in others, and can document its occasional expression with respect to the particular acts and ends concerned, I would claim it to be valid to investigate the relationship of that pattern of behaviour and its consequences in the perspective of a model of value-maximizing choice.

The issue of values

Any model of aware actors must provide as one of its major components some representation of their system(s) of codification and evaluation of goals and ends. As between the variety of possible abstract levels and concepts which were then and are currently in use, 'Models' seeks to develop one particular alternative: the concept of 'value'. I think perhaps I overestimated the potential power and adequacy of this particular conceptualization; but I see no justification either for the disabling imprecisions or the ideological condemnations to which it has been subjected by various critics and users.

The word itself is liable to invite usage for a considerable range of meanings. Values may refer to (i) standards or scales of evaluation; (ii) readings on such scales, i.e. amounts of worth; (iii) the qualities or even objects that are positively evaluated, i.e. personal characteristics and concrete valuables; or (iv) ideas of rightness and morality, i.e. how things should be or should have been (but admittedly are not): the ideals that man should strive towards. 'Models' unfortunately employs the term in all the first three meanings (as do most anthropologists including my commentators and critics). If one is aware of the distinctions, however, it is easy to separate these three levels in terms of context. In contrast to much anthropological literature, 'Models' does *not* employ the term value in the fourth sense; if this is recognized I think considerable confusion can be avoided.

Fundamentally, 'Models' sees values as standards held by actors which affect their behaviour by ordering their choices between alternatives. But my text sees this connection as unproblematical, and addresses itself mainly to the reverse question of feedback: what happens to values *as the result* of transactions. In other words, I ask how the conceptualization of alternatives may be affected by particular events and praxis, and how norms of exchange may thereby be marginally changed. This is carried as far as asking how over-arching principles of evaluation are systematized, i.e. how wider cognitive integration may be generated; but the process is emphatically seen as taking place in the context of a complex cultural 'reality' of standards and practices and does not claim to depict genesis of (the first?) values from (prevaluational?) experience (cf. p. 77).

Against my assumptions and discussion of values Paine (1974: 11-15) seems to argue that no concept of value can be developed without the moral component (iv) above. This leads him into a bi-polar distinction (or even, illogically, a continuum, ibid. p. 11) between 'intrinsic' values (=moral, not prostituted by transactions, nice) vs. 'extrinsic' values (=self-interested, transacted, not-nice). Quite apart from the unnecessary reifications entailed in his text, I think such a demarcation of a concept of value will inevitably prove confusing and infertile.[2] I think it essential that we specify our concept of values to refer to the standards of evaluation for what people want (and don't want) to have to *have* and to *be*, not the rules and codifications of how one should best (on a continuum from 'most politely' to 'most effectively') go about getting it. People obviously also codify notions of morality in this latter sense. But when doing so they run up against all the difficulties of taking due account of the concrete opportunity situations of different actors, the multiple consequences of acts, the un-certainties of probability and risk and of intention and awareness, the relative weight of short-term and long-term consequences, etc. The clarification of this immensely interesting field of questions is not furthered by creating a concept of 'values' which is useless for other purposes. 'Models' sets out to see how far one can get in analysing the actual patterns of choice and activity in a society by means of a rela-tively restricted concept of value.

On the other hand, I do not favour the attempt to narrow the con-cept even further by distinguishing 'values' (collective and objectivated) from 'preferences' (individual and motivating) along the lines ex-pounded by Evens (1977:582 ff.). To do so will not facilitate our hand-ling of the undeniable fact that people's appetites and interests are temporary and shifting so that 'preferences' vary not only from indi-vidual to individual, but also from moment to moment. It obscures the extra-personal, cultural and collective authority behind many pre-ferences actually practised by individuals. Finally, by locating prefer-ences in the individual, it tends to place 'values' somewhere else, in some reified macro-world and not in the attitudes and acts of indivi-duals. What I wanted to capture in my development of the concept of value was, among other things, the simple suggestion that people can come to realize that not only do those things they want, and will come to want soon, have value to them, but also some things which they themselves don't want, but which others want, likewise have value to them if those things can enter into their exchanges with others. This elementary insight is hidden by the dichotomization of preferences as individual vs. values as collective, and its implications for the dynamics of cultural integration is lost.

My general, underlying view of the place of values in relation to choice and action has itself, however, come under considerable attack. Kapferer (1976:3 ff.) articulates this by raising the objection that values may perhaps be constructed by the fieldworker ad hoc to explain any and every behaviour in agreement with his axiomatic maximization principle. Little remains of the methodology and fruitfulness of 'Models' unless such objections can be refuted. Firstly, one should note that the context of anthropological investigation is one where a multitude of behaviour and interaction must be provided with satisfactory meaning and purpose. It is highly unlikely that fictive ad hoc 'explanations' could serve for the broad range of activities and choices encompassed in an ethnographic description without becoming so diverse, and contradictory, as to merely add to the confusion, if not indeed be mutually falsifying. More importantly, I would argue that with values, as with so many other cultural things, we are in the fortunate position of having a multitude of sources of empirical data. If we conceptualize them as being only in 'people's heads', we cannot observe them; if we regard them as manifested in people's acts and statements our sources are legion. They appear as persistencies and consistencies in behaviour as between different contexts and opportunity situations, they are told by actors and spectators in explanation of choices made, and are heard advanced in sessions of collective planning. Values are depicted in tales and histories and affirmed in rituals. They are acknowledged in the admiration and condemnation expressed for the achievements of others; they provide the justifications for exultation, self-pity, appeals, etc.: they are referred to in quarrels, litigation, arbitration and judgment. No single one of these sources is adequate. We shall want to discover the different modalities in which different values are communicated in a particular culture; and we want to use such expressions as evidence for the values that are embraced and practised. But we run into the difficulty that their most explicit expressions are the most likely to be rhetoric or deception, requiring a special context for interpretation. My own view is that the most useful data come from those small and large crisis situations where the fieldworker has the good fortune to be participant observer, and so stands the best chance of becoming informed about the nuances of context which the actors regard as relevant. And the explanatory power of values is tested in the *diversity* of choice and action which they illuminate and explain, not the perfection with which they seem to fit one exemplary case.

The description of values found in a culture thus seems to me as capable of empirical substantiation as most anthropological statements; as components in a generative model they are no more suspect than the other elements. What then of the report of *changes* in values, i.e. changes in the priorities given to the securing of different alternative goals? Since such statements necessarily entail a comparison of then and now, the context as well as the standards of choice must perforce differ. Even where informants make explicit comparison, they will never have the option of facing the old context of choice with the supposedly new values, and demonstrating to a sceptical anthropologist what the result is, indeed, *different* choices predicated by changing values.

My exposition of the changing evaluation of hospitality, wealth and autonomy in politics and men's house feasting in Swat (above, pp. 53-5) has been used to raise this issue (Evens, 1977:592). My argument was twofold: (i) In the new situation, conceptual distinctions between a variety of alternative forms of wealth and consumption became alternatives in terms of practical choice and had to be given priorities or preference weightings. (ii) The fact that the frequencies of alternative choices changed through time leads us to ask whether opinions as to the relative attractiveness of the alternatives may not have progressively changed as a result of experience. Concretely, when big landowners became able to sell their crop for money, more and more of them chose to do so in the period, say, from 1944 to 1954. This allocation produced changes in the amount of personal wealth secured by chiefs, as the alternative good which they now might obtain instead of political power and autonomy. What value did the parties concerned place on the virtue of hospitality in this new and changing context?

The fact that more chiefs in 1954 than in 1944 chose to obtain personal wealth and rely on the Ruler's protection of their property is not, of course, ipso facto an indication that they do not value political autonomy. It may simply be the fact that such autonomy had become more difficult and costly to achieve. Germane to the issue is the fact that giving high priority to autonomy could be costly also in the old days. We have a number of life histories to show that ambitious chiefs in the 1940s placed such value on autonomy that they gambled on odds that almost justify a statement that they 'chose' death rather than abasement. By 1954 this was no longer so. Why? Because, as some reflective persons were prepared to explain, they had discovered that it was now possible to retain many of the advantages of elite land-ownership without independent political force, whereas before the two had been inseparable because the one predicated the other. The follow-ing are my grounds for concluding that hospitality was valued less than before. Its incidence in practice was decreasing. The costs of hospitality had increased since one could do otherwise with wealth. Benefits for the giver had been reduced, since hospitality - because it was a bid for political autonomy - drew selective countermeasures from the Ruler. Finally, benefits to the receiver of hospitality also decreased, since there was increasing chance that one would be called to fight against overwhelming odds for one's host. The general agree-ment was therefore emerging that lavish hospitality was not, in fact, such a good thing: both the potential givers and receivers had become disenchanted with that style of assertion and interaction. More careful and moderate ideals (which had always been encouraged by Islam, and were practised by religious leaders and the Ruler) were increasingly embraced by the general public in place of the previous admiration for the immoderation and flamboyance of extravagant chiefs. This change was occasionally deplored with wistful nostalgia by some, but was clearly conceived and accepted as sensible. In this straight-forward sense, there is evidence of a change of values, i.e. that the standards guiding people's choice in behaviour changed from 1944 to 1954 as a result of experience of what it entailed to *have* and *obtain* the qualities of wealth, hospitality and political autonomy in the world of 1954.

Values in this sense are thus synthetic accounts of an actor's or a group of actors' codification and ranking of a diversity of ends and goals, where the aspect of ranking is embodied in a praxis of choice. Values thus serve to identify, within a particular culture, the purposes and priorities which inform an actor's choices and organize his efforts. Such values, and the opportunity situations of the different persons and social groups in the society, should together explain the patterns of allocations that are made. These performed allocations, taken together, constitute the overt, surface structure which is aggregate social form.

Analysis in terms of such a concept of value thus achieves a synthesis of micro- and macro-levels which a normative perspective cannot provide. Note the difference in the force of a normative and a value-maximizing explanation on, respectively, micro- and macro-levels. On the level of any particular actor, it may be perfectly reasonable to say that he does something because it is normative, customary in the situation. By describing a particular act as normative, one relates it to a higher level of generality where, presumably, there are conceptual and institutional determinants for the pattern; and to say that a particular actor is observing a norm is therefore not a manifestly weaker insight than saying that the actor does as he does because he values the outcome that (he thinks) his acts effect. But if we move up to the level of prevailing patterns of behaviour among a population of actors, it becomes perfectly vacuous to try to explain the practice by saying it is the norm, it is regarded as proper by them, it is their custom. The appeal to values, on the other hand, retains its simple power: if the acts (seem to them to) serve particular ends which are valued in their culture, the whole pattern of 'typical' behaviour, as well as the individual cases, is explained by the existence of those values.

To serve on the macro-level, the normative perspective must be cast in an excessively idealist mode: one is driven to adopt the classical structural-functionalist position of social structure as a set of ideas which are reflected, indeed 'expressed', in the separate and collective acts of the actors. Alternatively, one may support an essentially similar construction by arguing that it is people's ideas only that matter, not their acts: empirical behaviour is to a large extent chaos anyway, and it is its social construction both in its 'as if' character and in its interpretation in terms of ideational schemata, which provides society with a, partly illusory, structure.

There is recognizably something to each of these arguments, but each also appears to have serious flaws as a dominant framework for understanding social action and society. The first version begs the question of what are the effective constraints that make individual actors conform to a norm; and it entails an unsatisfactory conceptualization of variation in terms of norm and deviance. Still more seriously, it assumes lightly that the activities of individuals will reproduce in the aggregate the actors' understandings of macro-institutional forms: that it is unproblematical for a plurality of actors who approve, say, of a lineage system, to produce such a system in fact. The second version strikes me as mainly unsatisfactory in assuming a basic insensitivity

of man to his environment of objects and events: it seems to deny the
possibility of falsification through experience ever affecting people's
cognitions. What is more, it also seems to posit that acts will have
no other essential consequences than their interpretation (cf. the discussion of saying vs. doing, p. 81 above). Both versions seem patently
inadequate in a world where people, at least sometimes, pursue covert
strategies and break rules, and where the turn of events frequently
confounds, frustrates, and disappoints us. Basically, I do not find the
normative construction true to life, either as I experience it or as I can
observe it closely and meticulously in any society with which I am
familiar. But how plausible, and how true to life, is the individualist,
selfseeking and maximizing perspective on man which purportedly
underpins the thesis contained in 'Models'?

The issue of maximization

Probably no other stereotype of the argument of 'Models', and some
of my other works, has occasioned more widespread reserve among
my colleagues than the imputation that it entails, or even extols, a
vision of man as a ruthless, opportunistic entrepreneur. In this matter
(as in most others) there is clearly a need on all sides both for receptiv-
ity as to what is actually being argued, and awareness of what one's
own reasoning entails.

Let us start where 'Models' begins, with the argument that there
must be a significant connection between values and acts: 'It is meaningless to say that something has value unless people in real life seek
it and prefer it to something of less value, in other words maximize
value.' People's wishful thinking, utopian dreams, and ideological
statements hold anthropological interest as mental constructs and may
serve as collective representations, but they cannot explain the shape
and direction of behaviour unless they also serve as values in the sense
advocated here i.e. to order and organize acts.

It should be clear that the expression 'to maximize values' in this
context does not entail a theory of decision-making, but intends
to direct our attention to discovery procedures which may ascertain
how 'people in real life seek it'. I do not think we best further this
by developing a typology of various formalized 'decision rules' (as
proposed by Skvoretz and Conviser, 1974:60 after Meeker, 1971)
and certainly not by searching for psychological assumptions that
will fill the gap between constraints and incentives and the observed

patterns of behaviour (Heath, 1976:27). What we need are aids to
identify the salient features of the *context* in which activity takes
place. For this we adopt the more flexible concept of 'strategy', which
will relate a generalized principle of maximization to the concrete context. Alternative strategies reflect not the adoption of alternative decision 'rules'; they are accommodations to the salient features of different concrete situations in which ends are being pursued.

Let me exemplify. If an actor is confronted with a reasonably
informed, selfseeking other on the issue of dividing a limited good,
it is good strategic sense to act so as to preclude the worst eventuality:
a mini-max principle can serve *because* alter can be assumed – or
feared – always to choose the option most favourable to himself and
thus, in such contexts, least favourable to ego. If alter may be expected
to seek to maximize his own net gain in a context where this does not
need to entail maximal loss to ego, it makes good sense to present
alter with the option of transactions. If there are grounds for trust
in fair play, and the context is one where cooperation would be productive, surely cooperation is the strategy, i.e. course, that will 'maximize'
ego's value benefits. If ego's choice will not affect the moves of alter,
i.e. the context is like a game against nature, then it makes sense to
take chances if the probabilities are favourable – but within limits set
by the amount of resources available to the actor which can buffer him
against total destruction in the case of loss. Thus there can be no question of analysing these different situations by employing any single
principle of maximization. What we do is to ask the question of how
alternative strategies – i.e. plans of procedure by a decision-making
unit – will affect the outcome for that unit in various concrete contexts, and so in each case discover which alternative will maximize the
chances for outcomes which the actor values.

Since we are here still in the stage of constructing models and transformation rules that apply to models, it might be profitable to return
again to the Theory of Games, referred to in my text as exemplary of
such analysis. Morgenstern himself makes two very clear and basic
recent statements in respect to this theory: 'In analyzing games the
theory does not assume rational behaviour; rather it attempts to determine what 'rational' can mean when an individual is confronted with
the problem of optimal behaviour in games and equivalent situations'
(Morgenstern, 1968:62). Furthermore, since the fundamental fact of
cooperation is that players in coalition can often obtain more than
they can obtain by playing alone, 'the conceptual structure is more

complicated than . . . the conventional view that society could be organized according to some simple principle of maximization' (ibid., p. 66).

Real life everywhere is also a great deal more complicated than any single segregated game. If we then employ transformation rules in our models of social organization which embody the kind of precise rationality of a strategic analysis – are we not then assuming precisely such rational behaviour on the part of those actors which our models purport to depict? Indeed, no, as I shall try to demonstrate at some length. To think clearly on this issue, we need to distinguish the levels of acts vs. aggregates, the different definitions of situations imposed by actors in terms of their understandings of different contexts, and the incomplete and provisional character of 'values' and 'integration' as used in this text.

Essentially, as Morgenstern points out, a more rigorous strategic analysis allows us to define what would be rational in a context with a certain structure (including a particular set of values).[3] Having made such an analysis we can make judgments about the *extent* to which people are acting so that they maximize certain values; inversely we can also judge what their values might be or what their imputation as to the structure of a situation must be, if a certain pattern of action were in fact rationally conceived. We are also able to simulate what the implications of rationality would be, for the actor and the aggregate, in situations with a particular structure.

Thus, what I am advocating is the use of models of strategy, not to replace our observation and description of decision-making, but to sharpen it. The model aids us in identifying the entailments of alternative acts in complex contexts, and in seeing possible constructions of purpose and value which may be served by the acts which we observe, and so facilitate our search for significant data. Whether a rigorous game construction also provides a generally plausible model for the reasoning employed in individual and collective decision-making is a different question – which we now should be ready to address. To do so, we must draw on observations of how decisions are arrived at in actual cases. As anthropologists we have field materials separately available to use for this purpose, and our knowledge of ourselves and our acquaintances. These latter ones are more useful than introspection alone, because we may be more prepared to recognize in them than in ourselves a characteristic indecision, and even irresolution, in the face of important choices. Quite clearly, actors do not regularly proceed to decisions through sustained, rigorous, and exhaustive analysis. Indeed the course of any particular set of events is often so unpredictable, and the factors affecting the outcomes so many, that it would be very costly in time and effort to do so. Collectives, being generally concerned with a much narrower range of interests and allocations, may be in a better position to perform such analysis, but are often limited by their internal organization in the procedures they can adopt and the decisions they can make. Generally, actors are guided by their own previous routines in similar situations, if they were not obviously disastrous, and by the approval and assurance obtained from others that a course of action is sensible. This usually means adopting a customary course of action. From a strategic point of view, this may in fact make rather good sense too: it reduces the need for information and enhances the predictability of outcomes, including the reactions to the event by third parties. These are considerations often forgotten or unrecognized by armchair theoreticians. They also provide a pragmatic rationale for conforming to norms, without an appeal to normative sanctions.

When people do agonize over choices, I expect this is more frequently because they do not know what they want than because they are speculating over the rationality of alternative means. One difference between games and real life is that, since actors have many and diverse simultaneous interests, real acts come to have so many relevant consequences, with various time depths and varying probabilities. Besides the pros and contras one may try to consider, one also knows there are an unknown number of other factors, perhaps completely dwarfing those one has taken into consideration. In this situation, the decision-maker may – perhaps rightly – feel that it is not his values, but the outcomes, that are unclear.

Yet people are constantly making judgments in life. They harbour net impressions of what would have to be immensely long and detailed ledgers of prestations in social relations; they have expectations and make plans in terms of these expectations, despite patently inadequate information on the state of the world. They are certainly not always looking to their own advantage in any opportunistic sense, but they are often taking note whether things are going well or poorly. They are realistically aware that if they do not, probably no one else will do it for them (except where they partake in relationships of incorporation, in which case the same reasoning holds true for the corporate group as actor), and there are always others who will take the advantage of them. Also, in every culture, some signals and situations are conventionally recognized by actors as setting the stage for protracted contests requiring strategy. Though these will not concern all forms of value, they will often concern forms that are given high priority because they are regarded as being highly critical for life and well-being. Such clearly demarcated contexts will also loom large in everyday existence because it is especially feasible for those involved in them to prepare elaborately for them beforehand, and gloat or commiserate over them afterwards.

These conventionally identified contests, as well as the management requirements of all orders of decision-making units, can usefully be subjected to rigorous strategic analysis. Such analysis will provide a check on which values are indeed being pursued; it will reveal the underlying structure and constraints on interaction; and it allows us to identify what would be rational strategies in a situation with that structure. 'Maximizing' thus remains a transformation rule applied in a model. But if the observed acts, not to speak of observed customs or patterns, seem irrational in terms of what such model operations generate, it makes good sense to wonder and search again (but *not* simply dream up a further value or circumstance) to discover whether values have been accurately identified, and opportunity situations correctly understood.

These steps in analysis thus emphatically do not entail an empirical assertion that the world is populated by perpetually rational but heartless entrepreneurs. Having, hopefully, laid this ghost, we may shift our attention to the aggregate level, to patterns of behaviour, institutionalized practice, and the relation between values and social systems.

Though 'maximization' does not provide us with a generally valid model for individual decision-making, it may still provide illuminating insight in the processes whereby institutionalized patterns of behaviour emerge. To clarify this argument from 'Models', I shall formulate two simple assumptions which derive from our definitions of values as standards for judging outcomes, for what is chosen and sought. These underlie the argument of cultural integration presented in chapter 3, above. (i) Where an actor adopts a course which comes close to the most rational strategy in terms of the values embraced by him, the chances are great that he will interpret the outcome as a relative success. It is reasonable to expect this to encourage him to repeat that particular strategy. (ii) Where another person does so, then to the extent that this becomes known to an actor and his circumstances replicate those of the other, that other will tend to serve as an example.

The implication of these assumptions is that in a range of variable acts, those forms will become ascendant as patterns which come closest to the rational solutions. Thus, the conventional patterns of behaviour in a population will move in the direction of what is strategically optimal for these orders of actors (the existing statuses, persons and corporate groups) in terms of their embraced values. The analysis thus is capable of 'explaining' customary patterns of behaviour by revealing the structure of rationality that underlies it. In this we have synthesized the basic processes that produce the integration between values and praxis, and thus between the evaluations of those forms of goods which are confronted and related in praxis.

It should be emphasized that these processes cannot be concluded to produce the best of all possible worlds. The relationship which they depict between values and social systems is *not* one where the latter is designed to maximize the former. Rationality remains associated with micro-level units of decision-making, not with overall systems. Thus the separate actors in social systems may repeatedly find themselves in situations where they unilaterally or mutually preclude each other from choosing the options which would be of most benefit to them separately and jointly. This will arise because of frequent discongruities and even antitheses between micro- and macro-levels of systems (cf. above p. 79); but it is also, surely, often the result of misconceived, or indeed noxious, values that are sometimes embraced and confirmed as parts of life styles and praxis.

Epilogue

The form which society and aggregate activity takes in any particular place, and the explanation of how such forms come about, were the foci of inquiry in 'Models'. The argument which was developed sought answers in an understanding of processes. Essentially, 'Models' sees social life being generated by actors who go about their activity by pursuing their interests fitfully, often thoughtlessly, and generally conventionally. Yet they are concerned about the outcomes of their efforts in so far as these affect themselves. In this concern their judgments are based on values which serve to organize choice and action by providing standards to compare different alternatives and outcomes, both prospectively and retrospectively. When doing so, people tend to maximize the amounts of value they obtain by pursuing benefits and avoiding losses and drawbacks inasmuch as they see a way to do so.

In many connections, each of these statements will be regarded as a truism even by the anthropological colleagues most critical of 'Models', and will be readily embraced by them as premises for understanding the actions of people they know and observe during their fieldwork. But when these premises are juxtaposed and their entailments explored, I mean to have identified a set of processes which provide a powerful source of patterning of institutionalized behaviour, social organization, and cultural ideas. My argument in 'Models', and in the present chapter, is that this will be so because the *aggregate* result of such orientations in the efforts of actors is to give marked direction to the incremental changes that affect such patterns. 'Models' particularly tried to identify those processes which entail

- a general patterning and standardization of the behaviour of interacting persons;
- a certain degree of sharing of values between them;
- and a certain degree of integration of values, i.e. interrelations between them whereby they come to constitute a relatively coherent and practicable life style.

People themselves experience and observe these regularities; and they conceptualize the emergent macro-patterns, often reifying them, speculating over them, and judging the desirability or not of various aspects of them. The polemical thrust of 'Models' is mainly that anthropologists have concentrated too much attention on such collective representation of macro-features, either studying them as objects torn loose from the contexts of interaction in which they belong, or fallaciously relating them to behavioural events as their causes rather than their reflections.

The general perspective of 'Models' might be restated slightly differently by saying that its analysis focuses on how acts reflect management choices, using the term not as metaphor but in the most generalized construction that can be placed on it. The analysis propounded in 'Models' directs our attention to such considerations as the source of most non-random features characterizing behaviour. To identify these sources, it is essential to recognize the great diversity of social entities invested with estates, assets, rights and duties, or other conceptualizations entailing management needs or functions. For any analysis, these must be correctly identified; and this is also a problem which actors themselves must face. That explains the fundamental place of social metacommunication in interaction, in terms of its importance for the actors in clarifying which units are involved, and maintaining such definitions of the situation. The perspective also alerts us to the great variability in the opportunity situations of actors arising from the material presence, absence or conditions of physical assets and props, as well as the 'as if' components of social dictates and demands. We also become better prepared to recognize in social life the various conflicts of interests that recurrently arise between different management units, and the bases for the regular dilemmas that arise within and between persons from how they are joined together for some management purposes and separated for others.

One aspect of the management perspective might be noted which was not exploited in 'Models' (but see Barth, 1978:264 ff.), which may possibly be of considerable potential: the presence of strategies regulating the latency and activation of persons' social identities and capacities. We are used to conceptualizing arenas, and other focused gatherings, and the implication is plain that actors will seek and avoid such occasions according to how well or poorly they are equipped, at any moment, to meet the demands which the occasion implies. But the mere congregation of people at any focused gathering also offers an opportunity to initiate *other* social activities, functionally irrelevant to the focus. Some such activities will prove to be practically and socially compatible with the developmentally primary focus, others will not. Aggregating such tendencies, we may speculate that (a) experience and routinization will generate institutionalized expectations which may profoundly shape social life in an area. On the one hand we may see cases of complex accretion of diverse activities into fiesta-like elaborations, on the other hand bleak and empty spaces and times, avoided by nearly all for nearly all purposes. (b) Thus also, the feasible alternatives for choice are profoundly pre-structured for participants: they must choose to expose themselves to, or entirely avoid, those whole packages of accreted options and activities, and have little realistic hope of presenting themselves as potential parties to only some components of institutionalized occasions. Thus major patterns of self-realization may be affected, whereby the characteristic features of identities and distinctions in life style – say between genders, age-groups, classes etc. – may be generated. In the present context, however, these last speculations should perhaps best be regarded as an aside, illustrating only what may be the main productivity of the perspective embodied in 'Models': how it alerts us to a wide variety of dialectics between event and aggregate, thought and action, process and emergent form.

6   On the study of social change*

The analytical contribution of modern anthropology to the understanding of social change has been limited, despite the fact that our
material is becoming increasingly rich with most dramatic cases of
change. I shall use the opportunity that a brief and general discussion
of the wide theme of social change offers to make a preliminary diagnosis of why this should be so, and to suggest certain requirements and
reorientations that I feel are necessary if we wish to remedy this situation. I shall argue in favor of (a) a greater attention to the empirical
study of the events of change, and a need for concepts that facilitate
this; (b) the necessity for specification of the nature of the continuity
in a sequence of change, and the processual analyses that this entails;
and (c) the importance of the study of institutionalization as an on-
going process.

We should not underestimate the effects on our discipline that
giving first priority to the understanding of change may have. There has
been a comfortable convention in social anthropology till now of treating 'social change' as if it were a topic of anthropological investigation
like 'religion' or 'domestic organization,' something that may be discussed in addition to, and preferably subsequent to, other substantive
fields in the description of social systems. But if we couch our description of these aspects of society as if we were dealing with forms that do
not entail and reflect processes, we cannot expect that the terms and
concepts we develop in this description will serve us with equal facility
in the description of changing forms.

To understand social change, what we need to do as social anthropologists is to describe all of society in such terms that we see how it
persists, maintains itself, and changes through time. This may mean
recasting many of our terms for the description of social systems, not

* Plenary address to the American Anthropological Association, 1966. Published
  in the *American Anthropologist*, 1967.

merely adding a chapter of additional data. To do the job of analyzing change adequately may mean that we will do some of the old jobs less adequately, or at least less simply, than we have been doing. To someone who does not share this priority, the efforts may look unnecessarily complicated and relatively fruitless. But for those who give the understanding of change high priority, it is wishful thinking to expect that we can build indiscriminately on all the concepts that our discipline has developed for other purposes.

Because of our general unwillingness to abandon well-established routines, studies explicitly addressed to the investigation of change have been prone to contain descriptions of a social system at two points in time – or even at *one* point in time! – and then to rely on *extrapolation* between these two states, or from the one state, to indicate the course of change. I feel that if we want to understand social change, we need concepts that allow us to observe and describe the *events* of change. Our contribution as social anthropologists must lie in providing such primary materials for understanding the processes; it lies in our powers of observation out there where change is happening today, and not in producing secondary data by deduction and extrapolation. If this means that we must recast our very description of social systems in order to accommodate these data about the events of change, that makes our task more difficult but also more interesting.

The reason for the social anthropologist's impasse when he tries to add change to his traditional description of social systems is found in the basic characteristics of the descriptive concepts we habitually use. We wish to characterize groups, societies, or cultures, and to do this we have to aggregate individual observations. We generally think of the procedure as one where we aggregate individual cases of behavior to *patterns* of behavior, specifying the common features of the individual cases. Such patterns we think of as customs: stereotyped forms of behavior that are required and correct. Some of us may choose to emphasize the *moral* character of customs (and thus the possibility of eliciting them directly from informants) rather than their *stereotyped* character, but in either case we feel that the two are connected. We then construct a system composed of such formal features, and characterize the whole system as one 'with' dowry, or 'with' cross-cousin marriage, or 'with' ambilocal residence.

This kind of morphological concept of custom as the minimal element of form has been fundamental to our thinking because it serves such a useful purpose. It allows us to aggregate individual cases into a macro-system and to maintain the connection between the two levels. We avoid the difficulties of some of the other social sciences of using different kinds of concepts for the description of the micro-unit and the macro-aggregate: a man 'gives' a dowry and a society 'has' dowry. A custom has morphological characteristics that are like those of an individual item of behavior, and on both levels we can use the same descriptive and characterizing terms. And so we can observe people practising the very culture that we abstract, whereas nobody practises socioeconomic class or gross national income.

But such a concept of custom makes the pattern as a whole un-observable, except as exemplified in the stereotyped aspects of each in-dividual case – the aggregate pattern can never be observed by measure-ment. A custom is revealed only in a series of more or less representa-tive exemplifications. And change in a pattern, or change from one pattern to another, is even less observable: there is no way to observe and describe an event of change, except perhaps in the field of legisla-tion.

A statistical view of the practice of customs does not provide a way out. We may observe breaches of custom – but is a breach of custom an event or change? We may even summarize a frequency, a rate of breaches of a custom; we will still know nothing about the probability or imminence of a change in the custom, or about the direction of change that frequent breaches signal.

I feel that we need rather to use concepts that enable us to depict the pattern itself as a statistical thing, as a set of frequencies of alterna-tives. If we, for example, look at social behavior as an allocation of time and resources, we can depict the pattern whereby people allocate their time and resources. Changes in the proportions of these allocations are observable, in the sense that they are measurable. New allocations are observable as concrete events that may have systematic effects and thus generate important change. And this view does not entail that we limit ourselves to the description of an economic sector of activities only; it can be applied to the whole field of social organization, to describe how people in fact manage to arrange their lives.

Sharp's classic description of the introduction of the steel axe among the Yir Yoront of Australia (Sharp, 1952) stands out as an illuminating case study of social change precisely because it adopts this perspective. It provides an understanding of change by explaining the changing bases from which people make their allocations. We see how Yir Yoront women no longer need to offer as much submission to their husbands because they no longer need to go to them to obtain an axe; we understand why people no longer allocate time and resources to intertribal festivals because they are no longer dependent on them to obtain their tools.

This way of isolating the underlying determinants of social forms, so as to see how changes in them generate changing social systems, implies a view of behavior and society that is rather different from what has frequently been adopted in anthropology. What we see as a social form is, concretely, a pattern of distribution of behavior by different persons and on different occasions. I would argue that it is not useful to assume that this empirical pattern is a sought-for condition, which all members of the community equally value and willfully maintain. Rather, it must be regarded as an epiphenomenon of a great variety of processes in combination, and our problem as social anthropologists is to show how it is generated. The determinants of the form must be of a variety of kinds. On the other hand, what persons wish to achieve, the multifarious ends they are pursuing, will channel their behavior. On the other hand, technical and ecologic restrictions doom some kinds of behavior to failure and reward others, while the presence of other actors imposes strategic constraints and opportunities that modify the allocations people can make and will benefit from making.

I would therefore argue that it is unfruitful to explain a social form, a pattern, directly by hypothesizing a purpose for it. Individual actors and individual management units have purposes and make allocations accordingly; but a social form, in the sense of an overall pattern of statistical behavior, is the aggregate pattern produced by the process of social life through which ecologic and strategic constraints channel, defeat, and reward various activities on the part of such units.

This analytic perspective stands in marked contrast to the anthropological predilection for going from a generalized type construct of a social form to a list of 'prerequisites' for this general type. Though these two exercises are so close in many formal respects, their objectives are strikingly different. In one case, a social form, or a whole society, is seen as a morphological creature with certain requirements that need to be ascertained, in the functionalist tradition, the better to understand how it is put together. In the other case, a social form is seen as the epiphenomenon of a number of processes, and the analysis concentrates on showing how the form is generated. Only the latter view develops concepts that directly promote the understanding of change.

I have been concerned recently to analyze the institution of the beer party in the society of the Fur, a village-dwelling population in Darfur province of Sudan that subsists mainly by the hoe cultivation of millet (ch. 9, pp. 157–8).

One may describe the norms or customs governing this institution and show how it organizes a group of persons around a joint task. Beer is supplied by a host, and the guests arrive to drink, sing, and work for the host. Some of the guests are there by invitation; many arrive unasked and unannounced, to share in the work and the beer and the company. In all these respects, one beer party is like another beer party, and this brief description summarizes the gross customary features of the institution. As far as changes in the institution go, all that the informants, or an anthropologist with longer field work in the area than myself, might be able to say is that beer parties are becoming fewer or more rowdy.

If one wishes to describe an institution as a pattern of the allocation of time and resources, one needs to specify the set of alternatives. In a beer party you can be *guest* or *host*, or you may choose to allocate your own labor directly to your own millet field. Different frequencies of these allocations entail different kinds of community life: although they may be looked at as behavioral outputs, their frequencies have structural implications for the society.

Thus, where there is a predominance of allocation of own labor to own fields, this entails a limited circulation of labor services in the community as a whole and a low level of neighborliness and community life. Differences in wealth are constrained by the range of the labor capacity of each cultivator-householder.

Where on the other hand there is much beer-party activity and reciprocity in the host-guest relationship, this maintains an egalitarian, communal peasant community through the constant circulation and redistribution of labor services and rewards.

But the actual extent of reciprocity also needs to be measured. If some consistently act more as hosts than as guests, they are transforming some millet into labor. An increased rate of nonreciprocal allocations of this kind leads to an increased social differentiation, where some simultaneously obtain both wealth and leisure; that is, it leads to change in the direction of increased social stratification.

One may therefore argue that these behavioral outputs feed back on the structure of the community itself. The ubiquitous beer-party guest, who is exchanging labor directly for beer, does not ask himself:

How will this allocation affect our system of social stratification? Yet his allocations, made on the basis of limited considerations, do in fact create directions and constraints on possible change. It is only through attention to the frequencies of allocations, by describing the pattern itself as a certain set of frequencies, that it becomes possible to observe and describe such quite simple events of social change. Because of an interest in observing events of change, a group of us in Bergen decided to turn our attention to the study of entrepreneurs (cf. Barth, 1963b). The choice was rather obvious in that entrepreneurs are clearly agents of change: they make innovations that affect the community in which they are active. Entrepreneurs are also much more common and active in some communities and societies than in others, and the dynamic character of some societies has sometimes been explained by the prevalence of entrepreneurs in them.

The anthropological study of entrepreneurs and entrepreneurship has characteristically sought to show the common characteristics of entrepreneurs that differentiate them from nonentrepreneurs, and thus the prerequisites for the emergence of entrepreneurship. What we did was to ask, not what makes the entrepreneur, but what does the entrepreneur make: what can one say about his enterprise, is it possible to characterize it as an event of change?

Now in retrospect, one might see several alternative ways of pursuing this question and simpler ways of handling it than the ones we adopted in that particular study. But what proved stimulating to us then and later was the way this question directed us to look for ways of characterizing and describing change itself, rather than the prerequisites for change. We attempted to characterize particular cases of entrepreneurial activity as new kinds of allocation. But since our major interest was not in an individual or a category of individuals, but in a social system, we had to go on to characterize this social system and show how the entrepreneurial activity in question was changing it. We therefore had to try to show the system of allocations in the entrepreneur's community and to place his new allocations in relation to these others. In this material and elsewhere (Barth, 1967) one finds that entrepreneurs effect new conversions between forms of goods that were previously not directly convertible. They thereby create new paths for the circulation of goods, often crossing barriers between formerly discrete spheres of circulation.

This activity cannot be without effect on the culture of the members of an entrepreneur's community. If we look for the bases on which people make their allocations in primary cultural facts such as people's categorization of different kinds of goods and their preference criteria for evaluating different outcomes of their allocations, then we are relating their choices to the cultural values or value orientations to which they subscribe. The entrepreneurial coup, where one makes one's big profits, is where one discovers a path by which something of little value can be transformed into something of great value. But looked at this way, entrepreneurial successes produce new information on the interrelations of different categories of valued goods. The information produced by such activity will render false the idea that people have held till then about the relative value of goods, and can reasonably be expected to precipitate reevaluations and modifications both of categorizations and of value orientations. In other words, it changes the cultural bases that determine people's behavior, and in this way entrepreneurial activity becomes a major wellspring of cultural and social change (cf. Barth, 1966, esp. pp. 16-20).

However, the main point in the preceding discussion is the most general one: I feel that it is important for social anthropologists to realize that we further our understanding of social change best by using concepts that make the concrete events of change available to observation and systematic description.

There is also a requirement of another order that needs to be observed in such studies. To speak about change, one needs to be able to specify the nature of the continuity between the situations discussed under the rubric of change. Change implies a difference of a very particular kind: one that results from an alteration through time and is determined by the constraints of what has been, or continues, in a situation. Let me use a very simple illustration. Imagine a situation where you stand looking into an aquarium, and you observe a fish. A moment later you find yourself looking at a crab in the same place where the fish was. If you ask yourself how it got claws instead of fins, you are implying a certain kind of continuity: this is the same body, and it has changed its shape. If, on the other hand, you say to yourself that this is the same aquarium, you are specifying another kind of continuity, implying a set of constraints that leads you to formulate other hypotheses about the dynamics of change in this instance. Different specifications of the nature of the continuity that ties two situations together in a sequence of change give rise to very different hypotheses about the mechanisms and processes of change. For every analysis, it is therefore necessary for us to make explicit our assertions about the nature of the continuity.

In physical anthropology, the principle of non-inheritance of acquired characteristics represents a step toward such a specification of the nature of continuity. And the increasingly rigorous study of change has only been made possible through the explicit assertion that what continues through time may be described as a gene pool, and that changes in form reflect changes in the frequencies of genes in the gene pool of the population.

In archeology, a hand-axe does not breed a hand-axe, and the typological vocabulary that seemed to imply this kind of continuity has largely been dropped in favor of an explicit recognition that the continuity is found in (a) the cultural tradition of the tool-makers. However, the constraints on the processes of change implied by this are very poorly understood. Perhaps for that reason, archeology seems so far to have been more successful when specifying other kinds of continuity, such as (b) the constancy of materials, implying constraints that help us understand courses of change in techniques and art styles, or (c) the continuity or slow change of environment, enabling archeologists to see successive cultures as changing adaptations to the environment.

In social anthropology, the specification of continuity is highly problematical. To formulate hypotheses about change, we must be able to specify the connection, that is, the processes that maintain a social form, an institution, or an organization. An item of behavior does not breed an item of behavior. What then is it that creates continuity of society from one day to the next?

Obviously, one can say that society is in the minds of men – as experiences and expectations. If forms of behavior can be described as allocations with reference to evaluated ends, then what persists in the minds of men can be understood as items of credit and debt, as prestations outstanding that make the actors pick up where they last left off. In more general terms, one can see a continuity of agreement between people about the distribution of assets – that is, about the location of rights in statuses distributed in the population. Underlying these one might expect to find shared cultural schemes of classification and evaluation.

But the aggregate pattern of behavior, the structure of society, is not determined by this alone, so this does not exhaust the factors of continuity. What people do is also significantly constrained by circumstance: a whole range of facts of life, mainly ecological, enters as components because people's allocations are adjusted and adapted in terms of what they experience as the observed outcomes of their behavior. The strategic constraints of social life also enter and affect behavior: people's activities are canalized by the fact of competition and cooperation for valued goods with other persons and thus by the problems of adapting one's behavior to that of others, themselves predictive and adaptable.

I would argue that since these various components are all involved as determinants of the forms of aggregate social behavior, consequently they must all enter into our specifications of the continuity connecting situations in a sequence of change; and any hypothesis about social change is inadequate unless it takes all these constraints of continuity into account. It may be a convenient shorthand for structural comparison to say that a matrilineal kinship system changes into a bilateral one, or that a lineage organization develops into a segmentary state. But such a formulation is *not* a convenient shorthand for the series of events of change that have taken place, since it begs the whole analysis by implying a naive and mechanical kind of continuity between the two forms, like that between the fish and the crab in the aquarium.

Let me illustrate what I mean by a simple example, again based on material from the Fur.[1] Fur household organization is one where each adult individual is an economic unit for himself: each man or woman produces essentially what he or she needs for food and cash, and has a separate purse. Husband and wife have certain customary obligations toward each other: among other services, a wife must cook and brew for her husband, and he must provide her with clothes for herself and their children. But each of the two cultivates separate fields and keeps provisions in separate grain stores.

This arrangement can be depicted as a system of allocations (Figure 6.1). A woman must allocate a considerable amount of her time, varying with the season, to agricultural production. By virtue of the marriage contract, she is also constrained to allocate time to cooking and to brewing beer for her husband. The husband, on his side, owes it to his wife to allocate some of his cash to consumption goods for her. Such patterns of allocation are thus one way of describing the structure of Fur family and household.

Some of these Fur couples change their mode of life and become nomadic pastoralists like the surrounding Baggara Arabs (cf. Håland,

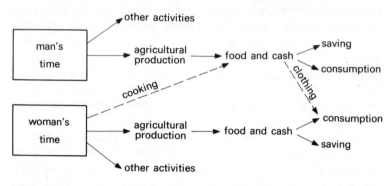

FIGURE 6.1

1967). Together with this change in subsistence patterns one finds a change in family and household form, in that such couples establish a joint household. Their allocations change, as compared to those of normal Fur villagers (Figure 6.2). The husband specializes in the activities that have to do with herding and husbandry, while the woman cultivates some millet, churns butter and markets it, and cooks food. They have a joint grain store and a joint purse and make up a unit for consumption.

In the anthropologist tradition, one might reasonably formulate the hypothesis that what we observe here is a case of acculturation: as part of the change to a Baggara Arab way of life they also adopt the Arab household form. This manner of describing the course of change implies a very concrete view of household organization as one of the *parts* of Arab culture, a set of customs that people can take over.

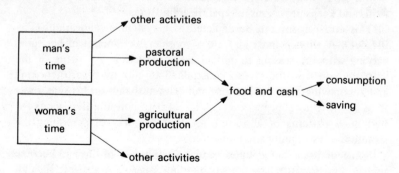

FIGURE 6.2

Fortunately, the ethnographic material provides us with a test case for the acculturation hypothesis: some Fur cultivators, in villages where they have no contact with Arab horticultural populations, have recently taken up fruit-growing in irrigated orchards as a specialized form of cash-crop production. Among such Fur too, one finds joint house-holds, but with a slightly different pattern of allocation (Figure 6.3). Here the conjugal pair make up a unit both for production and consumption, jointly cultivating the orchard and sharing the returns.

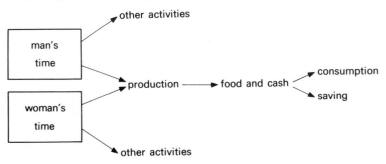

FIGURE 6.3

To maintain the force of acculturation explanation of the form of the nomad households, one would have to look for similar factors in the case of the orchard cultivators and hypothesize a change in values and acculturation to modern life among them. But it is difficult to see the sources of influence for such acculturation; more importantly, a restatement of the nature of the continuity provides opportunities for other kinds of hypotheses. If we agree that behavior in households is determined by several kinds of constraints, that all behavior is 'new' in that it constitutes allocations of time and resources made or renewed in the moment of action, and that households persist because their forms are recreated by behavior each day, then we need to ask what the other determinants of these allocations are. To explain a changing pattern of activities, we need not hypothesize changed categorizations and values: we can also look at the changed circumstances that may well make other allocations optimal when evaluated by the *same* standards.

Indeed, the traditional range of behavior and allocations in a Fur village indicates that the Fur do not subscribe to any kind of prohibition in joint conjugal households – such arrangements are just not very convenient. A fair autonomy of husband and wife is regarded as a good thing, and joint economic pursuits are a potential field for conflict. Moreover, the techniques of millet cultivation are such that persons work individually in any case; and where a person desires help during peak seasons, he or she can mobilize labor in bulk through a beer work party. In the case of irrigated cash crops, on the other hand, the horticultural techniques are such that it may be convenient to cooperate. Persons with neighboring plots often do so; occasionally, a husband and wife will also decide to cultivate a joint field – because they 'like' to work together and because they can partly take turns at irrigation, etc., partly cooperate.

The advantages of this jointness in cultivation are rather limited, only slightly reducing the labor input required for the same result, and few spouses choose to work jointly. But in a situation where one of the spouses can specialize in herding, the other in cultivation and dairying, cooperation offers great advantages. Similarly, where a pooling of labor in specialized arboriculture and fruit-picking gives far greater returns than millet cultivation, it is also clearly to the advantage of both spouses to go together over production and share the product jointly.

One may hypothesize a persistence of values in all these different situations: (a) a preference for husband-wife autonomy, and (b) a preference for the minimization of effort in production. How can spouses further these interests in different situations where environmental constraints change? Where effective production can be pursued individually, persons will be able simultaneously to maximize both interests. Where pooling of labor in orchards gives great returns with limited effort, this allocation on the balance gives the greatest advantage to both spouses. Where they thus have a joint share in the product, it is difficult and meaningless to divide it up when the mutual obligations of cooking and clothing tie the spouses together anyway for certain aspects of consumption – so joint households are generated. Finally, where complementarity and cooperation are not only advantageous but necessary, as in a nomadic setting, the necessary allocations will similarly create a joint household, organized on a slightly different pattern from that of the orchard owners. It is by considering *all* the factors of continuity in the situation of change – in this case both valuational and technical–economic – that we are in a position to formulate, and choose among, the full range of relevant hypotheses.

In this example, then, we find that change in household form is generated by changes in one variable: the relative advantage of joint production over separate production. This is hardly a surprising conclusion. But if we attack the problem in terms of a typology of household forms, we might be led to classify household type I (individual households for each person) and household type II (joint conjugal households) as very different forms and to worry about how type I changes into type II, which is like worrying about how the fish changes into the crab. Yet the situation is clearly not one where one household body changes into another household body: it is one where husband–wife sets, under different circumstances, choose to arrange their life differently. By being forced to specify the nature of the continuity we are forced to specify the processes that generate a household form. We see the same two people making allocations and judging results in two different situations, or we see a population of spouses performing allocations in a pattern that generates predominantly individual households in one opportunity situation, joint households in another. We are led to seek the explanations for change in the determinants of form, and the mechanisms of change in the processes that generate form.

In our efforts to understand social change, this general viewpoint shifts our attention from *innovation* to *institutionalization* as the critical phase of change. People make allocations in terms of the pay-offs that they hope to obtain, and their most adequate bases for predicting these pay-offs are found in their previous experience or in that of others in their community. The kinds of new ideas that occur can no more determine the direction of social change than mutation rates can determine the direction of physical change. Whatever ideas people may have, only those that constitute a practicable allocation in a concrete situation will be effected. And if you have a system of allocations going – as you always must where you can speak of change – it will be the rates and kinds of pay-offs of alternative allocations *within that system* that determine whether they will be adopted, that is, institutionalized. The main constraints on change will thus be found in the system, not in the range of ideas for innovation, and these constraints are effective in the phase of institutionalization.

The comparative rates of pay-off of alternative allocations, which determine the course of institutionalization, must be seen from the point of view of actors or of other concrete units of management that dispose over resources and make allocations. Individual actors will naturally make frequent misjudgments of what the pay-offs of their allocations will be; but as the outcomes become apparent through experience, they can be realistically evaluated. If the pay-offs are great, one can expect the behavior to be emulated by others; if, on the other hand, the results are not desirable for the actor, he will not be emulated, and he will also himself attempt to revert to older allocations. But the process of institutionalization is not simply one of duplication; the allocations of one unit can also have direct implications for other units. They may find their opportunity situation changed, not only through the possibility of emulation, but also through a new need for countermeasures or through new opportunities for activity. The aggregate patterns that can emerge in the population will thus be shaped by the fact of competition and the constraints of strategy. To depict these constraints on actors and the way they will determine the aggregate pattern of choices in a population, we need models in the tradition of game theory.

I do not wish to minimize the complexity of the dynamics of such change and adjustment. My main point is that most of the salient constraints on the course of change will be found to be social and interactional, and not simply cognitive. They will derive from the existing social and ecological system within which change is taking place. And finally, they can most usefully be analyzed with reference to the opportunity situation of social persons or other units of management capable of decision-making and action: the mechanisms of change must be found in the world of efficient causes. It should follow from this that though it may be a convenient and illuminating shorthand of culture history to differentiate between 'emergent' and 'recurrent' change, the mechanisms involved seem to be essentially the same: we must use the same tools to understand the continuities that constitute society in each case.

In summary, I should like to submit that this general line of analysis – which is being pursued in various ways by numerous colleagues in the United States and elsewhere – makes it possible for us to improve our analytic and predictive understanding of social change. I have had to harness it in this presentation to specific, incomplete, and doubtless in many ways inadequate exemplifications. But its essentials are a concentration on the observation of *events* of change and a specification of the nature of *continuity*: the constraints of the whole system that is changing.

Conversely, I would suggest that approaches that rely on typologies of overt social forms, or seek to characterize and compare different courses of change, will not provide as ready insights into the nature of social change.

7 Analytical dimensions in the comparison of social organizations*

A major aim of social anthropology is to provide a comparative perspective on social organization, particularly one that embraces all varieties of society from the simplest to the most complex. Such comparisons are fruitful because they lead to empirical generalizations, they expose analytical problems, and they allow for the falsification of hypotheses. To perform such comparisons, however, one needs to develop explicit typologies of social systems. Current trends in the analysis of society and culture would indicate the need for a typology which takes account of differences in the organization of encounters and allows for the exploration of interconnections between aggregate social forms and the construction of social persons on the micro-level.

In the following I shall discuss a few major dimensions of social organization capable of generating a fairly comprehensive typology of social systems. This I shall illustrate with some examples and substantive discussions; but the focus of the paper is on the clarification of analytical dimensions, not on the elaboration of a taxonomy.

The comparative analysis developed here thus does not proceed from a macro-view of societies through a comparison of substantive institutional structures. Rather, it seeks to penetrate down to modes of interaction in encounters, groups, and communities and to see if we can characterize how social systems differ in their basic organizational apparatus. If we seek to make typologies of the ways of constructing societies, rather than the overt structures of societies, we escape at least provisionally the vexing problems of delimitation and scale in the comparison; we no longer compare cases of society but kinds of social systems. In the latter part of this essay I shall return to the connection between membership size and the forms of organization, but the focus on encounters makes it possible to postpone this

* Reprinted from the *American Anthropologist*, Vol. 74, Nos 1–2, February–April, 1972.

discussion. We also escape at least some of the pitfalls of comparative method exposed by Leach in his contrast between comparison and generalization (Leach, 1961:2 ff.), since we will mainly be attempting to generalize some dimensions for comparing social processes, not to construct a taxonomy of institutional forms. To construct my typology, in other words, I seek generalizable features – the kind of abstractions that led to Tönnies' distinction between Gemeinschaft/Gesellschaft or led anthropologists to develop concepts like substitutability (Fortes, 1953) or multiplexity (Gluckman, 1955) to characterize a certain type of society.

A typology capable of being applied to anthropological material clearly must be compatible with basic analytical concepts in the discipline, particularly the concepts of *status* and *group*. The analytical discussion in this paper will expose certain basic difficulties in their use, but provisionally we may regard the concepts as unproblematical. Their still unworked potential has recently been demonstrated (Goodenough, 1965; Mayer, 1966). That this potential can be increased for typological purposes by a consistent emphasis on their system-oriented rather than ego-oriented application was exemplified by Nadel (1957, Ch. IV) in his exploration of 'The coherence of role systems'. Nadel seems to have articulated a general perspective, and been followed by many, in seeing social systems as basically constituted of a great number of abstractable elementary units of ascription which we, *pace* Nadel, may call statuses.[1] It has long been recognized (cf. Radcliffe-Brown, 1958) that such statuses always cohere in structured contexts which may be seen as *relations* or *persons* or *corporate groups* according to the aspect of social reality on which one choses to focus. Indeed, I should like to add a fourth 'natural' clustering of statuses in *careers*, to which we may have devoted too little attention apart from their standardized 'life cycle' form.

Most attempts at developing typologies on this basis seem to have concentrated on corporate groups, and then quickly to have foundered on the great empirical variety of such groups (see, e.g., *International Encyclopedia of Social Sciences*: Political Anthropology: Political Organization). Constructing a typology of groups seems to turn into a race with your own imagination, an improvisation of subtypes and additional types based on criteria fetched from outside a theory of social systems and descriptive of the hopeless variety of habitat and circumstance documented by the ethnographic record.

I would submit that these attempts fail because they fail to abstract one of the major dimensions of social organization: that of *tasks* and *occasions*. To subdivide and classify the flow of social events it is always necessary to specify not only persons, relations, and groups, but also the rules of relevance which actors impose on the situation. Though these often arise from necessities of a self-evident and common human kind, they are codified in ways which are peculiar to each case and cross-culturally highly variable. The events through which statuses, relations, and groups are made manifest also have their form determined by the actors' codifications of tasks and occasions – or, as Nadel puts it: social structures have jobs to do. The variety of circumstances and purposes, of 'jobs' cannot profitably be left out of the formal theory and then smuggled back in through concrete typologies, as, for example, by classifying corporate groups into subtypes according to the kind of activity they serve to organize. We should rather from the outset give equal primacy to each of the major axes of organization: the structures of statuses, and the delimitation of jobs.

To encompass these twin aspects of social organization in one frame of reference, we can utilize the perspective so vividly presented by Goffman (1959, 1961). For our gross typological purposes, it is sufficient to emphasize the concept of 'definition of the situation'. In arriving at a definition of the situation, actors reach certain agreements about the rules of relevance in a particular encounter, both with regard to what are the relevant capacities of the participants and what is the 'job' on hand, i.e. the occasion. This perspective opens very attractive possibilities for developing analytical concepts such as 'scene' and 'setting', and typological concepts such as 'forum' and 'arena' (e.g. Bailey, 1969); but these have still been very little exploited.

The important thing in the present context, however, is not to develop a substantive classification of activities into tasks, institutions, or types of occasions, but to use the concept to make a first step at characterizing *the way* in which members of a society organize their activity through the definition of situations. Thereby, we capture both the crucial aspects of social organization, viz. both the social structures and the jobs they do.

I shall attempt to substantiate this claim in the following paragraph. Very simply, we can visualize any society of which we are members as follows. Each of us is a compound person, the encumbent of many statuses. When we come into each other's presence we do so in a physical environment – one which we perceive selectively and classify culturally as a potential scene for certain, and only certain, kinds of activities. We add to these constraints, or modify them, by communicating with each other as to who we are and what we intend to do, and thereby we arrive at an agreed definition of the situation, which implies which status out of our total repertoire we shall regard as relevant and to what use we shall put it. The agreement will be workable only if all participants have a status in their repertoire which articulates with those of the others and are willing to act in this capacity. A definition of the situation thus implies the mobilization, as relevant and acceptable, of a *set* of articulating statuses. Through such understandings, social statuses are mobilized and activity ordered in the manner we can describe as social organization. Behind this creation of organized encounters, we can identify the interests and goals that set social life in motion: we can recognize social statuses as *assets*, and situations as occasions for realizing them by enactment. In part, people will seek out the partners and places that provide occasions for achieving this; in part, they will merely find themselves in the proximity of others who call on them to take social cognizance of each other.

This implies a particular view of the relation between the microlevel of separate social encounters and the macro-level of societal form, one which it might be well to make clear. I am not propounding a subjectivist viewpoint which denies the objective consequences of social acts or the existence of objective social and ecological macrofeatures which operate as constraints on behavior. What I am denying is the mechanical determination of behavior by these constraints. Human acts are predominantly shaped by cognition and purpose, asserted through awareness and voluntary behavior, i.e. through decision and choice. Regularities in multiple cases of choice are not satisfactorily explained by the demonstration of the presence of some objective circumstances alone, but require an account of how these circumstances are perceived and evaluated by actors. Their specific effects on social organization depend on the way in which participants in encounters accommodate themselves to such circumstances by taking them into account; thus they are present as part of the 'micro'-events of an encounter, as constraints on behavior, modified through the actors' definition of situations and considerations of choice. Only by showing how these codifications and evaluations are stereotyped and shared do I feel we have explained regularities in social behavior, i.e., aggregate features of society.

The feedback on societal macro-features which arises from the objective consequences of behavior, e.g. on the distribution of assets or facilities for control, is likewise neither explained by a denial of the objective consequences of acts nor by imputing purpose to all the unsought consequences of acts. An analysis requires the demonstration, for each connection claimed, of the particular mechanisms whereby such consequences follow.

I thus see encounters, constrained by circumstances and structured by common understandings between the participants, as the stuff of society. If you grant me that this is one way of looking at social life, my question will be: are the people in different societies equipped with structurally similar arrays of statuses, alters, scenes, and occasions through which they can define situations and structure interaction sequences, thereby generating the regularities in their encounters? Comparative material clearly provides *no* as an answer. Societies differ, as I shall try to show, in fundamental ways with respect to the elements of organization which they provide their members and by which these members create order in their social lives. And they differ not only in their status inventories, but in ways these statuses can be combined in persons and elicited by alters and the ways distinctive social occasions can be created. These differences would seem to provide a significant and fundamental basis for classifying and understanding different social systems.

To construct more exact dimensions for such a typology we need to look more closely at what I have referred to as status sets. The concept is an expansion of the dyadic social relationship to encompass any natural cluster of two or more reciprocally relevant statuses, exemplified by mother-child, or doctor-nurse-patient. It is meaningful, indeed possible, to differentiate status sets only if actors themselves distinguish between social situations that systematically elicit them as different sets, i.e. if alternative capacities exist for some of the persons which are elicited in other situations. Otherwise, all of the society would consist of only one set, making the term redundant.

Let us compare the two examples of status sets mentioned to note some dimensions of structural contrast. Mother is mother to (her own) children only; she is called so only by them and acts as mother only toward them. Nurse is nurse both to doctor and to patient, and must act very differently toward the two. Hers is a status with several roles, as first clarified by Merton (1957).[2] Which of these sectors of her rights and duties as a nurse will be activated mainly depends upon which alter in the total set her behavior is directed towards.

Yet, being mother also in fact implies relations to others, just as being nurse does; by virtue of motherhood a person should also be a party to relationships to husband and father-in-law and is liable to become mother-in-law and grandmother. Do all these statuses together constitute the set in the analytical sense? Are we just duped by a different convention of naming, where in our conventions of kinship terminology each role sector is given a separate term? Not quite, because, having indicated that the statuses involved are kinship statuses, we have implied a special kind of linkage whereby a number of statuses are connected so that being mother to a child you are also child to another mother, whereas being doctor to a nurse you are not also nurse to another doctor.

In other words, the concept of 'status sets' expounded here is not sufficient to describe the structure of social systems. Such systems also exhibit fundamental differences in the ways of constructing 'persons', or relevant sectors of persons. In the sphere of kinship each person is so composed as to produce, in conjunction with others, a particular kind of larger system which we may call 'replicating': if a person is A to B, he is frequently also B to another A, so most persons are indeed A + B. Kinship sets internally also show another special feature: any status can only be made relevant toward a particular kind of other – they can be depicted as dyads, and, given any particular interaction partner, there is no freedom to manipulate this component of the definition of the situation, only the task at hand remains open to negotiation and agreement. The hospital set, on the other hand, does not presume any other component of the definition of the situation: both the occasion and the relevant alters must be specified before predictable behavior will be generated.

These two systems imply very different organizations of activity. In the kinship system, most persons will perform most tasks, but toward different alters. The additional situational components determining what mother will do are in a sense secondary and are connected both with the scene and with what is instrumental in an environment. Nor can mother repudiate the relationship: the rights and obligations of the status set are always entailed in the interaction between these persons. Given the appropriate alter, there is thus really no alternative status than can be made relevant, and consequently no social interaction is necessary for the purpose of defining gross features of the situation. The fact that the main situation variable – the available alter – is incorporated in the status definition leads to the substitutability and multiplexity noted in such systems.

The structure of the hospital set, on the other hand, implies the existence of alternative sets and the possibility of interaction in terms of such sets; consequently, activity does not become organized until a gross definition of the situation, indicating the relevance of a particular (hospital) status set, has been reached. In systems of this kind, activity is organized so that any one person performs relatively few tasks, but does so toward many. The limiting case is the person who performs a unique combination of tasks and does so for all members of the society, being singularly unsubstitutable. This of course is the aspect of organization emphasized by the concept of organic solidarity. A wide range of implications of the contrast between these two kinds of system has been explicated by Lévi-Strauss (1963), suggesting that we are indeed dealing with two basically alternative and different societal types.

Three crucial dimensions which depict the organizational bases for such differences between social systems can be formulated as follows. A person, as a combination of statuses, can be said to have a certain 'repertoire' of statuses; different situational definitions bring out different components of this repertoire. Further, a total society may be said to be composed of a total 'inventory' of statuses – partly interconnected in sets, partly co-existing as alternative sets. Finally, 'social situations' are conceived in different societies as differently constituted and contrasted. The dimensions I propose for classification – not quantifiable in numbers but clearly measurable as contrasting orders of magnitude – are thus:

1 The 'inventory' of statuses in a social system: the total number of differentiated statuses known to the actors.

2 The 'repertoires' of persons: the sizes and structures of the standardized clusters of statuses that make up persons in the society.

3 The components used in the actors' 'definition of situations': what agreements are made about relevant status sets, occasions, and tasks.

A short comparative series of thumbnail sketches of empirical types may demonstrate the features brought out by these dimensions. I appeal to the reader's knowledge of the relevant ethnographies to elaborate and criticize the characterizations: they are included here merely to provide concrete referents for the typological terms.

1 Shoshonean or Bushman bands: (a) small inventory of statuses; (b) very small individual repertoires; (c) environment-oriented task organization. In these *elementary* social systems, each person would

seem to occupy a relatively indivisible position. There is thus no clear separation between a man's capacity as dominant adult male/husband and father/hunter/etc., and in all these respects he contrasts with a child or a married woman. Though such specially codified capacities change in a regular career pattern through a life cycle, they are at any one time unambiguously distributed on the local population, and interaction is predominantly organized by *one* dominant status set. Situations differ from each other mainly with reference to the definition of the task at hand, and this derives prominently from the opportunities offered by the immediate environment.

2 Australian societies: (a) larger inventory of statuses; (b) larger but highly repetitive individual repertoires; (c) partner-specific elicitation of capacities. These *replicating* systems show considerably greater complexity than Type 1, without, incidentally, being associated with more complex productive technology. Characteristically a person is the encumbent of status A *vis-à-vis* person one, of status B *vis-à-vis* person two, etc.; those persons may turn to him whenever they want prestations of kinds appropriate to statuses A and B respectively. With classificatory ascription of kin statuses, marriage-class organization, etc., the life cycle does not involve drastic changes in the constitution of the persons. Situations differ pre-eminently in terms of which personnel is present; therefore activities are organized through the process of seeking out specific partners, as well as by the definition of tasks.

Let me contrast these two types of simple societies with two types of complex societies, using the same dimensions:

3 Indian villages and regions: (a) large inventory of statuses; (b) large repertoires, which tend to be found only in a limited range of standardized constellations; (c) elaborate structures of occasions and tasks, signaled by complex idioms widely manipulated to define situations. These *involute* systems have occasioned considerable theoretical discussion, where also an attempt of mine to account for them in general terms related to those exercised here (Barth, in Leach, 1960) has been severely criticized (Dumont, in de Reuck and Knight, 1967). The issue, as I see it, lies in what has been referred to as the 'summation of statuses'. I find it necessary to distinguish the versatility of a person that comes about by his having a large, diverse repertoire of statuses, from the versatility that comes about by his occupying a status with a large diversity of rights and obligations. My argument, now and previously, is that these should be distinguished because they come

about in very different ways and exist in societies with very different constitutions and properties, although, from a certain perspective, they may appear phenotypically alike.

No one seems to disagree with the gross generalization that subcaste membership tends to imply standard constellations of capacities, i.e. standardized social persons. These component capacities of a person can be distinguished as separate statuses only if they can be shown to belong in different status sets. This requires that actors have ways of defining a social situation so that only one sector of a person is made relevant, that this sector articulates with a limited sector/status in an alter, and that the two or more parties need not involve themselves in interaction in other sectors. It is not possible in this way to elicit one such sector of 'father' and define situations so that no other inter-action involving other rights and duties of father will take place: father is one status. But it *is* possible to elicit one such sector of 'toddy-tapper', e.g. liquor seller, and allow only that status be relevant to interaction without becoming involved with the other statuses of toddy-tapper. In other words, toddy-tapper is a standard repertoire of statuses which may be activated severally and singly in distinct social situations and relationships. The fact that these statuses in Indian society tend to cluster in stereotyped repertoires has important implications for the form which interaction may take: it becomes *possible* to treat whole persons as standardized transactional partners; indeed, some parts of Indian social organization, such as, for example, the jajmani systems, are based on this fact. But the recognition that this is not necessary, that the Indian system is one based on large repertoires and not on a few wide and undifferentiated statuses, is important because it leads one to pose two central questions that would otherwise be meaningless: What maintains the stereotyped repertoires? What are the aggregate consequences of those processes, and of the presence of non-stereotyped deviance?

We know that the stereotyped repertoires are maintained by persons' own efforts and the sanctions of others and that they depend on a hierarchical concept of congruence within repertoires. A single pollut-ing status in a cluster has a contagion effect on the person as a whole, while a few more highly ranked statuses and capabilities give limited benefits when associated with the others. These premises have enor-mous implications for the social process, and thereby organize activ-ity in a characteristically Indian way: persons both seek, and avoid, occasions with elaborate care; they pursue a sensitive husbandry of social assets that channels community life and sustains complex cultural codifications for defining social situations.

The fact that people are capable of entering into limited interaction in a single status set, on the other hand, leaves a way open for persons to try to construct alternative repertoires, and through them to achieve cumulative results for themselves while at the same time creating new patterns in the society. Thus while a career for most persons involves a rather limited and predictable progression through successive life cycle phases, for some persons it constitutes a tactically ordered, innovative pattern with potential consequences for community organization. It is thus possible for the goldsmith to be a moneylender, the toddy-tapper to be a liquor salesman, the toddy-tapper (to his own and his customers' mutual advantage) to double as a moneylender until, one day, the toddy-tapper is a landowner. The local diversity and regional complexity of Indian society is usefully seen in this perspective: not as an ultimate 'explanation' of the creativity of the Indian tradition, but as a picture of the social organization, through which this tradition is consummated in behavior and thereby sustained and elaborated.

4 Modern western societies: (a) very large inventory of statuses; (b) very large individual repertoires (but each much smaller than the total inventory), highly diverse in their constellations; (c) swift and often transient definition of situation, great variation in degree of formalization between situations. A label for such complex though partially familiar societies is difficult to find; but, in view of the great range of opportunities they offer for diverse and voluntary articulation with a very large range of potential alters, we might characterize them on the basis of their most explicit and formalized kind of individual agreements as *contract* societies.

As to the social organization that characterizes them, different potentialities in these organizational elements are emphasized, in fact or description, in different accounts: (i) In an impersonal, urban environment the parties to different kinds of interaction are segregated, i.e. each status set involves a different personnel and the person moves in social space, articulating only in one limited capacity with any particular alter. The result of this kind of organization has been characterized as an open network and been associated with tendencies to subjective isolation and alienation. (ii) Perhaps more characteristic of the life situation of many members of such societies is the emergence of cliques and classes through a process whereby persons with partly similar repertoires seek each other out as interaction partners. Such partners will find that they potentially articulate in terms of a number of different status sets, and they seem to create opportunities for active switching between situation definitions rather than distinct fora for each separate set.

Yet, these sets and statuses retain some definitional distinctiveness, since two persons' repertoires never completely replicate each other, circles only partly overlap, and formal occasions with heavy constraints on switching are also maintained. The network pattern that results is more highly connected than in (i), but in my view the more significant aspect is the activity of swift and transient definition and redefinition of situations in encounters with the same personnel creating the many-stranded informalized relationships of friendships. These again, as in the discussion of caste, need to be categorically distinguished from the many-stranded relations between members of simple societies, because they are a part of very different total systems and are maintained by very different social processes, though showing clear features of overt similarity.

With respect to career forms, contract societies are characterized by variable and complex career structures in which sequences of statuses are assumed and shed by persons in patterns highly significant to the organization of society.

The thrust of this way of depicting society is generative, seeking to show how more complex features are aggregated from simple elements. It further assumes that this aggregation is, in real life, effected by the process of social interaction. The transformation rules of the model, leading from elements to aggregate social forms, must therefore be such as rest on concepts like strategy and resource management, choice and opportunity. These parts of the argument I have allowed myself to treat sketchily and implicitly, since they have been expounded at greater length elsewhere (Barth, 1966). I have concentrated rather on clarifying the elements on which the process acts. It should be noted that our empirical task is to identify and describe these elements, not to invent them. They are not heuristic devices or intermediate variables constructed to explain the recorded features of aggregate social form; on the contrary, once they have been specified they should also be available to observation as concrete features of actors and encounters on the micro-level. This opens the way for empirical testing of each main sector of the model: the elements, the transformation rules, and the aggregate forms. The use of such a model as a framework for comparative study should thereby become particularly fruitful.

This perspective, then, opens the way for identifying, in the constitution of persons and encounters, the correlates of major morphological features of the macro-system. A crucial concept in this connection is the concept of the *definition of situation*, which depicts how cultural factors of a variety of kinds are transformed by the actors into constraints which operate on the process of interaction. The comparison of some different types of society should have served to emphasize the great differences in the apparatus for defining situations which actors in different cultures have at their command. The means whereby actors can create social organization is by their conceptually differentiating kinds of social persons and kinds of occasions; it is their success in reaching agreement on some such distinctions that makes a degree of order possible. The conceptual tools at the actors' disposal for these purposes severely affect the kinds of social situations they can define and, thereby, the patterns of organization they can establish.

The poverty of components in the definition of situations in societies of types 1 and 2 I would connect with the totemistic use of *taboo* as a major idiom for defining social persons. While taboo is an apt mechanism for using distinctions in nature to create and define social distinctions, it simultaneously implies a denial that some of a person's identities can be latent and situationally segregated: taboos apply to whole, indivisible persons. During recent fieldwork in a marginal, newly contacted New Guinea community I was very struck, coming from work in more complex societies, by the constraints on status differentiation and the simplicity of repertoires which characterize a system of social differentiation based on taboo. In such systems, different personal capacities tend to coalesce; situational restrictions of relevance are difficult to conceptualize for actors, and the facility to switch between conceptually distinct definitions of the situation is lacking.

The most 'primitive' distinction in the definition of situations is that between the sacred and the profane. By means of taboos and other cumbersome and contrived idioms a supreme effort is made to conceptualize and distinguish the sacred situation from profane life. Perhaps some of our bewilderment with much primitive ritual stems from the fact that social anthropologists have not been sufficiently aware of this absence of sophistication in the manipulation of definitions of the situation within many native social systems. The organizational message of the idioms seems clear enough to us, and we are tempted to dismiss as 'redundancy' an elaboration of message which participants experience as highly necessary for so problematical a distinction. We generally meet members of such societies after a recent history of coerced contact has taught them to enter into interaction with strangers on the premises of the dominant Westerner and they have as individuals achieved some sophistication in switching between whole social systems. We must recognize the cultural limitations found in the traditional apparatus for defining social situations and analyze each system in terms only of those mechanisms on which it is in fact based.

In addition to the active manipulation of situations characteristically practised in many societies, some complex systems are also prominently organized by means of the special kind of situational distinction that separates bureaucratic and personal capacities. Complexity results in part from the *addition* of this organizational mechanism to the others; and different domains of social interaction within one population can become differently structured. Western society is thus simultaneously built on certain basic identities maintained by taboos (such as sex, and often confessional membership in universal churches), on a wide variety of statuses which are very freely manipulated situationally, as well as on offices of innumerable kinds which are delegated to encumbents who may act in these capacities only for certain purposes and may have prestige reflected on them for occupying the offices but do not command them as an integral resource. The social person in such systems is at best constituted as a highly stratified repertoire of statuses including imperative or inalienable identities, situation-specific capacities, and offices.

The incomplete and provisional typology of social systems sketched in this paper highlights the need for further analysis, in a common basic vocabulary, of the organization of encounters in a wide range of different social systems. The concept of the definition of the situation may be utilized to describe the limitations which different cultural traditions impose on the actors' control and ability to manipulate such definitions. One can thereby depict the essential duality of social organization as a simultaneous ordering of activity both in *relations* and *tasks*, and the great differences in how such ordering is achieved in different social systems. Empirical comparisons and analyses in this framework should contribute both to our understanding of the macro-level of social institutions and the micro-level of interaction.

To provide an adequate basis for comparative analysis, however, the framework that has been developed above needs to be relieved of at least two naive assumptions which have been implicit in my argument: (1) the empirical character of 'pure types', and (2) the irrelevance of scale. I shall try to show that these provisional simplifications can be eliminated without seriously complicating the analysis.

1 I have already emphasized that the typological dimensions developed in this paper do not apply to the description of whole societies as abstract entities but to the different ways in which social organizations are constituted. The evidence seems overwhelming that communities around the world differ in the way social persons are composed and social encounters are consummated. Yet it is not equally obvious how one could go about classifying the social life of any particular place with reference to the 'pure types' generated by a few abstract dimensions. As was perhaps first shown clearly in the 'Analysis of a social situation in modern Zululand' (Gluckman, 1958), social life at any one place encompasses elements of very diverse origins based on very different sanctions. This has partly come about through the colonialism and other spectacular expansionism of a particular, and many places recent, phase of history; descriptive accounts have often depicted this as the clash of two 'worlds' while concentrating on one or another of these worlds: the traditional or the modernized. But the life situation of any one person in the community is compound and confusing and is rarely composed of two such tidy sectors; also brokers and entrepreneurs by their activities create social systems that are compound in their very constitution. On a wider scale, such activity ties essentially all local communities together in a kind of complex global plural society, and every basis for isolating and classifying a part of this network seems to have been lost.

What then is the utility of the typological distinctions I have suggested between differently constituted systems? The fact of local variation remains and shows no sign of being ephemeral. Members of a Melanesian and an Indian and a Norwegian community may interact in ways that are similarly constrained by the rules and agents of modern bureaucracy or international business, but the ideas and capacities that they themselves bring to their life situation, and that they have confirmed and maintained in it, are radically different and variously generate social systems with elementary, replicating, involute or other characteristics. Our problem, in other words, lies in defining the kind of abstraction to which the typological properties of inventories, repertoires, and components for defining situations can be ascribed. Given the empirical continuum of one global society, these properties are most reasonably ascribed to systems of organization that have such separate identities as the actors themselves give them, and are often encapsulated one within the other (Bailey, 1957, 1960, 1969). Thereby we avoid the need to dichotomize modern and traditional institutional complexes, or to commit the simplification of distinguishing between total societies as distinct bodies of people. Rather, we can utilize the relative discontinuities in the networks and premises of interaction to delimit social systems within their larger environment. Such encapsulated systems can be characterized with respect to their internal constitution and workings, without ignoring the processes whereby they articulate with their environment (see especially Bailey, 1969:146 ff.)

The delimitation of the social system to which particular characteristics are ascribed thus needs to be analytically validated in each particular case. This requires a description of social organization in interactional terms. Such a description must rest on a demonstration on the one hand of the structure of encounters that provide the vessels for internal social activity and, on the other hand, the encounters and roles that effect boundary maintenance and brokerage. This should reveal the character of the discontinuities that separate embracing and encapsulated systems in terms of the social processes that maintain, and change, the institutional macro-systems. Eidheim (1971) presents one of the few case studies with such intentions (see also Barth (ed.), 1969).

2 By focusing the comparison on the way in which social interaction is constituted and channeled in different systems rather than on the institutional features of different societies, it is possible to ignore the question of scale in membership when constructing the dimensions for comparison. But it is of interest to consider the question of the organizational capacity of these different social systems with respect to scale. One tends to take for granted that simple societies cannot organize large populations – though it is difficult to demonstrate why this should be so. Conversely, there seem to be certain functional difficulties in maintaining the viability of small and peripheral communities in industrial societies. Building on the analytical framework developed here, such questions can best be approached through a discussion of *information*. I have spoken as if persons in social systems share codes and evaluations but have no significant previous information about each other – i.e., as if they have to arrive at a definition of the situation by signalling whenever they meet.

Firstly, codes may be imperfectly shared and only superficially understood, generating both unpredictability and dynamism as well as surface agreement. With respect to information in general much social interaction is in fact routinized in that previous information makes signaling unnecessary, and even may constrain or invalidate efforts to signal other definitions of the situation. The amount of such previous information that is needed, or tolerated, in any particular organization will depend on the constitution of that organization. On the other hand, the amount of such information that is actually available will depend in part on the size of the interacting population. The capacity of different social systems to organize societies of different scale, i.e. to order the life of different sized total populations, is thus closely connected with the amount of previous information about persons that is required for interaction. This again depends prominently on the techniques utilized by the actors to define situations. The story of Australian aborigines killing a stranger if they cannot establish a kinship connection with him (Radcliffe-Brown, 1913) indicates the necessity of certain vital items of information for interaction in such a society. Without information on moiety and class, or perhaps certain indicative totems, there is no way of ascribing any particular status and thus no basis for an ordered social interaction. A few such limited items of information, on the other hand, suffice to identify a whole social person and specify his relations to all available alters in a replicating type social system.

By contrast, the involute systems require more careful information management of members. Indian villagers may interact for certain purposes across caste lines without any previous information and merely through a preliminary signalling of caste identities. Such inter-action, then, may take place with a very great number of potential partners and can organize relations in a large-scale network. In other spheres of activity, more information is required before the suitability of the person as an interaction partner is established, as, for example, if the possibility of marriage is at issue. The widest potential scale of the kinship network is consequently much more limited than that based on some of the other status sets. The capacity of such a social system to organize large populations thus varies, in an immediate way, with the status sets and kinds of assets involved in the encounters. The limits of the more narrow range networks are set by the availability of information, while the wider scale networks are limited only by the limits of shared codes and evaluations. That the establishment and maintenance of such shared premises plays a prominent part in the life of these traditional civilizations has become very clear through studies in India (cf. Marriott, 1959 and Vidyarthi, 1961). For a variety of interactions in industrial Western society, no previous information is required, and the mere signalling of the presence of an asset as an object of transactions is sufficient to elicit a status set and organize an encounter. The social organization also contains a great number of functionally specific status sets in which one of the positions is open to near universal encumbency, as in the case of the doctor-nurse-patient set. Interaction is prominently organized by the fleeting mobilization of such sets by a multitude of otherwise anonymous persons who merely demonstrate their command of the minimal qualifications to be passenger, audience, citizen, etc. Such an organization has the capacity to structure immensely wide networks. The realization of this potential is further enhanced by the remarkable freedom of each individual person to accumulate information and act upon it by diversifying social relations and involving himself in deeper commitments with a particular alter based on this information. Whereas most societies require such information to be widely shared and legitimized, Western society largely allows it to be private and known only to the parties directly concerned, while remaining unknown to their many other alters. The contrast to other moderately large scale societies of involute type is striking, where an initial lack of information about a person gives him access only to a provisional 'stranger/guest' status, which, though limited in various ways, is multiplex and involves complex reciprocities of a problematical kind and also shared obligations in a wider community.

The effects of imposing a Western form of contract and situation-switching organization on a small scale population are however familiar and disastrous. The mere fact of limited personnel creates difficulty in maintaining an organization based on specialization and division of labor: the limitation of the total inventory of statuses that can be filled by the available members of the community here leads to a failure of vital functions. Small scale also has an immediate effect on the previous knowledge actors bring to their encounters. The overlap of personnel in different status sets leads to a surfeit of information and the coalescence of separate occasions: persons have difficulties segregating social situations and particularly separating out their bureaucratically defined capacities. Existing relations are made more constraining and given additional sanctions by the person's loss of freedom to withdraw from particular alters, while the safeguards to privacy which multiple potential partners and formal organizations provide in large scale communities are lost without the compensation of adjustments and tolerance which multiplex small scale organizations may provide. It has been suggested that a function of ritual in the social systems of small scale societies is precisely to overcome some of these difficulties (Gluckman, 1962:26). Most certainly the manipulation of the organization by situational redefinition and switching presupposes open networks and limited information, and is defeated by small scale (cf., e.g., Paine, 1957 and 1965 for an empirical description of these effects).

It should perhaps be emphasized that this perspective on scale does not attempt to derive structural principles by abstracting from network form. Rather, it seeks to identify the kinds of network that can be, and will tend to be, generated by actors interacting by means of certain organizational aids. I would argue that it is not necessary, or indeed possible, to reconstruct these organizational elements from a mere record of network form in a community. To provide such data in a systematic way is most difficult and in itself insufficient, whereas the organizational elements are more readily identified by a close microanalysis of encounters where the opportunity situation of each actor can be observed. The analytical perspective expounded here should provide an alternative and more feasible simulation-type approach to the analysis of networks, in place of structuralist macro-analysis.

This discussion of interaction under varying conditions of population size and organization also brings out another important implication of this comparative attempt: that the very concept of 'status' in these different social systems refers to rather different kinds of things. In the simpler societies status refers to a sum of multiplex capacities *vis-à-vis* alters with comprehensive previous information about a person. In involute systems it refers to a – perhaps compromising – component of a stereotyped cluster of capacities. In modern contract society it may refer merely to the ability to demonstrate *vis-à-vis* strangers the command of a very limited and specific asset. In other words it varies between being a total social identity, a compelling straitjacket, and an incidental option. The difference may be highlighted by the realization that a concept like that of role distance, based on the distinction between subjective self and objective status (cf. Goffman, 1961), which seems very useful and fundamental to an understanding of status in our society, becomes totally inapplicable in a social system of elementary type, based on only very few status sets. Comparability in terms of a concept of status is also seriously impaired by the presence or absence of modes of communication as different as face-to-face interaction, writing, and telecommunication, and fora as differently constituted as domestic units, lecture halls, meetings of parliament, and art exhibits.

With the tools so far developed, any attempt at all-embracing comparative exercises are consequently predestined to failure in a number of gross ways, but may yet be of some value in the anthropological debate. I would particularly emphasize the need, in any comparative reasoning, to cast one's analytical net somewhat wider than has been the practice and give attention simultaneously both to the wider organization of persons and of tasks and also to the structure of the encounters through which any interaction must be consummated.

8 Descent and marriage reconsidered*

A reconsideration of some of the themes from the debate on descent and filiation, so prominently shaped by Meyer Fortes over a number of years (Fortes, 1953, 1959, 1969) may serve as a fitting tribute to a teacher and senior colleague. My approach in the following departs from the main trend in this debate in two respects: I give greater attention to how native concepts and social groups are shaped by interaction and experience, rather than how they constitute cognitive schemata; and I introduce some further materials mainly on Middle Eastern systems, into the discussion. By these means I hope to contribute to the debate on the nature of kinship, descent and filiation, and to shed some light on the properties of the Middle Eastern systems.

The intent of Fortes' central original article (Fortes, 1953) was by the examination of a variety of new ethnographic materials to formulate a general understanding of the nature of descent and descent groups. These materials were heavily weighted towards certain African societies, and in retrospect we may see that some of the confusion and disagreement which those early generalizations engendered arose from empirical differences in the descent systems of different areas, i.e. from the common anthropological tendency to transform particular ethnographies to a paradigm of Man. This was first made clear by Leach (1957, last two paragraphs), a lead later developed by Schneider. The basic puzzle was that the classical descriptions (Evans-Pritchard, 1940; Fortes, 1945) depicted the segmentary structure as a logical entailment of unilineal descent, while later ethnographic accounts (of the 'alliance' systems of South East Asia) reported basic structural differences in such segmentary systems. In Schneider's formulation (1965a: 58)

---

* From Jack Goody (ed.) *The Character of Kinship*, Cambridge University Press, 1973.

138

Two different kinds of system, each made up of identically structured segments, are really at issue. In [the alliance] system, the segments are articulated into a logically interrelated system by the descent rule, the mode of classification of kinsmen, and the relationship of perpetual alliance between segments. In [the descent] system, segments are defined by the descent rule, exogamy, and the variable bounding of the segments in terms of specific functions (domestic, jural, political, residential, territorial, and so on).

From descriptions of some Middle Eastern societies (Peters, 1960, 1967; Lewis, 1961; Barth, 1959a; Pehrson, 1966) we may add a further kind of system. Here, segments are defined by the descent rule, but no rule of exogamy relates these segments in marriage exchanges with their social surroundings. Allowed or preferred parallel cousin marriage creates an individual network of kinship ties within and across segments, and the functions of different orders of segments depend on the variable limits of joint estates. These features have implications so that 'it is erroneous to regard Arab patrilineages as typologically one with the more commonly encountered exogamic patrilineal descent systems, for endogamy not only changes completely the relations between lineal components but alters the very internal structure of these groups' (Murphy and Kasdan, 1967: 2).

Problems have also arisen in the application of the descent concept to New Guinea Highlands societies (Barnes, 1962; for a summary of the subsequent debate see Strathern, 1969). At issue are the mode of recruitment to segments (by cumulative patrifiliation rather than descent according to Barnes, 1962: 6), the mode of articulation between segments (by locality; in accordance with descent dogma; by marriage alliance; by ritual exchange), and the ecological prerequisites of the social forms (the effects of density and land pressure). In attempts to accommodate these materials to a general anthropological vocabulary, or vice versa, distinctions have been made between how descent is applied by the actors themselves as (a) a principle of recruitment (b) a conceptualization of group unity (c) a statement of the proper composition of the group, and (d) a statement of the group's relation with other groups (Scheffler, 1965; but see also his different treatment of the question in Scheffler, 1966).

Where would such wider comparisons seem to bring us? We are faced with an increasing number of types of descent system in which the very concept of descent can imply a range of different things.

This outcome is characteristic of a tradition of anthropology which proceeds with each individual society as if it were dissecting an organism, and seeks to depict the morphology of the system by naming its parts, using concepts developed through comparative generalizations. This is the procedure so sharply criticized by Leach (1961: 2-3); to my understanding it is basic to a structuralism which starts with the empirical epiphenomena of behaviour and works through macro-concepts such as custom and institution to distil an increasingly abstract 'social structure' of which the empirical facts are an embodiment. In contrast to this mode of thinking, I should like to argue very simply that some empirical events are far more pregnant with consequences than others, and that we can construct stratified models of reality where some empirical features are singled out as the sources or determinants of a number of other empirical features. Thus, the practice of using unilineal descent as a principle of recruitment must necessarily produce groups with certain structural properties. Even though the specific consequences of this on other behaviour, will be affected by additional circumstances such as economic and political context, it remains essential to be able to show how this empirical process of recruitment generates other empirical features. I therefore see the task of analysis as one of locating such identifiable determinants and sources, and explicating the processes whereby their consequences ensue, rather than developing heuristic abstractions for describing structural patterns.

This indeed I feel has also been the intention of Fortes and Leach, among others, in their debate when they turn to the elementary kinship relations of father-child, mother-child, and spouses to find the sources of descent systems. Whatever they might claim to be doing, it has seemed to me that they are turning to real people, in real life contexts, to discover where the factors arise which generate the larger systems. But in wishing to go further and make this a crucial feature of anthropological model-building, I am forced to make clear what remains unclear in the structuralists' representations, viz: the dialectic between the concrete behaviour of persons, groups and categories on the one hand, and the collective institutions of culture and society that persist regardless of changing personnel. I must, incidentally, ask the reader's indulgence for the wide-ranging character of this discussion with the plea that, whenever one seeks to modify a theoretical framework, some previously simple points become unaccustomedly complex while some previously vague but complex questions become disappointingly simple.

To depict the connection between individual behaviour and collective institutions, it is necessary that one construct models with clearly differentiated micro- and macro-levels. I find it reasonable to see social institutions and customs as the outcome of a complex aggregation of numerous micro-events of behaviour, based on individual decisions in each person's attempts to cope with life. This is not to deny the existence of culture as a pre-established framework for choosing behaviour and interpreting experience – on the contrary, it is precisely to depict the interconnection of culture and behaviour that we need the models. Though every actor is dependent on his knowledge and codification, and hampered by conventional blinkers, there must none the less be a dynamic relationship between individual experience and learning, and the socially recognized collective facts which we call culture and institutions. The simplest form of this interconnection would seem to depend on sharing: individual behaviour produces experience, a confrontation with reality which may or may not seem consistent with preexisting conceptualizations and thus may sometimes tend to confirm, sometimes to falsify them. If a number of persons in communication share a similar opportunity situation, experience the same confrontations with reality, and have the same conceptualizations falsified, one would expect them to develop shared understandings and modify their collective culture and expectations in accordance with this. Obviously, this is not a complete theory of culture change, but may be sufficient for our purposes, as will emerge shortly. On the basis of it, we can ask specific questions about how such shared understandings emerge, and what their everyday relevance becomes. It is from this perspective I hope to elucidate the connections between descent systems and actual behaviour.

This simultaneous interest in (native) models and behaviour has been criticized as a 'failure to distinguish the segment as a conceptual entity from its concrete counterpart as a group' (Schneider, 1965a: 75). Success in making this important distinction must not prevent us, however, from constructing a model that contains both. I would criticize both Fortes and Leach not so much for being unclear on this distinction as for seeking structure and explanation too exclusively on the *conceptual* side of the dichotomy – the argument about descent often focuses mainly on the question whether it stands in conceptual opposition to affinity or to complementary filiation. Let us rather give equal weight to the aspect of confrontation with *reality* contained in any social experience. Given a certain pattern of membership in a descent group, to what groups and aggregations of actual people can the members of a descent group be counterpoised? And how does the social experience thereby produced affect the conceptualization of descent and descent group, and the social uses such group membership will be put to in the future? I am arguing essentially that we should consider the 'we–they' confrontation contained in the social interaction, and inspect how the experience of who 'they' are will mould the actor's conception of 'we'.

Now here is where some essential facts constrain us in our model building: through notions of incest and exogamy man makes an arbitrary and culturally varying, but fundamental, association between descent and responsibilities to dispose of women in marriage. It would be simple to construct a general model of unilineal descent alone, and see its implications of nesting segments, balanced opposition, etc. But people everywhere seem to see 'who they are' in terms of the whole kinship network, i.e. both with reference to relations of descent (or filiation), and marriages. Anthropology has been unable to produce a generally acceptable theory of incest and exogamy: we cannot say why persons everywhere in their choice of spouse must think of whose child they are. But the connection, variable in its particular injunctions as between cultures, is yet ubiquitous. When a group recruited by a rule of descent confronts a 'they' group, who 'they' are will be specified by the connected criteria of descent and marriage; and different marriage systems will therefore imply very different experiences of confrontation, and consequent images of the 'we' descent group.

Let me illustrate this by a straight-forward and extreme ethnographic case: the Marri Baluch (Pehrson, 1966). Here, a woman is disposed of in marriage by her closest adult male agnate or agnates. In return for a wife for its member, the extended household gives a brideprice, or a bride, in exchange. At the same time, marriage between close agnates, especially father's brother's children, is preferred. Now imagine the following situation, exemplified in Pehrson's field

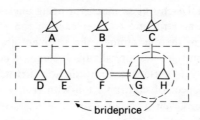

materials: The children (D-H) of three deceased brothers (A, B, C) form a minimal descent group. Marriage guardianship in the woman F is vested in her closest agnates, D, E, G, and H. G marries F in agreement with the preferred rule of marriage. He receives the bride; he and his brother pay the brideprice jointly. The recipients of the brideprice are his cousins, and he and his brother; i.e. G and H receive half shares in the brideprice which they themselves pay. Similar marriages have high frequency in the population, with a number of confounding effects (pp. 55 ff).

The conceptual distinction between parties giving and receiving a woman is clear enough, and where possible it is expressed physically as (the representatives of) two distinct descent groups facing each other (p. 115). But the concrete counterpart of the distinct groups will often fail to emerge, because persons belong equally to both categories; likewise the most elementary distinctions of kinship between agnates, matrilaterals, and affines will be confounded through the practice of such marriages (pp. 35 ff., 42). How different such experiences must be from those of the Kachin, where the wife-giving line materializes physically as a distinct group every time and all participants can see them as a corporeal reality, labelled by an unequivocal kinship term - different again from the Tallensi who can experience agreement about the presence of a group, but little agreement about who they are: matrilaterals, affinals, or unrelated.

The main thrust of the following argument is directed to show that this difference is not without effect on the meaning and relevance of descent: it affects the organizational potential of the descent structure, and the kinds of tasks and activities that are pursued by descent groups. Indeed, I shall try to show that this perspective can provide the basis for a comparative analysis of descent systems. This requires (a) concepts whereby one shows how descent rules and marriage networks produce structures with determinate organizatiohal potentials. But despite such potentials one cannot deduce from first principles the behaviour which will actually be organized by the structure in each case, i.e. whether the transmission of rights to real property, obligations in work groups, responsibility in feud, etc. It has been argued (Fortes, 1959 in 1970: 97; Leach, 1957 in 1961: 123) that to understand this, one must consider the political and economic context. But what determines which aspects of politics and economics are relevant? Different structures, as potential frameworks for the organization of activities, are more or less suitable for different tasks. We need to explicate how an aggregate of people come to use a certain structure for the organization of a set of tasks, i.e. we need (b) concepts to show the processes whereby tasks are codified and assigned to status positions in the structure.

This implies a perspective not unlike that of Fortes in his use of the concept of *domain* (Fortes, 1969: 95–100), whereby he distinguishes the normative concatenation of activity systems from their positional, structural aspect. I have argued elsewhere (Barth, 1966, and chapter 7 in this volume) that these are always connected dimensions of social organization, which both require systematic attention; and I have sought to identify them on the micro-level by the concepts of situation, occasion and task vs. status, status set and person. In one of Fortes' formulations, 'A social occasion, event or institution is not a hodge-podge of casually mixed cultural and structural elements; it has form and texture – that is, an internal structure. And this is because each element of status manifested in it carries with it (or we can turn this around and say is the outcome of) a specific context of social relations to which given norms and patterns of customary behaviour are attached' (1969: 97). In this light, a preliminary version of our question may be: 'What determines the content of descent relations?' – or indeed how is the content of any kinship relation determined?

One is led to pose the question this way because of the way we are used to identify kinship statuses. In most fields of social organization, the bundle of rights which composes a status gives, among other things, command over specific resources that provide the basis for enactment of its characteristic role: the feudal lord his land rights, the director his desk and telephone, the priest his temple. But what resources are given to a mother's brother? We identify a status as one of relevance to political structure because it gives command over political resources; thus we are not led to ask what determines the content of political relations because it is precisely in terms of their content that they are identified as political. But we recognize kinship statuses by a few diagnostic traits only; and so we can ask what determines the (rest of the) content of kinship relations. As Schneider points out in his discussion of the definition of kinship: '. . .it seems self-evident that there is more to kinship than meets the simple prerequisites of regulating sexual intercourse, socializing the young, caring for the baby. There are aspects of any kinship system that are so remote from such problems. . .that it is just not possible to account for them, or to hold them to be necessary, in such terms' (Schneider, 1965b: 88).

It looks as if, by dichotomizing status and task and putting our question in this way, we have manoeuvred ourselves into an impasse. I have chosen to do so to provide a basic paradigm of the process of institutionalization - i.e. how individual experience feeds back on cultural standardization - and thereby expose the kind of argument which may also facilitate the comparison of descent group organizations. Let us therefore focus for a moment on real people in an elementary kinship situation in Western society: one where relatively newly married spouses are pursuing the core activities of sexual intercourse, socializing the young, and caring for a baby. These tasks are assigned to a status set of husband/father, wife/mother, and child. This set is obviously for the newborn child the first set that he ever participates in. It can serve as a basis for interaction in a variety of activities, and will indeed tend to do so. If you look at what happens in such a social system of married parents and a child, you will see all sorts of role elaborations emerge as this triad copes with the daily problems of life; and they will organize all these new tasks in terms of the three statuses in the set, because they are what is relevant in the domestic situation. The child is, in other words, trained to participate in this status set; and it is the first he can handle. As he goes out into the world, and meets new kinds of problems, he will continue to appeal to the same status set. Faced with a new problem he will scream for mother, without asking whether it involves tasks organized in terms of kinship; in every community little boys go out every day and try to mobilize this basic kinship triad for new purposes. With growing social experience and competence they will start limiting themselves to doing so only where the status set is adequate or at least not grossly inappropriate. Obviously, the father-mother-child set is no good for organizing a group of boys for an egalitarian operation; for such tasks one must invent or borrow another organizational framework. But where the activity is one that can be adequately handled with the kinship statuses, I would expect them to be mobilized by numerous persons in similar opportunity situations, producing expectations and patterned ways of responding in alters. The roles in the set will consequently become more and more complex, compounded from different kinds of activities that do not have to do with sexual intercourse or socializing the young; and this organization of activities will become institutionalized as common, shared learning of how to cope with life.

What becomes kinship behaviour, in any particular culture, will thus constantly be under pressure of change from two combined sets of factors: one of which we may loosely call ecology - the concrete life situations that arise where purposes are pursued under technical and practical constraints, the other of which we may seek in the organizational capacity of kinship sets and relational networks. I do not claim that the full content of kinship relations can be deduced from these determinants; but I do claim to have pointed to mechanisms and processes which act on the tasks and obligations of kinship statuses and change them by cumulative increments.[1]

I should also perhaps point out that the reasoning expounded above bears little resemblance to Malinowski's type of biographical extension theory (Malinowski, 1929), since its crucial elements concern the transformation from status to role and the feedback of experience to routinization (see Barth, 1966: 1-11) and not the classification of variant cases with reference to prototypes.

Let me also seek to clarify the kind of analysis I am attempting by schematizing it, in contrast to a schematized version of structuralist analysis. This may be useful because my purposes are closely similar to theirs, my language is largely similar, yet some of the basic premises and analytical operations are drastically different. Let us limit ourselves to a simple, and hopefully not unacceptable, distinction between structural premises, social patterns, and individual cases of behaviour, belief, or action. As I understand the procedure of many British social anthropologists, these three are connected in linear fashion. In terms of the anthropologist's model, structural premises explain social patterns which in turn explain, and are exemplified in, individual cases. In terms of the anthropologist's investigation, it proceeds the opposite way, from individual cases to social patterns to structural premises, which

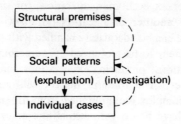

once they are discovered provide the key to model building. The type of model I am seeking to construct is one based on a micro-macro distinction, as follows: the crucial explanations lie in the transformations between these two levels: (i) how individual cases are generated

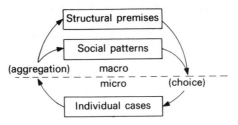

by choices constrained by empirical social patterns *and* structural, or as I should prefer to say, cultural premises, and (ii) how these individual cases are aggregated through interaction to social patterns and through reality confrontation, learning and sharing to cultural premises. The 'premises' and 'patterns' are only connected through behavioural ('micro') events, not directly in terms of homology and structural fit; the social patterns (e.g. a concrete empirical network of marriage relations) have a primacy in explanation equal to that of structural or cultural premises (e.g. a rule of exogamy).

Let us then pursue the analysis of descent systems in this framework. We have asked what determines the organizational potential, i.e. the structure, of a descent system. This potential derives essentially from the form and scale of the unambiguous status sets defined by descent available for use by the individual actors. We are, in other words, focusing first on the right-hand side of the model: the options presented by the system to the actor. The particular rules of exogamy will obviously have an immediate impact here: within the bounds of exogamy there will be a complete orderliness in the distribution of kin statuses on persons so that only a limited range of consanguines are found within the exogamous descent segment. Positive marriage rules will also create a type of order in patterning the overlap of consanguines and affines. But indeed, since *any* distribution in fact constitutes a pattern, it is the whole concrete network of pre-established marriages to which we should give our attention, not the general rules, since these consummated marriages will determine the total kinship composition of groups to which ego belongs or is confronted, and thus furnish premises for his own actions and understandings.

In Middle Eastern communities with patrilineal descent organization, the ordering effect of exogamy extends only to lineals and first order collaterals; thus no cousin is prohibited. A positive *right* to marry FaBrDa has been reported from many areas; however, since this refers to a specific genealogical relationship it should not be regarded as a positive marriage rule. Whether the explicit right is formulated or not, the actual frequency of such marriages, as a sub-category of descent group and family endogamy, is high. Crude counts vary from around 10 per cent (Ayub, 1959; Khuri, 1970) and 20 per cent (Patai, 1965), in some communities up to 30 per cent (Barth, 1954; Pehrson, 1966). There has been some useful discussion of the significance of such percentages (Ayub, 1959; Gilbert and Hammel, 1966; Goldberg, 1967, Hammel and Goldberg, 1971), clarifying how they combine the effects of local endogamy and postmarital residence with the effects of a specific preference for the particular relative FaBrDa. However, in the present context we are concerned with the frequency of the event and its implications, not its causes. These are only exacerbated by its association with rates of descent group endogamy of 40–80 per cent, and even higher rates of 'family' and 'village' endogamy.

As a result of such marriages in the past, paternal and maternal ascendants merge, and numerous affinal relations obtain between fellow descent group members. As noted above, this does not seriously inhibit the conceptual distinction of agnates from matrilaterals, or affinals. What it does, however, is effectively to inhibit any attempt to give this conceptual distinction any systematic behavioural content, i.e. make it the basis for any task organization. If my FaBr is my WiFa, and also a matrilateral relative, it is very difficult to act towards him in terms of these separate statuses, sometimes treating him as a mother's relative, sometimes as father-in-law and sometimes as agnate. The probability of our elaborating behavioural distinctions between these as separate roles is certainly minimal; the probability of our glossing over distinctions is considerable. Thus marginal modifications of behaviour would not lead to the emergence of distinctions in role capacities. And even if we did develop a task organization on this basis, it would not be capable of emulation by my brother, who has not married our FaBrDa, or my neighbour, whose father-in-law is his MoBr, or a stranger.

Considering now the left-hand side of the model, we are concerned with the aggregation of individual experiences and learning to collective and shared cultural premises. In our present case, it is obvious that the actual distribution of related persons in status sets differs so between actors that their opportunity situations are drastically discrepant and they can reach no effective agreement as to what represents useful and workable discriminations. In other words, the standardized organizational potential of kinship, given such a network of marriages, is very limited. The only possible agreement that can emerge, the only collective behavioural solution that is possible in such a system, would be to regard kinsmen of all kinds as essentially similar. And this indeed is true for most aspects of customary behaviour in the Middle East. Specific rights and obligations (inheritance, responsibility for homicide, etc.) are variously allocated, but the general obligations and expectations are of the same kind e.g. as between WiFa, FaBr, Fa and even $MoBr^2$ (see below) – in contrast to most of the ethnographies in our comparative literature. It is thus possible for Khuri (1970) to detail the basic compatibility of agnate-affine role combinations and conclude that 'given the specifically recognized family relationships in the Middle East, the practice of marrying the parallel cousin contributes to more harmonious relationships between the members of the consanguine group who at once become also the in-law group' (p. 606). Equally, one may reverse the argument in agreement with the view of role formation pursued above, and point out how this codification of kin and affinal roles agrees with what the model would predict from the limited organizational potential of the actors' actual relationship network.

Next, let us consider the political confrontations that take place between the larger descent group to which an actor belongs, and the 'they' group to which it is counterpoised. It is my thesis that the actors' experience of this opposition will affect the cultural codification of the meaning and content of descent. Detailed analyses from different parts of the Middle East document again and again that such political confrontations do not in fact follow a simple segmentary charter of fusion and fission (e.g. Barth, 1959a; Peters 1967; Aswad, 1971). There are limited situations, such as in the allocation of usufruct rights to jointly owned land, when a nesting hierarchy of segments is made tangible; but even then the actual politics is of a more complex nature. In the majority of confrontations involving related parties, the opposed units are not unilineal descent segments but *factions*, built on bilateral and affinal relations, friendship and opportunistic alliances as well as a selection of agnatic relations. As shown most clearly in Barbara Aswad's recent study, the main schisms of descent groups occur between close collaterals, in her case even full brothers; and these schisms serve as a focus for the alignment of others – not without regard to segmental position, but transmuted by cognatic and affinal ties created in part by FaBrDa marriage. Thus, twisting an Arab proverb which describes situational fusion and fission, she points out how 'In reality it is more correct as follows: "Me against *some* of my brothers, me and *some* of my brothers against *some* of my cousins, me, *some* of my brothers and *some* of my cousins against *some* outsiders." Another proverb, "The enemy of my enemy is my friend", is closer to the actual segmentation' (1971: 82). The prototypical opponent to which the whole 'we' descent group is counterpoised, is characteristically composed of strangers: armies, caravans, city-ruled police, nomads for the villagers, villagers for the nomads, other ethnic groups, other religious communities, unrelated neighbours. In *this* opposition, the basic essence of agnatic descent, involving as it rightly should close inmarriage, can be fully experienced as an ideal. The words of a Baluch leader summarizes this shifting, ambiguous character of unity and division: 'As close as the nail is to the flesh, so close are the men of our lineage to each other' (Pehrson, 1966: 57).

This view also provides us with the key to the other main feedback: how the choices of actors become such as to recreate the social patterns, here particularly the marriage network, that defines some of the features of the system. Unless the distribution of marriages is perpetuated, the premises for role solutions and agreements will change. In the case of exogamy and positive marriage rules, it is sufficient to demonstrate the perpetuation of the rule; in the case of the basically statistical pattern of the Middle Eastern system one needs to show the basis for the perpetuation of a range of choices. If we are not unduly distracted by the large and confusing literature seeking to explain FaBrDa marriage, but retain the wider perspective adopted here, this is not very difficult. In agreement with authors cited above (Barth, 1959a: 40; Peters, 1960: 44; Aswad, 1971: 48) it must be recognized that FaBrDa marriage is one of an arsenal of possible moves for securing social position. When, as is inevitable, opposed interests emerge between close collaterals, some of them will seek to align by marriage (whether to close the rift or to bolster themselves by the support of *other* collaterals in the face of the rift), and it is precisely their view of what is involved in descent and in affinal relations that makes this move attractive and effective. At the same time, it is also necessary to establish new alliances, and to renew old ones (i.e. with matrilaterals). Thus the mixed nature of the total marriage network will be perpetuated, and the same premises for experience be provided.

On one point the literature on Middle Eastern societies frequently presents material which seems discrepant with the general argument advanced here, *viz*: the special role of matrikin, and especially MoBr, as indulgent, warm and supportive relatives in contrast to patrilaterals. Informants from many areas give expression to this view, and in the anthropological tradition we might seek to understand it (i) as the result of an extension of sentiments from Mo to Mo's kin or more generally (ii) as the behavioural expression of a basic dichotomy between agnates and matrilaterals. I see no way of refuting such explanations in the present context; but my own argument has been based on the behavioural impracticability of such simple cognitive schemata and so my argument is in danger of falsification unless it can accommodate these data. Rather than appeal to concepts like complementary filiation or generalized exchange, I have to show how the standard experiences of actors could sustain an agreement about these special qualities in matrilaterals, and the feasibility of a specialized task allocation to MoBr.

To see this, we need to consider degree of closeness as a general kinship dimension. If ego's obligations and loyalties to all kinsmen are essentially similar, they will need to be practised with some general rule of priority based most easily on a scale of close vs. distant. Such a scale is clearly formulated by Middle Eastern informants and obtains not only for agnates, but for all kinsmen, to whom it can be applied egocentrically without difficulty also in a disordered system such as is generated by frequent endogamous marriages. The fact of patrilineal genealogies and joint estates for large agnatic collectivities, however, has an effect on this. Persons will know of many more agnates because of standardized genealogies and specific common interests; in cases where both agnatic and matrilateral distant links to a person are known, moreover, the former take precedence over the latter. In effect, a person will 'have' few matrilaterals and many agnates; all the matrilaterals will be 'close' while agnates will be both 'close' and 'distant'. I would argue that statements about the greater degree of intimacy with matrilaterals than with agnates reflect this fact.

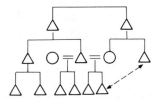

Consider next the special position of MoBr. Even where he is also an agnate, he will be a 'close' relative as MoBr and a more 'distant'

relative as agnate. In the nesting hierarchy of agnatic segmentation – important because it defines units with joint property, and thus sets of potential rivals – we find the series (a) brothers (b) half-brothers (c) father's brothers and father's brothers' sons, and (d) father's father's brothers' sons – the first possible slot that may contain a MoBr. In the schisms that divide close collateral rivals a MoBr will *always* be in a structural position where he can serve as an ally on the pattern 'the enemy of my enemy is my friend'; thus the character of this particular relative (but not 'matrilaterals' or 'cognates') as an elective, close and supporting person can be agreed upon by all actors. Finally, the position of MoBr as politically close by choice (he might align equally with any rival brother, or his other sisters' sons) is consistent with the existence of 'close non-relatives' – friends and allies without kin ties can also choose to establish stable relations involving all the prestations and loyalties of close kinsmen. Thus the politics of kinship merges fully with the politics of non-kin relations in this kind of descent system.

Let us briefly mark some contrasts with other, better known, descent systems in terms of their organizational capacities and implications. In systems characterized by unilineal descent and exogamy, as described from many parts of Africa, one obtains total order and agreement among agnates (to exemplify with the patrilineal case). This affects the organizational potential both of the agnate/matrilateral distinction, and of the segmentary hierarchy. As to the first, it makes possible a clear dichotomy of claims and behaviour towards the two: a number of tasks may be differentially allocated to each, and they can be consummated in behaviour between whole persons without any confounding effect. Thus, a wide variety of special privileges towards matrilaterals, as described for different African societies, is fully capable of realization and general confirmation among actors. However, with marriage scattering in unsystematic fashion outside the descent group, they form, as Fortes emphasizes, an individuated network. Thus while there can be general agreement within a descent group as to *what* the obligations to matrilaterals are, people cannot agree *who* they are. For joint purposes, descent group members must disregard these kinds of relations (or pretend that they are indeed agnatic, when grafting takes place). This means that matrilateral relations can be made a vessel for the organization only of some kinds of tasks, and not for the collective concerns of the agnates. Agnatic relations, on the other hand, will have a greater organizational potential; not merely are they suitable for collective tasks, but the unequivocal organization of persons in a major structure of nesting segments gives a distinctive organizational scheme for such collectivities in situational fusion and fission. The ethnographies described how this is directly reflected in obligations and in consummated behaviour, e.g. in politics – in contrast to the individuation of the close-distant scale in Middle Eastern systems producing more complex patterns of politics. The contrast of such systems to the alliance system of S. E. Asia is equally clear. A positive rule of marriage assures the concordance of kinship status and affinal status, the unilateral rule implies that affines are divided into two, each with a categorical relation to ego's descent group expressed, among other things, in kinship categorization. Not only are wife-giving and wife-receiving groups real, tangible collectivities who can appear *en masse* or be represented; since there can be full agreement between all descent group members as to who they are, the relationship can be used to organize collective tasks and collective concerns of agnates. It is this increased organizational capacity, in relation to 'local descent lines', which was so brilliantly demonstrated by Leach (1951); he also makes very clear how the behavioural content carried in such relations is not predetermined by the structure: 'With Kachin type marriage the relationship between wife giving and wife receiving groups is asymmetrical; hence differentiation of status one way or the other is more likely than not... (But) one cannot predict from first principles which of the two groups will be the senior' (1961 edition, p. 102). In the absence of such entailment, however, we need to identify the reciprocal influences of structure and behavioural content in terms of the processes whereby these are effected, and this is the focus of my present thesis.

Lévi-Strauss (1966) provides a discussion of Crow/Omaha systems which invites an analysis along similar lines. He points out very appositely that such terminologies seem to imply marriage patterns whereby new connections must be sought in every marriage, and kinship and affinity become mutually exclusive ties (p. 19). What might be the organizational potential of such systematic discriminations that differentiate members of own descent group, members of the other parent's descent group, and affines? Lévi-Strauss gives a hint by describing the system as resembling 'a pump which requires an external supply to draw upon according to its needs, and an outlet through which to restitute the by-products of its on-going operations' (p. 19). With such a process scattering the matrilateral and affinal bonds and connecting

each person in idiosyncratic ways, how much political or other collective content can these relations be given?

On the other hand, it is not clear what empirical cases we have for
such a form. Surveying the well-described societies with Crow/Omaha
features, and Murdock's classical summary of variations (Murdock,
1949: 240, 247), no common gross features emerge that might indicate
political implications of an exogamy-based process such as Lévi-Strauss
sketches. On closer inspection (pp. 306, 307) even the evidence for a
characteristic association of Crow/Omaha systems with these extensive
exogamic injunctions seems to fade. Thus the very source which Lévi-
Strauss cites on the Hopi (Eggan, 1950: 121) reminds us of the contradictory evidence, including the probable positive practice of cross-
cousin marriage. It would clearly be premature on the basis of such
uncertain evidence to try to characterize the actual operation of descent, and its effects on the actors' codifications, in a Crow or Omaha
'type' system.

It remains for me to suggest how the Middle Eastern concept of
descent reflects the gross features of the actors' experience of life with
kinsmen and strangers, and the occasions when descent groups are
mobilized and descent group identity is activated. Let me emphasize
that nothing that is said below denies the existence of a fundamental
ideology, which can easily be elicited from informants, of transmission
of substance and intangible qualities in the male line, the irrepudiable
primacy of obligations between lineal male ascendants and descendants,
and the joint fund of honour and shame between males so related.[3]
This also provides the ideological underpinning for the transmission of
property and other rights and obligations in the male line. But it does
not provide a sufficient basis for deductions about the ideology involving collaterals, or shareholders in joint estates, and thus the actors'
descent concept, it is my thesis that this, like all other concepts, will
emerge through a dialectical process of confrontation with the reality
it is used to designate. With the Middle Eastern codification of all kinship and affinal relations as essentially 'of the same kind', the range
of what will be experienced as *distinctive* for agnates becomes limited.
One can identify two dominant kinds of precipitate from the flow of
experience. (i) Whereas other kinsmen are 'close', many agnates are
'distant', yet tied together in important concerns. Relations to agnates
are therefore characteristically formal, jural, obligatory, and limited,
often expressed by the concept of *haqqi*, implying 'legal' and 'imperative'. The sanctions behind them are public rather than emotionally

internalized; trust is limited in proportion to degree of interdependence and rivalry is precariously controlled. (ii) Descent group affairs focus on property and the control of territory: they relate to a particular joint tangible estate. Among agricultural people, and to some extent pastoralists, this implies common residence and thus local community; but this is an artifact of land tenure rather than a direct effect, or obligation, of joint descent. Thus on the one hand where it dominates land tenure and settlement, descent may be identified as the source of all community life and all kinship, in opposition to outside threats by strangers and unrelated neighbours. On the other hand where joint landed estates disappear (by subdivision, administrative fiat, etc.) as is happening through most of the Middle East, most of the distinctive activities organized by descent are discontinued and descent groups disappear, since there is nothing in the organization of intimate kinship behaviour that sustains or generates them. In contrast to some authors who seek to derive the nature of Middle Eastern political systems from the descent system (Murphy and Kasdan, 1959, 1967), I would thus seek the determinants of descent group formation in political, and economic, factors. Indeed, it seems appropriate to characterize the content of descent relations as part of politics rather than kinship; and where the territorial estates at the base of these politics are removed, the whole unilineal organization disappears and kinship and local life take on a highly bilateral character. This would seem to contrast clearly to other unilineal descent systems with exogamy and/or positive marriage rules, which also tend to be sustained by their intimate kinship functions and often other joint concerns.

The main argument of this paper may be summarized as follows: in my view, the very extensive debate on descent and filiation, which has raged among anthropologists of various persuasions, has not produced adequate generalizations or a comparative understanding of descent systems. This is mainly because it has been unjustifiably simplistic in its view of the relationship of native concepts and social life: in part it has focused on these concepts *in vacuo*, in part it has assumed an easy identity between native concepts and their social expression. In a world where actual life often confounds logical dichotomies, falsifies ideological premises, and makes behavioural impossibility of embraced obligations, this is inadequate. We must construct models which capture more of the dialectical relation between concepts and norms, and social reality.

In the preceding pages I have tried to sketch some parts of such a model, focusing on the analysis of Middle Eastern descent systems in a comparative perspective. In analyzing descent and related native concepts, I have consequently asked how they are confronted with reality in terms of the descent groups that emerge and the features of the other groups to which they are counterpoised. In this we find that some culturally important premises, such as the primacy of the common identity of the male line, are retained although their implications for collaterals and the agnatic group are contradicted by the realities of rivalry, schism and factional alliance based on other kinship ties. Other conceptualizations are made ineffectual in real life, such as the dichotomy of agnate vs. matrilateral in a disordered endogamous system. Yet other culturally desired and pursued goals, such as the defence of agnatic solidarity through the retention of the women of the descent group, have unsought and unseen consequences in weakening the distinctiveness of agnatic bonds by generalizing kin obligations.

To isolate some of the processes whereby these connections are effected, I gave attention to some different kinds of content, in terms of tasks and circumstances, which may characterize relations, and the organizational capacity of different descent systems for such different tasks. I argued that this organizational capacity of descent groups is determined *both* by the descent concept in a narrower sense, and by the marriage pattern. In this connection it may be important to emphasize that an aggregate pattern of choices represents a structural determinant of the same order as e.g. a rule of descent, since it is a constraining 'given' in every person's life situation and canalizes his choices (*pace* Schneider 1965a: 76). Our perspective in analysis must be one of elucidating feedback (and consequent stability or change) in ongoing systems, and not the genesis of society from *logos*.

In conclusion, I might suggest that attempts to clarify and refine the anthropological concept of descent as a central analytical concept will hardly meet success, since it straddles so many analytical levels and encloses so diverse feedback effects. We might do better to regard it as an important member of that large vocabulary of concepts which we employ in our efforts to make adequate cultural translations, and rely on terms of greater specificity as analytical tools.

9   Economic spheres in Darfur*

This paper contains a concrete account of the main structure of the Mountain Fur economy. It also pursues an argument of greater generality concerning the use of the concept of spheres in the analysis of an economic system. Concretely, I try to show in what sense the flow of goods and services is patterned in discrete spheres, and to demonstrate the nature of the unity within, and barriers between, the spheres. I point to the discrepancies of evaluation that are made possible by the existence of barriers between spheres, and to the activities of entrepreneurs in relation to these barriers. To give the material, I also have to give a sketch of some important institutional complexes that constitute especially significant factors in determining the structure of the economy. Basic to the whole analysis is the view that the demarcation of spheres must be made with respect to the total pattern of circulation of value in an economic system, and not merely with reference to the criterion of direct exchangeability.

Physical background

Jebel Marra is a mountain massif located about 13° N. and 24° E., close to the centre of the African continent. The area is relatively self-contained, and is isolated by deserts to the North and East, arid and sparsely populated plains to the West, and the Bahr el Arab to the South. From a plain of about 2,000 to 3,000 ft in altitude the mountain rises to nearly 10,000 ft and creates an environment rather different from the surrounding savannah belt of the Sudan: despite a dry season from October till May there are perennial streams and stands of large forest. The mountain, particularly on its lower slopes, supports a dense population of Fur-speaking hoe agriculturalists, living in hamlets

---

* Reprinted from *Themes in Economic Anthropology*, ASA Monographs no. 6, London: Tavistock.

or villages of up to 500 habitants (for general background, see Lampen, 1950; Lebon & Robertson, 1961).

Subsistence

The crops cultivated on the Jebel Marra form two agricultural complexes: summer rainland crops, and winter crops on irrigated land. The predominant staple is bulrush millet (*dukhn*) grown on dry terraces and completely dependent on summer rains. Millet fields are prepared and hoed during May-June, the seed is sown as the rains start, and repeated weeding is required until harvest-time in September. The fertility of the soil is prolonged by periodic fallow periods, but extended use leads to impoverishment and final indefinite abandonment to bush.

In rocky fields, and inside the compounds, tomatoes are also grown in the summer, following their introduction by Egyptian troops some hundred years ago. Occasionally, wheat is also cultivated on the dry terraces in the summer, as a final crop before the fields are laid fallow. Low terraces by streams, on the other hand, are artificially irrigated and used for the cultivation of onion, garlic, and wheat in the dry winter season. Whatever manure is available is used on these fields; and they are not normally ever left fallow. In the summer, special crops of chillies, herbs, and potatoes are grown in these fields without irrigation. Scattered among the compounds are also a fair number of cotton bushes. To an increasing extent, irrigated lands are also being developed as orchards, containing limes, lemons, oranges, mangoes, papayas, guava, and bananas.

Of domestic animals, the most important is the donkey, on which the population depends for practically all heavier transport. Pigeons are kept by most families; goats are kept in small numbers for meat, with a negligible yield of milk. Cattle are kept by some, mainly for resale; they are not locally bred or milked. Swarming termites, locusts, wild figs, edible grasses, honey, etc. are collected and contribute significantly to subsistence.

Institutional forms

Besides this geographical and ecological basis for the Fur economy, there are also some basic institutions in Fur culture which may be regarded as primary, and from which forms in the economy may be derived. These relate to the size and composition of households, the forms of ownership of land, values concerning labour and reciprocal obligations, and the organization of weekly markets.

1 First, the units of management need to be identified – the unit which organizes production and consumption and holds a separate 'purse'. In this respect, Fur society is extreme and simple, in that every individual has his own farm plots, his own grain stores, and his separate budget. Domestic units are not primary economic units; though marriage implies certain reciprocal obligations and services, it does not imply a joint household.

Husband and wife each cultivate separate fields and store their produce in separate, adjoining grain bins in their joint hut. Neither spouse is allowed to take grain from the other's store, nor are they obliged to give any foodstuffs to each other. The economic obligations in a marriage mainly concern services: the wife must provide the husband with female labour, especially for cooking and brewing beer (from the millet he supplies from his stores); the husband in return provides the wife and her issue with clothing – predominantly, and formerly almost exclusively, spun and woven by the man himself. Some spouses elect to work one or several fields jointly, and most do assist each other somewhat in cultivation; but this does not alter their basic independence as units of economic management.

Children are fed by their mother from her stores. Boys remain with their mother till the age of eight to ten years; then they leave their home village to live as wandering scholars, attending the schools of Koranic teachers (*Fakki*) and supporting themselves by begging. After three, four, or five years they pass a religious examination with the last teacher they have been attending, and return to their village, where they start cultivating fields of their own. Until marriage, they depend on a mother or a sister for the female labour of cooking and brewing. The father, and other close relatives, are obliged to assist the boy in providing a bride-price; but he alone is responsible for his own needs. Daughters, on the other hand, remain at home until marriage and, until that time, may either work together with their mother or cultivate separate fields but pool their produce.

In other words, economic activities are characteristically pursued by single individuals, though in a matrix of obligations, mainly of providing labour, to persons in specified kinship positions.

2 This means that every person must obtain individual access to the basic means of production: land. The rights over land are institutionalized as follows:

Territorial rights are associated with descent groups of a non-unilineal kind – large blocks of kinsmen, with an endogamous tendency, often spoken of as patrilineal in form but in fact of a much looser structure allowing membership 'through our grandmothers'. This looseness in structure is possible only because the groups are non-corporate – their joint rights are vested in a title-holder, who represents the kin group in question and is responsible for its joint estate.

His responsibility consists in essence in allocating usufruct rights to fields. Such rights are given to individuals and are usually retained by them until use of the land is discontinued – i.e. the usufruct rights do not lapse when fields are left fallow in a systematic rotational pattern, only when they are abandoned. However, inside a community, it is regarded as every individual's right to obtain the land necessary for subsistence. When need arises, and when there is no unused land available, usufruct rights may be revoked and some land taken from those who have plenty and given to those who are in need. The title-holder is the person with the power to revoke such rights and redistribute the land of his descent group. Because the argument from relative need is accepted, he will be obliged to allocate fields alike to members and non-members of the 'owning' group; and the distribution of plots shows little correlation with the distribution of the users' descent-group rights.

The rights of the cultivator as *user* as distinct from *owner* are expressed in the symbolic prestation of one pot of beer to the title-holder after each harvest – a custom that is not consistently practised but is universally regarded as correct and proper. No rent in kind or services, or other obligations, are required from the cultivator.

The more shifting nature of cultivation on the unirrigated lands assures a fair circulation of usufruct rights in the population. There is some tendency for children to take over the dry farms cultivated by their parents, especially for daughters to succeed on the death of their mother; but there does not seem to be any question of the lineal transfer of usufruct rights over several generations. In the case of the irrigated lands, however, no periods of disuse intervene, and usufruct rights come up for redistribution only on the death of the cultivator. The argument of need is used to justify a reallocation of rights to small onion plots, but most of the irrigated land tends to remain in the same hands, and there is an increasing tendency, with the growth of irrigation agriculture, for title-holders to monopolize this resource (see below, p. 175).

None the less, the main picture remains that land, as the main productive resource, is made available to all without any significant rent or other counter-prestation.

3 With every individual so characteristically constituting a separate unit of management for economic purposes, the predominant pattern of labour tends to be one where every person uses his or her own time to work for the direct satisfaction of his own needs. By Mountain Fur conventions, it is furthermore shameful to work for wages in the local community, though a few men have experience as migrant labour elsewhere. None the less, there are institutionalized opportunities for both symmetrical and asymmetrical transactions involving labour, and there are some kinship and neighbourhood obligations which commit fractions of a person's time and effort.

The Fur institution that facilitates labour exchanges is the beer party. This takes several forms, exemplified by informal reciprocal help, work parties with many participants, and house-building parties. In the simplest form, two or more friends may decide to work together for company, in which case they jointly cultivate each other's field in turn, he whose field is being cultivated providing a pot of beer for their joint consumption. Larger work parties may be arranged in a similar way, but without the obligation of reciprocity: a man will announce his intention a few days in advance, have a large amount of beer prepared, and ask his friends and neighbours to come to the work party. Besides those who are invited, any person who wishes may join the party and drink beer in return for working. In these cases, the beer must be plentiful and is supposed to compensate for the work being expended; when the beer is finished, the work party disperses. Finally, house-building has a communal and reciprocal character; a day is announced for the work - first one for the women, who plaster the hut walls, then for the men, who build the roof and thatch it. On the appointed day, kinsmen and neighbours who have been invited are obliged to come, bringing with them the materials that are needed in the building. Large amounts of beer must again be provided by the host, and other persons may join in the work, in which case they pay a 'fine' of 2 piastres (about fivepence) for not having brought building materials.

Close kin of the house-builders, especially brothers and sisters, also assist by supplying one or several pots of beer at such occasions, as well as by working themselves and egging on the other guests to work well. A person's freedom to allocate his own labour is thus restricted by some commitments, and his opportunities for disposing of it on the Fur labour-for-beer labour market are restricted by the number of occasions offered by work parties in the local or adjoining villages. These are, however, very frequent in the larger communities; and with the above reservations one may say that essentially, a person's time is his own, to use for labour in his own fields or to exchange for beer on a local, relatively open, labour market. The reciprocities that limit a person's freedom on this market derive from obligations of mutual sociability, i.e. they are associated with the 'party' and not the 'work' aspect of the work party. Labour is seen as adequately compensated for in beer, and there is no restriction that each person's input of work and of beer into the system should be equivalent. This fact, together with the considerable degree of freedom allowed persons in choosing partners and occasions for transactions, means that we are dealing with a *market* for the exchange of labour and beer. The fact that persons also enjoy the 'party' aspect of the work party does not affect this argument.

4   Fourthly, the Fur have a well-organized system of marketplaces, which facilitates a great number of economic exchanges. The medium of exchange used at these markets is, and has for a long time been, money issued in the Nile valley. Previously, cloth may have served as a medium of exchange.

Each marketplace is active one day, or in a few cases two days, a week. They are spaced at a distance of 15 to 20 km from each other on the perimeter of the mountain, so that every community is within walking distance of at least one marketplace, enabling people to attend the market and return home the same day. Particularly in the slack agricultural seasons, markets are visited by large numbers of people, amounting to several hundred through much of the day.

Villagers bring all varieties of agricultural produce to the marketplace, though millet, being very bulky and heavy in proportion to its value, is rarely marketed. Most producers bring only small quantities, since they sell only to obtain cash for specific purchases, though some, anticipating a good price or because of acute need, may also bring larger quantities to sell in bulk. Occasionally, cattle or goats are also brought for sale by their owners. Craftsmen, who form a small, discrete population of male smiths and female potters, also bring their products for sale, and the smith sets up a small anvil for incidental repairs. Finally, travelling pedlars, most of them Arabs but some Fur, set up shops in booths or on mats from which they sell imported industrial consumer goods, particularly cloth, utensils, sugar, etc.

Numerous middlemen appear and mediate the flow of trade while seeking profit, either by speculating in rising prices through the day, or by accumulating products in bulk for transport and re-sale at communication entrepots 50 to 100 km away. Each will specialize in one or two products – garlic, onions, dried tomatoes, or wheat – buying from the individual producers and accumulating for re-sale on the spot, or for transport. Middlemen also buy the livestock, slaughter and partition it, and sell it in small portions to local consumers. Some sales of fresh vegetables, fruits, and other garden produce also take place directly from producer to individual consumer.

Some women also brew beer and bring it for sale in the marketplace. Though there is no dearth of buyers, especially as the afternoon wears on, the sale of beer is regarded as immoral and the women who do so are looked upon as immodest. This may be both because the making of beer is an intimate female service appropriate only in a close, domestic context, and because beer, as in a work party, is a festive idiom of cooperation and companionship and not appropriate as an object of commercial bargaining.

In the marketplace, then, individual villagers are able to exchange their agricultural products for tools and utensils, cloth, and a variety of other consumer goods which they do not themselves produce. They do so by freely switching between the statuses of buyer and seller, and must deal with factors of supply and demand and with fluctuating prices measured in a monetary currency.

Economic spheres

The facts presented so far invite the use of a concept of economic spheres. They suggest the existence of two discrete spheres of exchange in the Mountain Fur economy: one that embraces a large variety of material items, including also a monetary medium, and is associated with the marketplace facilities; and another that exists for the exchange of labour and beer. The two spheres are separated by the sanction of moral reprobation on conversions from labour to cash and from beer to cash. They thus would seem to fit well the definition of spheres given in Bohannan and Dalton (1962, p. 8), i.e. they each constitute a set of freely exchangeable material items and services. They also would seem to exhibit the feature of hierarchical ranking: conversions in the one direction are frowned upon; i.e. the sphere containing labour and beer would be regarded as the higher, that associated with the monetary medium the lower.

However, such a model is inconsistent with some of the empirical material. Thus some highly prestigious items of wealth, such as swords, are obtained in the cash sphere. Furthermore, the bridewealth for a wife is composed predominantly of cash and items from the cash sphere, and this would indicate a high rather than a low rating for the cash sphere.

Nor can one argue that these are the effects of breakdown associated with the introduction of money. Cash had been used in the Fur area long before colonial times, and the system described here is in this sense a traditional and relatively stable one in which cash is an integral part. If a concept of spheres is to be useful for the analysis of this system, the hierarchical assumption is best dismissed.

What is more, it is difficult to relate the labour-beer sphere significantly to the cash sphere by any patterned channels of conversion. On a more fundamental level, I would argue that a separation of spheres based on the criterion of exchangeability alone gives an unnecessarily inadequate representation of the structure of the economy. The concept of spheres has much greater analytic utility if it relates to all forms of circulation and transformation of value, whether by exchange, production, inheritance, or other means.

I shall therefore try to depict all the standard choices of alternative allocations of resources open to the units of management in the Fur economy, and to delimit the significant spheres with respect to the total pattern of circulation or flow of value. The units of management are single individuals, whose basic problem is to transform their own efforts into a range of items that satisfies their own consumption profile. The institutional forms I have described above may be regarded as the main facilities or means at their disposal to achieve this transformation; and the description of the economy is simplified by the fact that persons have approximately equal access to these facilities.[1] It is further simplified by the fact that, as members of a relatively homogeneous society, their habits and appetites are similar, except for the male–female differences which mainly reflect reciprocal obligations in marriage.

An attempt to aggregate the allocations of the whole population of management units, giving a picture of the *village* economy, is therefore unusually simple in this case. In the cash sphere, as long as there is no shortage of land, the village economy can be represented as the *sum* of decisions of management units, since these units do not seriously compete for resources and their activities do not have any great impact on market prices. Aggregating the decisions in the millet–beer–labour sphere is more difficult, since any transformation by a management unit of its beer into labour presupposes the presence of persons willing to exchange their labour for beer. The simplest procedure is to assume a certain supply of labour and beer and to see how the allocation decision of one member unit might affect the availability of these forms of value on the market, and possibly also affect the relative 'price' of each as measured in terms of the other. Some of these problems are taken up below in the section on management and stratification (pp. 171-2) and in connection with new uses of labour and possible responses to this (pp. 173 ff.).

The pattern of standard alternative choices for a Fur management unit can thus be represented as in the diagram. With the reservations noted above, this may simultaneously be regarded as a model of the village economy as a whole. The remainder of this paper is essentially an exposition of this diagram followed by a discussion of its implications.

Patterns and alternatives of allocation

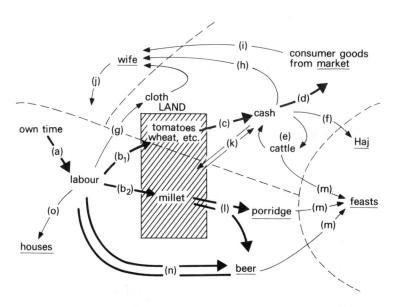

FIGURE 9.1 The pattern of standard alternative choices for a Fur management unit

(a) The input into the economic system is the person's own time, used as labour. All self-supporting persons in the society must and do have the basic skills necessary to cultivate the main varieties of crops, and to trade.

(b) To start production, a person next needs access to land. This is obtained either from a parent or close relative with plenty, or from one of the title-holders in the village. Every individual needs to obtain plots of several kinds, suitable for different crops and uses. A configuration of sizes and types of farm implies an allocation of labour to alternative products: millet, and some onions, for basic subsistence, and readily marketable crops such as tomatoes, wheat, garlic, onions for cash needs. The balance struck between these two categories of products depends on the person's obligations: women, especially those with small children, concentrate more of their effort on millet, while men, especially those with plural wives have greater need for cash to meet the obligations of clothing their families, and to save towards bride-wealth for themselves or their sons.

In the course of the year, every person will need to cultivate at least one farm in each category. One may choose to distribute the labour so that most work falls in the rainy season on millet and tomato farms, leaving much time in the winter for threshing, house-building, and trading, or to allocate the labour more equally between summer and winter crops. Individual skills and preferences, and established usufruct rights to irrigated land, will influence these allocations.

(c) Tomatoes and wheat are produced exclusively for the market, since they are used hardly at all as food by the Fur; garlic, onions, etc. are partly for own consumption and partly for sale. The weekly marketplaces are available to transform these products into cash. Cash again is used to obtain a variety of consumer

(d) goods from the market. In 1964 the annual cash needs of men in the prime of their lives was estimated by informants, and reported for themselves, to be about £8; that of women only £1, £2, or £3. The rate of consumption in the cash sector has, however, been increasing rapidly over the last years.

Also purchased for cash are tools – a relatively minor expense; donkeys, of which every man wishes to own one, and young cattle. These last are bought from Baggara Arabs when they are

(e) about two years old, for about £6. They are then kept for some years, tended by the children of the owner, till they are ready for sale as meat on the market at the age of 5 or 6 years, when they bring about £11 or £12. No breeding or milking takes place, but the manure that accumulates where the animals are stabled at night is valued and used in the irrigated fields.

Livestock thus constitute a possible field of investment, if one has the children to tend them. Otherwise, the possibilities for investment of cash in productive enterprises are extremely restricted. Cash savings are useful as a store of wealth to secure against crop failure or sickness in the future; and amounts up to several hundred pounds are accumulated by some. But for most people who dare not use such savings for speculation and trade on the market, they remain inactive wealth, buried in a pot under the floor of the hut, and are not used as capital. A few villagers choose, usually fairly late in life, to use such savings to

(f) perform the *Haj* pilgrimage to Mecca. The returned Haji tends to take little part in village affairs, and so this conversion of wealth to rank has limited consequences in the Fur system.

(g) Men may somewhat reduce their cash expenditures by weaving cloth for their families rather than buying it. Cotton for such thread may be bought, or produced by the man himself. He spins it by hand while walking or sitting idle, and weaves it on a horizontal loom which, though nominally it may be owned by someone, is in fact used communally by all.

(h) A major cash expense is that of bridewealth, involving various traditional prestations to the wife and to her bi-lateral kinsmen totalling about £35 in value. This expense is borne by the groom and his father. Most of it is given in purchasable objects (donkeys, cattle, swords, cloth) or their cash equivalents. Two lengths of cloth must, however, be produced by the groom himself and given to the bride's parents. For the rest of their married life, the husband is further obliged to provide his wife, and small children,

(i) with basic necessities from the market.

(j) In return, the wife must provide female services of sex, cooking, and brewing of beer.

(k) The other main kind of crop is millet. Some people find that they, in their initial allocation of labour (b), have struck an inadequate balance between production of cash crops and of millet. This can be corrected in the marketplace: not infrequently, people run short of millet and have to buy some before the next harvest;

while a few find that they have an excess which it is more convenient to store as cash than as grain. Much of the Marra mountain
seems to be rather too high to offer optimal conditions for millet,
and there is doubtless an overall import from lower-lying, surplus-
producing areas.

(l) Millet is used for porridge and beer. Independent estimates in connection with sample budgets indicate that on an average about
one-fifth of the total grain production goes into beer – more in
the case of men, somewhat less in the case of women.

(m) Most of the porridge is consumed directly. On special occasions,
however, connected with funerals and memorials for senior deceased relatives, or the life-crises of junior relatives, feasts are given
at which porridge is also served to invited and uninvited visitors. At
most feasts, beer is also given, and occasionally cattle are slaught-
ered. Such feasts bring honour to the person who gives them; but
as they are given in the name of another person and are not formalized in grades or titles, it would be inappropriate to regard them as
'feasts of merit' in any real sense; and their effects on the political
influence of the feast-giver seem to be minimal.

Beer-making is a rather complicated procedure which stretches
over several days, and the product does not keep for long; so most
households are unable to have beer available regularly for home
consumption. Most of the beer produced thus enters the circuit of
(n) feasts and work parties, especially as a reciprocal in exchange for
labour, as discussed above. Besides being used to mobilize labour
in millet cultivation, where the large, uniform fields invite the
use of communal labour, such beer-for-labour exchanges are used
(o) in house-building. Indeed, a final marriage obligation, after a
period of successful marriage, is the building of a hut by each
spouse for his or her parallel-sex parent-in-law, using only labour
mobilized by beer in a kinship/friendship network, and associated
with special festive customs, dances, and songs.

Possibilities for growth

The diagram thus depicts all the main forms of goods and services in
the Mountain Fur economy, how they are produced and how they can
be exchanged for each other – i.e. it depicts the flow of value through
the system. The whole system is seen from the point of view of an
ordinary villager, not a craftsman or a market-place speculator; and it

presupposes the ecological and institutional facts outlined in the first part of the paper.

From the point of view of each individual unit of management, the central purpose of economic activities must be to direct the flow of his own assets in these various channels in such a way as (i) to achieve maximal increase in them while (ii) obtaining a balanced distribution of value on the various consumption items of market goods, porridge, beer, housing, *Haj*, and feasts. The balance in question is determined by each person's consumption profile.

Some general characteristics of the economy stand out very clearly in this diagram; most clearly, the limited possibilities for cumulative growth. Such growth possibilities depend on a recognized channel for reinvestment and will show up in the diagram as possible *circles* of flow, permitting what might most vividly be described as *spirals* of growth (Barth, 1963, p. 11). Only three such circles are present: (i) labour-cash-crops-cash-wife-labour, (ii) cash-cattle-cash, and (iii) labour-millet-beer-labour. The first of these circles is apparent rather than real; and all have built-in brakes which prevent them from serving as true spirals of growth.

As for the labour-cash-wife-labour circle, this is controlled by a number of factors such as the availability of marriageable women, the acceptance of the marriage offer by the woman and her kinspeople, and the ultimate limit of four legal wives. Of more immediate relevance, however, is the fact that the labour obtained from a wife is not of the same kind as that invested in work on the cash crops. A woman's labour obligations to her husband concern the special female services only; as a cultivator she is independent, and the cash crops which she cultivates are her own, not her husband's. Though spouses often work together in the field, this is on a reciprocal basis. Thus, plural marriages will not only deplete a man's savings, but also increase his cash expenses without providing him with any source of labour, from wives or from children, which he can use in the production of cash crops. There is thus no opportunity for cumulative increase of assets in this circle.

The cash-cattle-cash circle, on the other hand, offers a genuine circle for investment and increase provided that (otherwise essentially unusable) juvenile labour is available in the domestic unit. However, the erratic supply of young cattle constitutes a brake on systematic investment: there are no markets to facilitate trade in such animals, and the supply depends entirely on the whim of the Arab nomads, who offer the beasts for sale individually through random contacts and only in response to unforeseen and urgent cash needs. In a complete census of one mountain Fur community of 212 adult householders, one person owned 5 cattle, the rest fewer, and most of them none. Though restricted in this way, profits in this particular spiral are none the less frequently cited by villagers as the source of accumulated savings.

The labour–millet–beer–labour circle is the most clearly marked one in the economy. But it also has characteristic built-in brakes. General notions of reciprocity are not effective, as noted previously; but there is a tendency for labour efficiency to correlate negatively with the size of the task: the larger the field, the more beer and the more people are present, and the more quickly does the whole occasion degenerate into a pure drinking party. The host tries to control this tendency by bringing out his beer a little at a time; but if he is too careful people will leave the site in protest.

Furthermore, the circle is essentially a closed one: millet is not treated by the Mountain Fur as a cash crop, and so wealth once in this circle remains within it, and a person's incentive to try systematically to accumulate in a spiral is limited by his view of his possible consumption needs or appetites for porridge, beer, and thatched huts.

Spheres and barriers

The items labour, millet, porridge, beer, and houses are thus closely interconnected, and most nearly constitute a sphere in terms of exchangeability. By also considering other regular modes of circulation, especially that of a production in which the factor of land is freely available, the interconnectedness of these items is more adequately depicted. It should be noted that all items are *not* freely exchangeable for each other, e.g. labour cannot be obtained in exchange for millet. But through the brewing of beer, labour is mobilized in direct proportion to the millet invested and there are no significant restrictions on the volume or timing of this transformation – i.e. it is present in the system as a constantly available possible allocation of the resources in question. It thus seems most meaningful to classify these items together as constituting a single economic sphere, and to demarcate such spheres by criteria of freedom of allocation and the facility with which each item or form can be transformed into any other.

The concept of spheres, then, serves to summarize the major structural features of a flow pattern. In this case, most items fall by such criteria clearly in either of two main spheres, that of labour, beer, etc.

and that associated with cash. In addition, the diagram depicts conversions to *Haj* and feasts, in a sphere related to rank and influence that has no clear feedback into the economic system, and also some conversions into a sphere of kinship and affinal ties, represented here by wives as the only item with a significant, though limited, feedback on the labour side of the economic system.

The barriers between spheres, in this view, are barriers to ready transformation, i.e. all the factors that impede the flow of value and restrict people's freedom to allocate their resources, and reverse these allocations. Thus the allocation of cash to the purchase of a ticket to Mecca is a conversion to another sphere, since this amount of value can never be transformed back into cash. An allocation of labour to millet cultivation is likewise an allocation of resources to a non-cash sphere; because of the items in this sphere millet is for reasons of price and competition not a marketable cash crop, porridge has no buyers, the sale of beer is regarded as immoral, and the labour obtained for beer cannot be sold and has traditionally been used only in millet cultivation and house-building. Houses, finally, are not sold, because of the difficulty of finding buyers.[2] The barriers that prevent or restrict flow between spheres are thus compounded of a variety of factors, only some of them of a moral or socially sanctioned nature.

Management and stratification

Successful management consists in allocating labour wisely to the two main spheres, and steering one's assets through the channels of each sphere in such a way as to maximize increase. In the cash sphere, this involves agricultural skills and an adequate programming of labour input in terms of the changing requirements of hoeing, watering, guarding, and harvesting – and, in the case of tomatoes, also of drying the crop. Besides, relative gains or losses result from the choice of different alternative crops in different years, as a result of fluctuations in weather conditions and market prices. In general, cultivators seemed to feel that weather fluctuations were unpredictable; and many also seemed to choose their crops on a conventional or habitual basis, without reference to prognoses of changing prices. A steady rise in the price obtained for tomatoes over the last years none the less has resulted in a very considerable increase in the quantity of tomatoes cultivated.

Finally, the time of marketing affects the price obtained. Thus the price of onions sinks, when the new crop comes in, to less than half

of the peak price that obtains in early winter. Persons with cash resources to cover current expenditure are thus able to postpone their
crop sales and reap the greater profits.

The linear character of the flow channel in the cash sphere does
not give much scope for management finesse, and only in the small
cash–cattle–cash circle can careful saving and investment produce
bonuses of any importance. Not so in the millet–beer–labour sphere,
however: systematic management of millet cultivation and beer–labour
mobilization is the cornerstone on which the prosperity of most villagers is based.

Let us first look at the direct relation between labour input and
production. The millet-growing season extends over approximately
seventy days; including the preparatory period of terrace-mending and
hoeing, and the considerable concluding labour of threshing and win-
nowing, nearly six months are probably needed to produce a final
harvest of reasonable size.

Villagers estimated that a woman with no cash-cropping commitment in the summer season should be able to produce at least 100
mīd (1,000 lb), by her own labour. As a daily rate this would correspond to more than 1/2 *mīd* (5 lb), per working-day.

Alternatively, much of the labour may be done with the aid of
work parties. At such parties, the hosts generally estimate that a large –
about 30 litre – pot of beer provides enough beer for six men for one
day. By the brewing techniques generally used in the Marra mountain,
millet produces about six times its own volume in finished beer. One
mīd (corresponding to about 5 litres) of grain thus makes about 30
litres of beer. The daily consumption of beer per man in a work party
is thus approximately 5 litres, corresponding to 1.7 lb millet.

Given an adequate store of millet, a person can thus mobilize labour
at a cost of some 1.7 lb millet/day/man and apply it to a task that produces an average of some 5 lb millet, or three times the cost, per work-
day. A reasonably skilful management in this flow circle thus secures a
person an adequate supply of millet from a relatively small labour
input. The person who cannot husband his resources, and whose thirst
or hunger tempts him to join work parties so as quickly and directly
to transform his labour into beer, will constantly be on the losing end
of the deal. In Mountain Fur villages, the population thus has a tendency to fall into two strata: a majority of moderately prosperous
persons, and a fraction who, because of disease, age, or bad management, have inadequate grain stores, and who supplement their food

resources by frequent participation in work parties, thus serving as a labour reserve for the more prosperous villagers.

Discrepancies of evaluation

I have argued elsewhere (pp. 50 ff.) that the barriers which separate spheres and limit the amount and occasions of flow between them will allow considerable discrepancies of evaluation to persist as between items located in different spheres. Such discrepancies may be discovered when barriers break down and new patterns of circulation are made possible, in which cases an increased flow may force people radically to revise their evaluations (see p. 176 below, on the value of land). Alternatively, these discrepancies may be demonstrated where it is possible to construct some common denominator, or co-efficient, for comparing evaluations in one sphere with those of another. In the present case, such a common denominator may be constructed on the basis of the market price of millet – an 'imperfection' in the separation of the two major spheres, brought about mainly by the activities of travelling merchants who bring millet in from the adjoining ecological zone, but also occasionally by the sale of millet raised by the Mountain Fur themselves.

The price of millet in 1964 ranged from 4 to 6 piastres, i.e. around an average of 1 shilling per *mīd* (10 lb) of grain. We thus get the equations:

10 lb millet = 1 shilling = 30 litres of beer = 6 man days,

or 1 man day = 5 litres of beer = 2d. worth of millet.

This evaluation of what a man-day of labour is worth in beer may be compared to that obtaining in the cash sphere. The Sudan Forestry Department, and some other public bodies, make relatively unsuccessful attempts to recruit local labour in Jebel Marra. Their basic wage offer has been about 10 piastres = 2 shillings a day, or 12 times the value of the millet which a man demands for participation in a work party. Yet it has proved very difficult, especially in the initial years of recruiting in any one village or locality, to entice people to take work. Privately, I found that an arrangement for having fresh water brought to my hut, at the rate of about 1d. per 12 litre pot, was impossible to maintain because the women in the neighbourhood were dissatisfied with the rate of pay – the equivalent of half a day's 'millet pay' for 20 minutes' work. Admittedly, in these equations I have ignored the value of the labour of brewing – as indeed I suspect that the Fur themselves, particularly the men, would do if they were to attempt the comparison. But this additional factor is far from sufficient to make good the discrepancies. Likewise, one might argue that the Fur idea that it is shameful to work for a wage should be represented as an additional cost for a man entering a wage contract; and that this constitutes the balancing factor. The empirical facts would, however, rather suggest that these costs are not so very great, since once the Fur are given enough opportunities to work for wages so that they discover the advantages of these wage rates, they eagerly accept the contracts, as in some of the Jebel Marra foothills areas. No matter how one chooses to represent it, there does seem to be a very great discrepancy between the values placed on beer and labour, and those placed on money.

Innovating activity

So far I have discussed the economic activity of persons within the traditional framework of alternative allocations. But to the extent that the individual units of management really attempt to maximize their assets, they will assert a constant pressure on this framework, and will seek ways of utilizing new opportunities where they are apparent and not blocked by unreasonable risk factors or supervening social sanctions.

The most general change that is taking place along these lines in the Jebel Marra is a progressive increase in the range of crops cultivated, and a certain change in the whole agricultural regime because of the increasing importance of tree crops. This development has been initiated by some modest agricultural experimental stations, but is sustained without any supporting agricultural extension work. The development of orchards is leading to derivative changes in the views on land-ownership and tenure rights. Finally, in a few localities one can also find some truly entrepreneurial undertakings where new strategies of management and channels of conversion are being exploited. The forms which these changes take are to a marked degree determined by the economic system outlined above, and give further perspective on its structure.

Orchard development

The development of orchards requires irrigated land - i.e. the tree crop is an alternative to the irrigated winter cash crops. Such a tree crop takes four years before it gives a significant product; however, in the intervening period the fields may also be used to raise an irrigated onion crop, so no significant loss of current production is suffered during the transition. The fruits are marketable for cash – limes, lemons, oranges, and mangoes particularly for export; papaya, guava, and bananas mainly for local consumption. The ease of production, and the relatively low value of the fruit in the case of limes and lemons, make them less attractive under present circumstances, whereas some varieties of oranges have been spectacularly profitable.

The labour to establish an orchard comes in addition to that normally required, since other cash crops must be cultivated to cover current expenses until the trees start producing. The development of an orchard thus requires an extra input of labour; and this has generally been done by the innovators with the aid of work parties, utilizing surplus millet for beer. A precedent is thus established for the use of beer-mobilized labour in the cash-crop sphere. So long as a person's millet resources are large enough to provide simultaneously for the other current uses, there are no sanctions against such an allocation; but it requires careful management, i.e. a successful large production of millet by beer work parties in the year preceding the orchard development. Perhaps for this reason, only the quite successful and prosperous have embarked on this production beyond the occasional planting of single trees. In the localities of fieldwork, the first orchards were planted in a village adjoining the foothills zone in 1956, in a high mountain village not till 1962. The mature orchards give large incomes with little input of labour, individual properties producing £20 to £30 worth of fruit annually.

Land rights

This change in agricultural regime has created some uneasiness with regard to land-ownership and usufruct rights. The principle of individual ownership to (wild) trees is established and recognized. The trees which a person plants will according to this principle be his, no matter who owns the land on which they grow. However, an orchard on irrigated land becomes so dense that it shades other crops and monopolizes that land. A person who obtains usufruct rights to irrigated land to which he has no title can thus, by planting an orchard, render it useless to all others for an indefinite period. Some men who held titles to land on behalf of their descent group were, in 1964, quite concerned over this, and pressed for the general acceptance of a rule forbidding the planting of orchards on borrowed land. Some few of them, on the other hand, had been quick enough to evict other users in time to secure ample areas for their private orchard developments.

Others, who had no such titular rights, wished to obtain the exclusive access to irrigated land that would make the long-term investment of orchard development a safe proposition. In the most sophisticated areas, a few sales and purchases of land had taken place by 1964, tentatively establishing truly private ownership to land. Both parties to such transactions were quite uneasy about the deal, the sellers because they were alienating rights which they held in trust for larger kin groups (and only those who belonged to nearly extinct, or emigrated, kin groups were willing to consider sale at all), the buyers because they felt that the price was excessive.

Indeed, the prices demanded are an extreme illustration of the discrepancies of evaluation that can obtain where the items, in this case land and cash, have not been in circulation in the same economic sphere. I recorded those few transactions of this kind that had taken place in one community. The first sale took place in 1961, when a field was sold for £17. The buyer planted orange trees, and proceeded to cultivate onions in the three transitional years. For these onion crops he obtained £27, £22, and £25, respectively. He expected his first proper yield of oranges to bring a larger income. He was personally no longer in doubt that the transaction had been to his advantage; but he failed by this argument to convince his friend to purchase a field for £30 which had regularly been giving an onion crop worth more than £15 annually. The man in question was willing to offer £25, but would not go higher – not because he did not have the money, but because he felt that, surely, no piece of land could be worth that much. One must assume that an increasing number of such transactions will progressively lead to a general revision of relative evaluations.

Entrepreneurial activity

On purely logical grounds I have argued elsewhere (pp. 56 ff.) that entrepreneurs will direct their activity pre-eminently towards those points in an economic system where the discrepancies of evaluation are greatest, and will attempt to construct bridging transactions which can exploit these discrepancies. The social factors which produce a reluctance to sell land serve as a general impediment on entrepreneurial activity in this field; besides, the profits connected with such transactions are long-term. But the disparities of evaluation between the cash and the millet-labour-beer spheres offer opportunities which have recently been discovered and exploited by a few entrepreneurs. The problem, when an entrepreneurial adventure consists in breaking through the barrier between spheres, is that of reconversion of assets without loss - i.e. that of locating channels that allow a circle of reinvestment and growth (see above, p. 169, and Barth, 1963b, p. 11).

Returning to the diagram the possibility of such a circle is apparent in the combination of channels (k) - (l) - (n) - (b₁) - (c). Concretely, what happened, apparently for the first time in 1961, was that an Arab merchant who regularly visited the marketplaces on the northern fringe of the Marra mountain, asked for permission to spend the rainy season in a village, and asked for an area of land on which to cultivate a tomato crop. He brought in his wife and settled her in a hut, and he bought a large amount of millet in the lowlands to the north-east, where the price is very low, which he transported in on his donkeys and camels. From the millet, his wife made beer; this beer he used to call work parties, applying the labour to the tomato cultivation. Without any significant labour input of his own, he thus produced a large tomato crop, which he dried and transported to el Fasher for sale after the end of the rainy season. On an investment of £5 worth of millet, he obtained a return of more than £100 for his tomatoes.

In 1962 and 1963, more merchants, and some local people, adopted the same strategy with results nearly as spectacular. The precedent of orchard labour showed the way in which assets in the beer-labour circle could be converted to the cash sphere by being used in the production of cash crops - a conversion that takes advantage of the disparity in the beer versus cash evaluations of labour. The reconversion of assets from the cash to the non-cash sphere through the purchase of millet again takes advantage of a favourable disparity of evaluations, and is particularly simple for a trader with access to lowland markets.

The profits on trade and transport of the products also enters into the enterprise of the merchant given above. The case of one of the first local men to attempt the scheme is therefore of special interest. On the local market, he purchased:

50 *mīd* of millet at 6 piastres per *mīd* - 500 lb millet:	£3	0	0
Also, for the main work party feast, 1 goat for 40 piastres:	0	8	0
Total labour costs:	£3	8	0

He had all the labour in the tomato field performed by work parties. The value of the tomato crop, ready for sale within about five months, was £38 – profits based entirely on production and conversions within the local economic system.

Again, one must assume that this situation is unstable: a re-evaluation as between spheres may be precipitated by this flow of value across the boundary, whereby evaluations in the two spheres are brought more closely in line. Alternatively, the critical conversions may be blocked: by a refusal to give land for cultivation to the entrepreneurs, or by the discontinuation of the beer-for-labour exchanges on anything but a reciprocal basis. There is some evidence for a trend in each of these directions, but as of 1964 no effective reaction blocked these enterprises. However, the increase in wage-labour opportunities which will probably take place will no doubt also affect this situation by making it more difficult to mobilize labour for beer on a non-reciprocal basis.

Concluding remark

In each major section of this description of the Mountain Fur economic system I have sought to make explicit the analytical steps that I have taken, and to give the argument a general form. It should therefore be unnecessary to formulate any extensive conclusion. One general feature of this analysis might however be noted. By discussing alternative allocations in terms of 'flow', and describing the concrete factors and barriers that channel this flow, one performs an analysis that is particularly useful for the study of change, and for short-range prediction. The model is, in this respect, amenable to developments and manipulations which a more strict structural representation would not allow. This increases its adequacy for the description of what is in fact taking place in the Jebel Marra area, and should also enhance its interest to economists.

10   Competition and symbiosis in North East Baluchistan*

The present paper may be regarded as a brief exercise in the ecologic analysis of the human population of an area. I wish to make two general points, neither of which is original, but both of which are all too frequently overlooked in anthropological literature: firstly, that an adaptation involves people not only in a relationship with the natural environment, but also in relations of competition, cooperation and symbiosis with each other which may profoundly influence the structure and distribution of groups. Secondly, that in a human adaptation, cultural factors such as systems of politics and property, and demographic factors, are as vitally involved as are the more commonly considered technological factors. Because it is brief, this paper will have to be conceptual rather than documentary. The material for the exercise is drawn from data on Marri Baluch collected by the late Robert N. Pehrson in 1955, and in part by myself in 1960.[1]

The geographical area with which we are concerned encompasses c. 10.000 square kilometres of barren mountain plateau in West Pakistan, around latitude 29° N longitude 69° E. The land rises northward from c. 600 to 1.000 m. altitude, criss-crossed by mountain ranges with peaks up to 2.500 m. altitude. The dominant subsistence of the area is based on wheat, and the herding of sheep and goats.

The area is occupied by three major and several minor ethnic groups: *Marris* – a Baluchi-speaking tribe of herders and cultivators, *Powindahs* – various Pashto-speaking tribes of pastoral nomads, and *Kakars, Lunis* etc. – Pashto-speaking agricultural tribes. Besides, one finds members of a Hindu merchant caste, speaking *Hindko; Loris*, a group of gypsy tinkers and musicians; *Jatt* camel herders; and *Sindhis*, the agricultural population of the adjoining plains.

The adaptations, territorial distributions, and movements of these groups differ. Kakar, Luni, and other agricultural Pathan tribes live in

---

* First published in *Folk*, 1964.

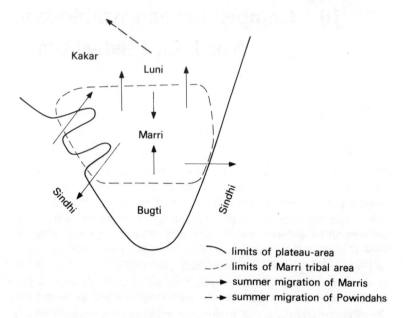

the northern part of the area, in large sedentary communities. The Powindah pastoralists spend the winter season in large, fairly permanent camps in the northern area; in the summer they travel far into Afghanistan on a pastoral migration. The third major group, the Marris, exhibits a highly varied pattern of adaptations and movements.

Some Marris live an entirely sedentary life in relatively large villages, with a predominantly agricultural economy. Such permanent settlements are found only in the southern part of the area; i.e. there is a clear geographical boundary between the territory of sedentary Pathans and that of sedentary Marris. Most Marris, however, have a mixed economy of agriculture and herding, and live in small, mobile communities, occupying tents at least part of the year. Some of these camps move only locally, within a perimeter of c. 20 km radius. Others exhibit a seasonal cycle of movement, but this may take several different forms, as schematized in the map. Thus in the summer, there is an exodus of camp groups northward from Marri into Pathan country, and a return southward in the winter. Other camps move eastward or southwestward into the Sindh plains in the summer. There is also a tendency for camps to shift in the summer into the valleys of the central Marri area, both from the northern and the southern areas. Finally, some camps winter in the plains west of Marri country, and spend the summer in the northwest Marri area or southwest Pathan area.

These distributions and movements cannot be satisfactorily accounted for by environmental factors. The periodicity whereby Powindahs utilize the northern pastures in the winter, and some Marris do so in the summer, depends in part on differences in the tolerance to heat and cold of Powindah and Marri strains of sheep. But the southern boundary of Powindah distribution, corresponding to the boundary between sedentary Pathan and Marri territory, does not relate to any apparent ecologic barrier; besides, it has proved unstable over time, shifting northward (Barth, 1964). Marris report on more reliable summer monsoon rains in the central parts of their territory as the reason for the seasonal shift towards the centre by some camps – but why then do other camps move in the opposite direction? Factors affecting the balance of economic importance between different subsistence forms, and restrictions and opportunities arising from the activities of other groups, must be invoked to explain these movements.

Basically, this requires an approach which takes total ecological systems into account. Whether the term is used explicitly or not, such an approach must make use of the concept of *niches* – positions in a biotic food web, or, from man's point of view, potential sources of organic energy. Ecologic relationships exhibit systematic features mainly because organic energy is limited and vital to all animal forms; an ecologic system may be depicted as a pattern of flow of organic energy. In such a pattern, each niche offers a certain amount of energy which can be exploited. Patterns of activity of an animal species, and the restraints on its distribution, may be understood with reference to the niche or niches it utilizes. Likewise, the numbers and density of an animal species are restricted by the carrying capacity of niches through a Malthusian control on population.

Human groups are ultimately subject to these same biological controls, but their exploitative activity is culturally conditioned. This opens greatly increased possibilities for variety in the niches that are utilized; it also makes possible the incidental exploitation by members of a society of niches which do not have, or no longer have, any significant carrying capacity. Various activities can be, so to speak, subsidized from the surplus energy obtained from other niches, as are for example fur hunting, through exchanges in a market economy, or trout fishing, as an exhausting but enjoyable leisure-time activity. There are not, as in the animal kingdom, the automatic controls that tend to regulate the balance between the rate of production of any particular niche, and the pressure of exploitation on that niche. Only by the addition of cultural restraints, such as patterns of exclusive ownership to productive resources, or monopolies on certain trades, may the exploitation of certain vital niches be subjected to such restraining balances. We may therefore conclude that under pressure of human population, niches whose exploitation has been highly profitable will lose their subsistence importance unless there are culturally determined processes of *exclusion* of persons from their exploitation.

A consideration of these cultural factors, which affect the patterns of exploitation under varying conditions of pressure, is necessary when we are concerned with the mechanisms of adjustment between human numbers and the carrying capacity of niches. The stability of the subsistence patterns, and thus of any culture or society based on those patterns, depends on the effectiveness of such mechanisms. By means of them, fluctuations or progressive changes in population, produced by natural fertility and mortality rates, can be 'corrected' and the rate of exploitation controlled, not by the ultimate adjustments of birth and death rates, but by imposed bars and incentives. These will mainly relate to recruitment patterns and involve monopolies on property or activities, supported by culturally determined views on legitimacy and thus ultimately by political sanctions. The familiar case in some European societies of the rules governing entailed estates preventing the fragmentation of land and maintaining a privileged class despite conditions of population growth illustrates concretely the kind of mechanisms we are concerned with.

An understanding of these mechanisms is necessary for the explanation of the distribution and movements of peoples in the Pathan-Baluch borderland. A time perspective also allows us to see the trend of change, and understand how the present patterns have emerged.

The three major ethnic groups show the following basic pattern: sedentary Pathan tribes concentrate on agricultural pursuits and Powindah nomads utilize the grazing areas as specialized pastoralists, whereas Marris have a traditional dual economy, most Marris engaging in both agriculture and herding. In the northern part of the area, settled Pathans and nomad Powindahs can thus utilize the same territory, since they exploit two different basic niches; because of their mixed economy, Marris alone exploit both niches in the south. The Marri tribe has a centralized organization which has proved militarily superior to that of the highly segmentary Pathan tribes, and has enabled Marris slowly to encroach on Pathan lands through conquest. However, this territorial expansion has not at all been sufficient to offset the increase of population, from c. 20,000 in 1850 to 60,000 in 1950.[2] Consequently, the pressure on resources has increased, and the circumstances have been created under which cultural mechanisms of adjustment between people and resources become of signal importance.

Marris monopolize both grazing and agriculture in the Marri Area; thus while Hindko traders and Lori gypsies are freely allowed to pursue their subsistence there, other ethnic groups who subsist by agriculture or herding are found only in small numbers, as labourers and clients of Marris. However, the rights by which a Marri is permitted to cultivate and to graze his herd, respectively, in Marri area are different. Pasture rights are held collectively by the whole tribe: any Marri may utilize pastures throughout the tribal area. This permits the flocks to congregate where pastures are available, and may be regarded as an adaptation to conditions of variable and irregular rainfall.

The right to cultivate, on the other hand, is held by smaller groups; for agricultural purposes the tribal lands have been subdivided and exclusive rights to each valley or plain vested in a tribal section. Within each such section, rights are held jointly, and equal shares of agricultural land are allotted to each male member of the section, for a decennial period. At each reallotment, adjustments are made for births and deaths in each family, and thus every male is guaranteed an adequate area in which he may cultivate for the next ten-year period.

With a growing population, the area of fields will increase: new land must be ploughed to give every man the fields that he needs. With the population densities that have characterized these parts of Baluchistan till now, this has been readily possible: within the land of every section, more fields have been carved out of the formerly fallow area. In other words, as far as agriculture is concerned, the carrying capacity of the niche can be increased as the population increases, within the traditional framework of ownership – each man will continue to have sufficient fields which it is his exclusive right to cultivate for the allotment period.[3]

Grazing resources, on the other hand, are adversely affected by population growth. The number of persons who share in grazing rights increases, while the actual grazing area is decreased by the expansion of agriculture. Moreover, the ownership pattern is one which precludes an optimal policy of herd/pasture management and balance – no man has exclusive rights to any part of the pastures, and an opportunistic policy of maximal extraction is most advantageous from the point of view of the individual herd-owner. Thus, in Marri area, the pressure on pastures increases, the carrying capacity is overstepped and resources partly exhausted. There is no possibility for specialization since no-one can be excluded – every Marri household has unrestricted pasture rights and will wish to have a share in the product of the niche, both to balance their diet and to augment their income. Thus as population increases, the relative contribution of pastoralism to subsistence decreases, and all households will uniformly be forced by the scarcity of pastures to reduce their stock and rely more heavily on agriculture. At the same time, there will be pressure on Marri herders to look for possible pastures outside of the Marri area.

Any overspill southward is blocked by the presence of another Baluch tribe, the Bugti, with an economy like that of the Marri and experiencing the same pressures. Between these two groups, there is consequently a relationship of comprehensive competition and enmity.

Eastward, and in the south-west, in the plains of Sindh, on the other hand, certain opportunities for a symbiotic relation can be found. In the late spring and the summer, there is a seasonal need for labour to assist in the harvest and to clean and repair the irrigation channels. This labour need constitutes a kind of niche which some Marris exploit. They can move in with their animals, which are encouraged to graze on the stubble of the harvested fields in recognition of the value of their manure, while the owners may earn an income in cash or kind as seasonal labour. This permits them to increase their flocks, as the density of pastoralists is lower in these agricultural areas. On the other hand, it interferes with the Marris' own agricultural activity, and seems to be mainly attractive to the impoverished who have difficulties in saving or securing sufficient grains for seed.

Another niche is open, by default so to speak, in the territories to the north. Sedentary Pathans dominate this area, but keep relatively few animals, concentrating on agriculture. This may be by choice, or may reflect the balance of power between them and the strong, wealthy Powindah tribes who enter the area in the winter and then monopolize the pastures. In any case, a symbiotic division and specialization is accepted by both groups, permitting each to exploit its own niche.

Moving in small camps outside their own tribal area, Marris are inferior in power to both these groups; they cannot seriously compete with Pathan villagers for the control of land, nor can they invade the Powindahs' pastures; though intermittently when the whole Marri tribe has been mobilized, the control of areas along the borderline has been progressively wrested from Pathans. However, whereas Pathan agriculturalists have a continuous interest in their territory, Powindah nomads utilize the pastures only as a winter base. Most of the year they spend on their pastoral migration into Central Afghanistan. During this period, their winter areas are essentially vacant, and potentially available on an individual basis to the small, weak Marri camps. They can gain access to these pastures only with the consent of the village Pathans; but these are prevented by the periodic presence of the Powindahs from keeping the necessary animals to utilize the pastures themselves, and are willing to let for the summer the pasture areas which they dominate. Thus through contracts with village headmen, Marri herders are able to move into the vacant pastures.

One might think that this would be a less advantageous pattern of pastoral nomadism for the Marris than would be the utilization of their own tribal pastures – after all, in Pathan country the not inconsiderable payments for grazing rights (a minimum of one animal of every 25 for every new territory entered) are additional costs on the pastoral enterprise. However, the conditions of ownership and contract have counterbalancing advantages. By a combination of fear amongst most Marris of the extortions of Pathan villagers, and tacit understandings between the wealthier, regularly visiting Marri herders and the village headmen giving them first right to pastures, a much lower density of pastoral camps is obtained and relatively exclusive pasture rights secured for the visiting Marri herder. Because of the nature and circumstances of ownership and contract, the over-exploitation which characterizes Marri pastures are thus avoided; and the security and possibility of systematic husbandry and pasture utilization, which are denied a Marri herdowner on his own, communal tribal lands, can be obtained by a lease-like contract with Pathans. Thus indeed one discovers that most of the wealthy Marri herd owners are found, not utilizing their own tribal pastures, but as migrant strangers in Pathan territory, paying a rent for the pastures on which their flocks depend.

The available data are insufficient to form even an approximate picture of the relations and controls on the western boundary of the Marri area, where some Marris seem to pursue a kind of miniature Powindah-like pattern of migration, only one step hotter: between winter pastures in the hot plains, and summer pastures in the Powindah winter areas. Nonetheless, the main parts of the Marri migration puzzle may now be put together, and the constraints which produce this pattern understood.

The summer movement north or south towards central Marri areas will characterize those camps that pursue a mixed economy of the traditional pattern, though their movements will be increasingly restricted as population increases and agriculture becomes proportionally more important. The summer migrations into Sindh reflect a symbiotic relationship with the agricultural population there, and are mainly attractive to Marri households with little capital and a relatively large labour capacity. Competition with a similar Baluch tribe prevents Marris from penetrating southward. The northward summer migration reflects a situation of competition with Powindahs and opportunities for a partial symbiosis with the Pathan villagers of the north, and is mainly attractive to herders with a large capital investment in flocks. Thus, a consideration of the systematic relations of niches and populations, the constraints of ownership forms, and the variations in capital and labour resources between households, will explain what seems initially a most bewildering pattern of movements.

Moreover, a time perspective and greater attention to cumulative trends and elementary rates, such as population growth, opens intriguing perspectives. To pursue them, one would need carefully collected and evaluated quantitative material, and until such material is available conclusive analyses cannot be made. But if interpreted with reference to the kinds of cultural mechanisms of allocation and exclusion illustrated above, they should materially enhance our understanding of social and cultural change. I should emphasize that these 'mechanisms', though they profoundly affect the relationship of populations to their environment, would not seem readily to be the object of conscious adaptation, and certainly not amenable to the kind of progressive modification that characterizes technological change. Perhaps precisely for this reason, they may be particularly significant factors in the explanation of the success or failure of societies and cultures through time.

11   A general perspective on nomad-sedentary relations in the Middle East *

General argument

To analyze nomad-sedentary relations we need a model that exhibits the crucial features of these relations, so that we can compare their variations under a unified perspective. Various alternatives present themselves: (a) We can depict nomadic society in its relation to its total environment. Sedentary peoples and societies are part of this total environment, and the nomads' relations to them are revealed as part of an ecologic, economic, or political analysis. (I have adopted this general viewpoint in my analysis of the Basseri of South Persia, Barth, 1961.) (b) We can take a more explicitly symbiotic view, and seek to analyze the interconnections of nomads and sedentary as prerequisites for the persistence of each in their present form.

Both these perspectives are problematical for comparative work because the features they bring out are specific to particular cases, and the general framework provides only an opportunity to identify similarities and differences. How does this help us to understand the sources from which such similarities and differences derive? To make analytical comparisons, we need to identify some crucial variables and observe their impact on the system as a whole. Thus we should develop a model whereby we can characterize the difference between nomads and settled along some common dimensions, and then seek to discover how variations in the characteristics of either group along these dimensions affect the larger system of which they are part. In most cases, the contrast between nomad and settled rests both on their distinctive territorial patterns – shifting vs. sedentary – and on their distinctive subsistence patterns – pastoral vs. agricultural. (The aberrant cases – nomadic non-pastoralists, like gypsies, or sedentary non-agriculturalists, like fishermen – need not concern us now, but may become crucial

* First published in C. Nelson (ed.) *The Desert and the Sown: Nomads in the Wider Society*, Berkeley, University of California Press, 1973.

187

test cases later.) The two characteristics are clearly functionally connected; yet they may be quite independent in their analytical consequences.

Let me suggest that it is perhaps not the distinction nomadic or
movable vs. settled that provides the vital focus for understanding the
relations between the two groups but rather the differences in their
systems of production, in terms of which they adapt and exchange and
articulate. Let us therefore provisionally focus on the differing character of pastoral and agricultural activities. (c) We can focus not on two
kinds of society, but – initially – on the total activities of a *region*. If
we stop for a while thinking basically of *groups of people*, and think
instead of *types of activity*, we can then disaggregate the activities that
take place in a region into some middle-range sub-systems which are
systems of production, or 'productive regimes' (see Knutsson, 1970 and
Geertz, 1963). In the traditional Middle East we will see respectively
pastoralism, agriculture, crafts, trade, etc. Coon (1952) has made us
aware of how these often seem to define community types; let us first
look at them rather as separate, internally organized activity systems,
somewhat in the manner in which the economist speaks of 'sectors' of
the economy. This will ultimately bring both nomads and settled populations in a region under a common perspective, whereby we can see
how they relate to each other in terms of dependence, dominance,
and stratification. Having analyzed their characteristics, we may then
be able to understand the dynamics of each such sub-system or regime.
Only then do I propose that we look at the overall social organization
that ties one or several such regimes to a persisting social unit and a
community type. We can then ask what the dynamic implications are
for those communities of the productive regimes under which they
exist, and we can analyze the interconnections of the communities of
the region in terms of these dynamics.

In developing the present argument, I am working on the hypothesis
that the pastoral regime of production has essential properties which
contrast with the other productive regimes of a region, and which in
various modulations determine the form and relations of nomads,
dependent on this regime for their maintenance, to the other population sectors of the region.

The basic argument of this paper is thus built in strata which, it is
hoped, become increasingly empirically adequate as we go along. I am
simply trying to set up the dimensions for comparison, and sort out
their implications step-by-step.

Basic characteristics of the productive regimes

To develop this argument, I shall first focus on the pastoral regime in terms of the nature of pastoral *capital*, and the options it provides for the person or group that makes management decisions (cf. Barth, 1964). The notable features are (a) that saving and investment are *necessary* under all circumstances – the herd capital is perishable and must be replaced – and (b) such investment is *possible* without benefit of any economic institutions, since one of the main products of the herd is lambs/calves, etc. Contrast this with the conditions of production in an agricultural regime where (a) land is essentially imperishable and cannot be consumed by the management unit except by benefit of elaborate economic institutions that facilitate its conversion to food; and (b) land cannot be increased by investment of its product (crops) except where economic institutions exist to effect its conversion.[1]

The consequences of these basic differences in productive regime are striking, particularly with respect to the growth potential of the units of enterprise that engage in them. Expansion of the enterprise must depend on increased investment in one or several production factors (including technical innovation). Enterprise in the pastoral sector is always faced with the possibility of rapid growth (or decline) regardless of what the public economic institutions and facilities may be, because part of its product comes automatically in the form of capital gains, which only an active management decision to slaughter will remove from reinvestment. Enterprise in the agricultural sector, on the other hand, has no such ready way of growth; unless special institutional public facilities for conversion exist, it will stagnate from lack of investment opportunities. Obviously, different agricultural societies have developed different institutional facilities which serve with varying success to increase investment and growth in agricultural enterprises. These institutional complexes may take the form of Feasts of Merit, in which food is converted to rank. They may make possible the conversion food → warriors → land by conquest in anarchic feasting societies. They may allow for the conversion food → labor → land, for example, in slave societies with low population density, or crops → exchange media → capital goods and land in elaborate market systems. Of special interest in the Middle East is capitalization and intensification of agriculture by the conversion food → labor → irrigation investment → new or increasingly productive land. The existence of either or several of these complexes will in a direct way modify the properties of capital in the agricultural sector by modifying the options open to management. They will thus affect the dynamic potential of agricultural activity, so the picture will rarely be that of an unmodified pastoral buoyancy and agricultural stagnation. But in any real-life situation, one would expect some trace of the contrast to remain between a pastoral potential independent of any collective economic institutions and an agricultural sector dependent on the proper functioning of such institutions and hampered and canalized by their specific forms. To understand the balance between these two sectors in a particular situation, we thus need to note the particular properties of these institutional facilities.

Relation of household units to the major regimes

We have focused so far on the activity system of each regime and the enterprise that may be based on each. But to what extent such activity systems are organized as specialized socioeconomic enterprises is an entirely open question of social organization. In most societies they are not, and the activities are pursued by multi-purpose households, often involved in the activities of several regimes simultaneously.

Some Middle Eastern nomads are, as we know, organized in households wholly or predominantly basing their livelihood on the pastoral regime. It should follow from the preceding argument that groups of such households will always have the potentiality of economic take-off: in prosperous times their enterprise will expand, their capital will increase, their economy will grow. Compare this to the classical peasant situation as described from many parts of the world: households are tied to an agricultural regime with blockage against reinvestment and growth, with a fraction of the product constantly tapped off by a tax or rent system, and with population growth and household subdivision dissipating whatever small surpluses may temporarily appear (cf. Wolf, 1966).

On the other hand, many households practice a mixed economy based on a combination of agricultural and pastoral regimes. We need materials to analyze the transfers of capital and product between these two sectors of the household economy achieved by adjusting consumption and allocating labor internally in the household. The variety of such adaptations in the Middle East should not be underestimated. In some cases they are readily recognizable in various forms of seasonal transhumance; in most cases we may expect long-term pulsations, with groups shifting between a pastoral and an agricultural role.

So far, I have argued only in terms of management *options*, and not considered the social characteristics and wider contexts of the persons or groups who constitute the management units, and how these affect the decisions made and policies pursued. To understand the position of households with mixed economies, as compared to those tied closely to only one type of regime, it is useful to anticipate this broader discussion somewhat. Growth does not result from the existence of an investment option, but from actors' choosing that option. In the case of households based entirely on pastoralism, I have described elsewhere (Barth, 1961 and 1964) the way the operation of such enterprises leads frequently to a compulsive husbandry of capital, saving, and investment. Essentially, because of the insecurity of the capital and the expenditure of labor being directed predominantly to capital maintenance, there is no cut-out of productive effort when a threshold of results is reached - a nomad's day never ends. One can see the signs of this very widely among nomads, from the 'overstocking' of African pastoral areas to the relentless flock-building of reindeer nomads.

In the case of households with mixed economies, on the other hand, I would guess that 'the Sahlins effect' (Sahlins, 1972) of the domestic mode of production frequently makes itself felt. The buoyancy of the pastoral sector in their economy may make such mixed-economy farmers more prosperous than their more purely agricultural fellows, even if they tend to occupy much more marginal areas. However, left to their own devices, they do not pursue growth relentlessly, but are happy to remain small farmers once a certain level is reached. When is this so; what kind of organizational superstructures might weld mixed farmers together, or exploit them, for expansive purposes; and when do they themselves, despite a domestic organization of production, choose to maximize capital growth? These become crucial (and so far unanswered) questions in the kind of comparative perspective outlined here.

We also need to consider the administrative and technical circumstances under which irrigation enterprises prosper and grow. The present intensification of irrigation agriculture in the Middle East is not entirely unprecedented, and we need to consider what have been the bases for similar sectorial take-offs in previous times. Indeed, it may be a characteristic of the agricultural sector that, during phases of technological change or smooth administrative and institutional functioning, it is characterized by growth periods that in their aggregate size and implications are quite breathtaking as compared to events in the nomadic sector.

Finally, any analysis of the balance between peoples of the pasture and peoples of the sown must take account of the other, often subsidiary, regimes of trade and transport, crafts, and warfare – the last involving military technology, geography, and mobilizable population mass. In this provisional discussion, however, I shall simplify the model to concentrate essentially on the two major sectors of pastoralism and agriculture only.

Macro-organization: the connection between groups or entities and their supporting regimes

From first principles it is apparent that social macro-entities such as ethnic groups, communities, tribes, or classes have no necessary one-to-one relation to pastoral or agricultural regimes of production. The divisions between such entities may or may not coincide with the lines of distinction between these regimes. Thus pastoralist may be merely an occupational category, as is trader or craftsman in many societies, or it may be descriptive of whole tribes or peoples. What are the conditions under which a social entity in a region has a special linkage with a particular type of productive regime, and what are the dynamic consequences of such linkage on the persistence and/or change of the entity or group? Essentially, I am proposing that the relations and dynamics of such groups may derive from what may be described as their mode of production,[2] within a larger regional economy.

Let me illustrate the point with a generalized, relatively categorical example. If we compare most East African Nilotic and Nilo-Hamitic societies with societies previously called Hamitic kingdoms (e.g. Rwanda, Burundi), we will find in both regional economies without market facilities for transforming capital, and containing agricultural and pastoral sectors. Where both these kinds of activity are pursued by households with mixed economies, as among the Nuer, Karamajong, etc., we generally find egalitarian, homogeneous societies. Where each sector is monopolized by a discrete ethnic group, I would argue that it is well-nigh automatic and inevitable that the pastoral group, favored by the inherent potential of the pastoral regime of production, will have the advantage over the agriculturalists, and by virtue of their mode of production become the dominant group. This dominance of the pastoral group within kingdoms is of course well-established in the descriptive literature concerning East Africa. What inequality we see is not the instituted effect of past acts of conquest, but the continuing effect of the inherent growth potential of pastoral production tied to a self-perpetuating group (cf. Maquet, 1968). If the social organization is such as to allow occupational specialization, but no ethnic division, a class division should emerge inevitably, favoring the controllers of pastoral capital. Only social institutions effectively preventing such specialization, or directly counteracting the growth potential of pastoral capital, could prevent the development of gross social differences.

What I am proposing, then, so as to bring nomadic and sedentary populations into a common analytic framework and understand the forms and variations in the relationships between them is (a) to look at them as participants in a common regional economy; (b) to understand the character of the productive regimes that each is associated with; and (c) to analyze the class relationships between them. This we can do without wedding ourselves to any preconceived schemata, but simply by inquiring systematically into the facts in each case. I would expect us to find, in varying degrees, depending on the factors noted above which affect the balance between the pastoral and agricultural sectors, that the growth capacity of the pastoral enterprises gives them an advantage over the agricultural enterprises, so that there is a tendency for an income flow to be set up from the agricultural to the pastoral sector. This is not the whole story, but let us stop there for a moment. *If* such an income flow is set up, it would lead, by steps that it should not be necessary to spell out, to an accumulation of wealth and influence in the hands of the pastoralists, and to a system of stratification in which they predominate.

The situation in the Middle East, however, is far more complex and variable than this, for two main reasons. Not only do market and other economic facilities exist that allow various types of reinvestment in the agricultural sector, and thus a highly variable balance of advantage between the two sectors, but also pastoralists are related to the peoples of the sown in other ways than through the food market – i.e. they are their customers for specialized services and luxury goods, they participate in their religion and high culture, they aspire to their wealth, power, and status. Moreover, all is not just domestic economy and markets: there is an ever-present taxing state structure which initiates and controls production and trade, at least in some kinds of goods. The regional picture of growth within sectors and flows of surpluses between sectors can thus only be depicted by a detailed analysis of the interplay of a variety of factors, but nonetheless it may derive its main dynamism from the two contrasting modes of production.

The basic pattern in the Middle East might be sketched as follows: On the domestic level, within local areas, an income flow tends to be set up from agricultural units to pastoral units, sustaining a local dominance by the pastoralists. However, cities with their urban elites, controlling the state apparatus, also prey on the cultivating households, and they do so by very effective and stable force and control, making peasants of the cultivators and drawing a substantial tax flow from them. Through this there is a tendency for the peasant households to be ground down even further by debt burdens to middleman entrepreneurs.

These state systems, however, have great difficulties controlling and dominating nomadic pastoralists, who may choose among several strategies in their accommodation to the state: submitting to it in return for peace, withdrawing and defending themselves from it to avoid the tax drain, or seeking control by attempting conquest of the whole state apparatus. But any rising local elite of pastoralists, no matter what policy they choose vis-à-vis the state, tends to be drawn into the wider system of stratification obtaining in the region as a whole, and therefore to embroil themselves in competition with urban elites – perhaps reversing income flows and dissipating advantages that have been won.

Thus we might be able to account for the seesaw of power between nomad confederacies and irrigation states, and the expansion and contraction of city bureaucracies vis-à-vis tribal marches and freelands that have characterized most Middle Eastern regions by such an analysis. But to do so, we would need to reorganize and probably supplement the available materials on social and cultural variation in the area.

Some questions from the Middle Eastern material

The universal integration in the Middle East of the pastoral and agricultural sectors of production into one regional economy is evidenced by the basic similarity of the diet consumed in tents and in villages, which is composed of both agricultural and pastoral products (see Arensberg,

1965 and Barth, 1960). In this respect the nomads of the Middle East seem to be similar to the nomads of most areas, though some East African cattle people and some North Asian herders may be exceptions. As for the growth capacity of the pastoral enterprise, this will surely vary according to ecologic circumstances, but can safely be assumed, at least for long periods, to be positive. Given these two circumstances, we would expect to find long-term trends in exchange relations and capital accumulation that favor the more pastorally oriented sector of the population, and particularly full-fledged pastoral nomads, leading to the dominance of such groups in local systems of stratification.

Such indeed has been the case at various times and in a great number of *local* situations. Characteristically, if one analyzes the elites in small towns, villages, and the countryside in the traditional Middle East, it is nomads – and traders – who have been actively upwardly mobile, while cultivators form the stable bottom of the pyramid, and landowners (in part) occupy the top positions, but are sustained there by stagnated enterprises. However, we must take into account a third circumstance: the existence of state structures with a sedentary base. These state structures pursue strategies that interfere with the 'free play' of economic processes. States have a 'nomad policy', whereas nomads, since the days of the Mongols, can hardly be said to have an 'agrarian policy'; they merely benefit from the buoyancy of their aggregate household economies. This lack of a long-term policy means that nomadic success and growth will need to be followed by diversification if the nomads are to have any hope of long-term political success. Pastoral growth and dominance, unless checked by other factors, will sooner or later evoke state countermeasures designed to contain, exploit, or destroy pastoral nomad ascendancy. The centripetal conquest of the state apparatus by a particular nomad tribe, as frequently seen in Persian history for example, would not change this, since the formerly nomadic dynasty would have the same interests as the previous controllers of the sedentary state – at least vis-à-vis all tribes but their own.

The balance between the pasture and the sown, as found in any particular region of the Middle East, should thus be understandable in terms of the following basic factors:

1 The local possibilities for profit conversion to investment and growth in the agricultural sector of the economy, producing a local sedentary elite with specific interests and capacities. This will affect

the nature and magnitude of the pastoralists' advantage, but for most places and times leave them dominant. The extent of dominance by the pastoralists will then depend on

2 Negative feedback relating to the growth of influence by the pastoral sector of the population:

  (a) *Ecologic controls*: Herd losses and other disasters leading to collapse of established control, or population growth leading to over-pressure and impoverishment (see the various mechanisms affecting population balance in Barth, 1961).

  (b) *Internal stratification*: Processes whereby wealth above a certain threshold is dissipated within the pastoral sector through feasting, warfare, and other elite consumption.

  (c) *Regional stratification*: Processes whereby wealth, often in support of elite personnel, flows from the pastoral sector to the sedentary centers to sustain claims to rank in the larger cosmopolitan state.

  (d) *State countermeasures*: Actions to contain a local pastoral elite, to exploit it, to drain its wealth, or to eliminate the group when the costs of controlling it are too high.

Some of these factors may be illustrated with material from various Iranian-speaking groups. In this south central Asian area, the last-resort attempts by states to put down nomads are familiar, tempered in Afghanistan by the ethnic association of most nomads with the precariously dominant group in a plural society (cf. Ferdinand, 1959).

Looking at the southern chain of peoples – various Kurds, Lur, Bakhtiari, Boir Ahmed, Qashqai, Khamseh, various Baluch, the Ghilzai-Powindah cluster –it is apparent that in many regions we find a fusion of pure pastoralists and mixed farmers in part-nomadic tribal units. Only some few Kurds (Hakkari, Jaf), the Khamseh, and the Powindah stand out as fully pastoral nomadic tribes. The rest seem to exemplify the situation where a locally dominant pastoral sector is controlled mainly by factor (b) above – the dissipation of wealth as an effect of internal stratification –though doubtless (as in the case of the Bakhtiari and Qashqai) competition for cosmopolitan rank also plays a part. Clearly, attention must be paid to the consolidation of mixed farmers into strong tribal polities, such as in parts of Kurdistan and among southern and central Pathans, where specialized pastoralists (Hakkari, Jaf, Powindah) seem to be in a position similar to that of the Basseri and other Khamseh – transients without local dominance.

There is a need for comparative material from other parts of the

Middle East, particularly on the local vs. cosmopolitan question of pastoral dominance - e.g., Arabian bedouin, Touareg, etc. - and how these might be understood in terms of the negative feedback noted above. Also, the social correlates of the pastoral and the agricultural sectors in the economies of Cyrenaica and the Maghreb seem unclear. I hope that the framework sketched here will provide illumination on some major historical puzzles, such as the virtual disappearance of pastoral nomads from India after a long period of apparent importance, or the insignificance of true pastoral nomads on the cultural history of Europe. At present, however, we are particularly in need of closely reasoned analyses of a variety of local nomad-sedentary systems to test hypotheses of the type advanced here. Though data for such analyses can still be gathered (and historical materials can be exploited), it should be noted that the modernization of a regional economy through full monetization of the factors of production, and the introduction of new investment alternatives in industrial enterprises, so changes the picture as to completely eliminate the patterns that have dominated the Middle East till now, and that have been the focus of this exploratory analysis.

12   Ethnic groups and boundaries*

This collection of essays addresses itself to the problems of ethnic groups and their persistence. This is a theme of great, but neglected, importance to social anthropology. Practically all anthropological reasoning rests on the premise that cultural variation is discontinuous: that there are aggregates of people who essentially share a common culture, and interconnected differences that distinguish each such discrete culture from all others. Since culture is nothing but a way to describe human behaviour, it would follow that there are discrete groups of people, i.e. ethnic units, to correspond to each culture. The differences between cultures, and their historic boundaries and connections, have been given much attention; the constitution of ethnic groups, and the nature of the boundaries between them, have not been correspondingly investigated. Social anthropologists have largely avoided these problems by using a highly abstracted concept of 'society' to represent the encompassing social system within which smaller, concrete groups and units may be analysed. But this leaves untouched the empirical characteristics and boundaries of ethnic groups, and the important theoretical issues which an investigation of them raises.

Though the naïve assumption that each tribe and people has maintained its culture through a bellicose ignorance of its neighbours is no longer entertained, the simplistic view that geographical and social isolation have been the critical factors in sustaining cultural diversity persists. An empirical investigation of the character of ethnic boundaries, as documented in the following essays, produces two discoveries which are hardly unexpected, but which demonstrate the inadequacy of this view. First, it is clear that boundaries persist despite a flow of personnel across them. In other words, categorical ethnic distinctions

---

*   'Introduction' to Fredrick Barth (ed.) *Ethnic Groups and Boundaries*, Boston: Little Brown & Co, 1969.

do not depend on an absence of mobility, contact and information, but do entail social processes of exclusion and incorporation whereby discrete categories are maintained *despite* changing participation and membership in the course of individual life histories. Secondly, one finds that stable, persisting, and often vitally important social relations are maintained across such boundaries, and are frequently based precisely on the dichotomized ethnic statuses. In other words, ethnic distinctions do not depend on an absence of social interaction and acceptance, but are quite to the contrary often the very foundations on which embracing social systems are built. Interaction in such a social system does not lead to its liquidation through change and acculturation; cultural differences can persist despite inter-ethnic contact and interdependence.

General approach

There is clearly an important field here in need of rethinking. What is required is a combined theoretical and empirical attack: we need to investigate closely the empirical facts of a variety of cases, and fit our concepts to these empirical facts so that they elucidate them as simply and adequately as possible, and allow us to explore their implications. In the following essays, each author takes up a case with which he is intimately familiar from his own fieldwork, and tries to apply a common set of concepts to its analysis. The main theoretical departure consists of several interconnected parts. First, we give primary emphasis to the fact that ethnic groups are categories of ascription and identification by the actors themselves, and thus have the characteristic of organizing interaction between people. We attempt to relate other characteristics of ethnic groups to this primary feature. Second, the essays all apply a generative viewpoint to the analysis: rather than working through a typology of forms of ethnic groups and relations, we attempt to explore the different processes that seem to be involved in generating and maintaining ethnic groups. Third, to observe these processes we shift the focus of investigation from internal constitution and history of separate groups to ethnic boundaries and boundary maintenance. Each of these points needs some elaboration.

Ethnic group defined

The term ethnic group is generally understood in anthropological literature (cf. e.g. Narroll, 1964) to designate a population which:

(a) is largely biologically self-perpetuating; (b) shares fundamental cultural values, realized in overt unity in cultural forms; (c) makes up a field of communication and interaction; (d) has a membership which identifies itself, and is identified by others, as constituting a category distinguishable from other categories of the same order.

This ideal type definition is not so far removed in content from the traditional proposition that a race = a culture = a language and that a society = a unit which rejects or discriminates against others. Yet, in its modified form it is close enough to many empirical ethnographic situations, at least as they appear and have been reported, so that this meaning continues to serve the purposes of most anthropologists. My quarrel is not so much with the substance of these characteristics, though as I shall show we can profit from a certain change of emphasis; my main objection is that such a formulation prevents us from understanding the phenomenon of ethnic groups and their place in human society and culture. This is because it begs all the critical questions: while purporting to give an ideal type model of a recurring empirical form, it implies a preconceived view of what are the significant factors in the genesis, structure, and function of such groups.

Most critically, it allows us to assume that boundary maintenance is unproblematical and follows from the isolation which the itemized characteristics imply: racial difference, cultural difference, social separation and language barriers, spontaneous and organized enmity. This also limits the range of factors that we use to explain cultural diversity: we are led to imagine each group developing its cultural and social form in relative isolation, mainly in response to local ecologic factors, through a history of adaptation by invention and selective borrowing. This history has produced a world of separate peoples, each with their culture and each organized in a society which can legitimately be isolated for description as an island to itself.

Ethnic groups as culture-bearing units

Rather than discussing the adequacy of this version of culture history for other than pelagic islands, let us look at some of the logical flaws in the viewpoint. Among the characteristics listed above, the sharing of a common culture is generally given central importance. In my view, much can be gained by regarding this very important feature as an implication or result, rather than a primary and definitional characteristic of ethnic group organization. If one chooses to regard the culture-bearing aspect of ethnic groups as their primary characteristic, this has far-reaching implications. One is led to identify and distinguish ethnic groups by the morphological characteristics of the cultures of which they are the bearers. This entails a prejudged viewpoint both on (1) the nature of continuity in time of such units, and (2) the locus of the factors which determine the form of the units.

1 Given the emphasis on the culture-bearing aspect, the classification of persons and local groups as members of an ethnic group must depend on their exhibiting the particular traits of the culture. This is something that can be judged objectively by the ethnographic observer, in the culture-area tradition, regardless of the categories and prejudices of the actors. Differences between groups become differences in trait inventories; the attention is drawn to the analysis of cultures, not of ethnic organization. The dynamic relationship between groups will then be depicted in acculturation studies of the kind that have been attracting decreasing interest in anthropology, though their theoretical inadequacies have never been seriously discussed. Since the historical provenance of any assemblage of culture traits is diverse, the viewpoint also gives scope for an 'ethnohistory' which chronicles cultural accretion and change, and seeks to explain why certain items were borrowed. However, what is the unit whose continuity in time is depicted in such studies? Paradoxically, it must include cultures in the past which would clearly be excluded in the present because of differences in form – differences of precisely the kind that are diagnostic in synchronic differentiation of ethnic units. The interconnection between 'ethnic group' and 'culture' is certainly not clarified through this confusion.

2 The overt cultural forms which can be itemized as traits exhibit the effects of ecology. By this I do not mean to refer to the fact that they reflect a history of adaptation to environment; in a more immediate way they also reflect the external circumstances to which actors must accommodate themselves. The same group of people, with unchanged values and ideas, would surely pursue different patterns of life and institutionalize different forms of behaviour when faced with the different opportunities offered in different environments. Likewise, we must expect to find that one ethnic group, spread over a territory with varying ecologic circumstances, will exhibit regional diversities of overt institutionalized behaviour which do not reflect differences in cultural orientation. How should they then be classified if overt institutional forms are diagnostic? A case in point is the distribution

and diversity of Pathan local social systems. By basic Pathan values, a Southern Pathan from the homogeneous, lineage-organized mountain areas, can only find the behaviour of Pathans in Swat so different from, and reprehensible in terms of, their own values that they declare their northern brothers 'no longer Pathan'. Indeed, by 'objective' criteria, their overt pattern of organization seems much closer to that of Panjabis. But I found it possible, by explaining the circumstances in the north, to make Southern Pathans agree that these were indeed Pathans too, and grudgingly to admit that under those circumstances they might indeed themselves act in the same way. It is thus inadequate to regard overt institutional forms as constituting the cultural features which at any time distinguish an ethnic group – these overt forms are determined by ecology as well as by transmitted culture. Nor can it be claimed that every such diversification within a group represents a first step in the direction of subdivision and multiplication of units. We have well known documented cases of one ethnic group, also at a relatively simple level of economic organization, occupying several different ecologic niches and yet retaining basic cultural and ethnic unity over long periods (cf. e.g., inland and coastal Chuckchee (Bogoraz, 1904-9) or reindeer, river, and coast Lapps (Gjessing, 1954).

In one of the following essays, Blom argues cogently on this point with reference to central Norwegian mountain farmers. He shows how their participation and self-evaluation in terms of general Norwegian values secures them continued membership in the larger ethnic group, despite the highly characteristic and deviant patterns of activity which the local ecology imposes on them. To analyse such cases, we need a viewpoint that does not confuse the effects of ecologic circumstances on behaviour with those of cultural tradition, but which makes it possible to separate these factors and investigate the non-ecological cultural and social components creating diversity.

Ethnic groups as an organizational type

By concentrating on what is *socially* effective, ethnic groups are seen as a form of social organization. The critical feature then becomes item (d) in the list on p. 200 the characteristic of self-ascription and ascription by others. A categorical ascription is an ethnic ascription when it classifies a person in terms of his basic, most general identity, presumptively determined by his origin and background. To the extent that actors use ethnic identities to categorize themselves and others for purposes of interaction, they form ethnic groups in this organizational sense.

It is important to recognize that although ethnic categories take cultural differences into account, we can assume no simple one-to-one relationship between ethnic units and cultural similarities and differences. The features that are taken into account are not the sum of 'objective' differences, but only those which the actors themselves regard as significant. Not only do ecologic variations mark and exaggerate differences; some cultural features are used by the actors as signals and emblems of differences, others are ignored, and in some relationships radical differences are played down and denied. The cultural contents of ethnic dichotomies would seem analytically to be of two orders: (i) overt signals or signs – the diacritical features that people look for and exhibit to show identity, often such features as dress, language, house-form, or general style of life, and (ii) basic value orientations: the standards of morality and excellence by which performance is judged. Since belonging to an ethnic category implies being a certain kind of person, having that basic identity, it also implies a claim to be judged, and to judge onself, by those standards that are relevant to that identity. Neither of these kinds of cultural 'contents' follows from a descriptive list of cultural features or cultural differences; one cannot predict from first principles which features will be emphasized and made organizationally relevant by the actors. In other words, ethnic categories provide an organizational vessel that may be given varying amounts and forms of content in different socio-cultural systems. They may be of great relevance to behaviour, but they need not be; they may pervade all social life, or they may be relevant only in limited sectors of activity. There is thus an obvious scope for ethnographic and comparative descriptions of different forms of ethnic organization.

The emphasis on ascription as the critical feature of ethnic groups also solves the two conceptual difficulties that were discussed above.

1 When defined as an ascriptive and exclusive group, the nature of continuity of ethnic units is clear: it depends on the maintenance of a boundary. The cultural features that signal the boundary may change, and the cultural characteristics of the members may likewise be transformed, indeed, even the organizational form of the group may change – yet the fact of continuing dichotomization between members and outsiders allows us to specify the nature of continuity, and investigate the changing cultural form and content.

2 Socially relevant factors alone become diagnostic for membership, not the overt, 'objective' differences which are generated by
other factors. It makes no difference how dissimilar members may be
in their overt behaviour – if they say they are A, in contrast to another cognate category B, they are willing to be treated and let their
own behaviour be interpreted and judged as A's and not as B's; in
other words, they declare their allegiance to the shared culture of A's.
The effects of this, as compared to other factors influencing actual
behaviour, can then be made the object of investigation.

The boundaries of ethnic groups

The critical focus of investigation from this point of view becomes
the ethnic *boundary* that defines the group, not the cultural stuff that
it encloses. The boundaries to which we must give our attention are of
course social boundaries, though they may have territorial counterparts. If a group maintains its identity when members interact with
others, this entails criteria for determining membership and ways of
signalling membership and exclusion. Ethnic groups are not merely or
necessarily based on the occupation of exclusive territories; and the
different ways in which they are maintained, not only by a once-and-
for-all recruitment but by continual expression and validation, need
to be analysed.

What is more, the ethnic boundary canalizes social life – it entails
a frequently quite complex organization of behaviour and social relations. The identification of another person as a fellow member of an
ethnic group implies a sharing of criteria for evaluation and judgment.
It thus entails the assumption that the two are fundamentally 'playing
the same game', and this means that there is between them a potential
for diversification and expansion of their social relationship to cover
eventually all different sectors and domains of activity. On the other
hand, a dichotomization of others as strangers, as members of another
ethnic group, implies a recognition of limitations on shared understandings, differences in criteria for judgment of value and performance, and a restriction of interaction to sectors of assumed common
understanding and mutual interest.

This makes it possible to understand one final form of boundary
maintenance whereby cultural units and boundaries persist. Entailed
in ethnic boundary maintenance are also situations of social contact
between persons of different cultures: ethnic groups only persist as

significant units if they imply marked difference in behaviour, i.e. persisting cultural differences. Yet where persons of different culture interact, one would expect these differences to be reduced, since interaction both requires and generates a congruence of codes and values – in other words, a similarity or community of culture (cf. Barth, 1966, for my argumentation on this point). Thus the persistence of ethnic groups in contact implies not only criteria and signals for identification, but also a structuring of interaction which allows the persistence of cultural differences. The organizational feature which, I would argue, must be general for all inter-ethnic relations is a systematic set of rules governing inter-ethnic social encounters. In all organized social life, what can be made relevant to interaction in any particular social situation is prescribed (Goffman, 1959). If people agree about these prescriptions, their agreement on codes and values need not extend beyond that which is relevant to the social situations in which they interact. Stable inter-ethnic relations presuppose such a structuring of interaction: a set of prescriptions governing situations of contact, and allowing for articulation in some sectors or domains of activity, and a set of proscriptions on social situations preventing inter-ethnic interaction in other sectors, and thus insulating parts of the cultures from confrontation and modification.

Poly-ethnic social systems

This of course is what Furnivall (1944) so clearly depicted in his analysis of plural society: a poly-ethnic society integrated in the market place, under the control of a state system dominated by one of the groups, but leaving large areas of cultural diversity in the religious and domestic sectors of activity.

What has not been adequately appreciated by later anthropologists is the possible variety of sectors of articulation and separation, and the variety of poly-ethnic systems which this entails. We know of some of the Melanesian trade systems in objects belonging to the high-prestige sphere of the economy, and even some of the etiquette and prescriptions governing the exchange situation and insulating it from other activities. We have information on various traditional poly-centric systems from S. E. Asia integrated both in the prestige trade sphere and in quasi-feudal political structures. Some regions of S. W. Asia show forms based on a more fully monetized market economy, while political integration is poly-centric in character. There is also the ritual and productive cooperation and political integration of the Indian caste system to be considered, where perhaps only kinship and domestic life remain as a proscribed sector and a wellspring for cultural diversity. Nothing can be gained by lumping these various systems under the increasingly vague label of 'plural' society, whereas an investigation of the varieties of structure can shed a great deal of light on social and cultural forms.

What can be referred to as articulation and separation on the macro-level corresponds to systematic sets of role constraints on the micro-level. Common to all these systems is the principle that ethnic identity implies a series of constraints on the kinds of roles an individual is allowed to play, and the partners he may choose for different kinds of transactions.[1] In other words, regarded as a status, ethnic identity is superordinate to most other statuses, and defines the permissible constellations of statuses, or social personalities, which an individual with that identity may assume. In this respect ethnic identity is similar to sex and rank, in that it constrains the incumbent in all his activities, not only in some defined social situations.[2] One might thus also say that it is *imperative*, in that it cannot be disregarded and temporarily set aside by other definitions of the situation. The constraints on a person's behaviour which spring from his ethnic identity thus tend to be absolute and, in complex poly-ethnic societies, quite comprehensive; and the component moral and social conventions are made further resistant to change by being joined in stereotyped clusters as characteristics of one single identity.

The associations of identities and value standards

The analysis of interactional and organizational features of inter-ethnic relations has suffered from a lack of attention to problems of boundary maintenance. This is perhaps because anthropologists have reasoned from a misleading idea of the prototype inter-ethnic situation. One has tended to think in terms of different peoples, with different histories and cultures, coming together and accommodating themselves to each other, generally in a colonial setting. To visualize the basic requirements for the coexistence of ethnic diversity, I would suggest that we rather ask ourselves what is needed to make ethnic distinctions *emerge* in an area. The organizational requirements are clearly, first, a categorization of population sectors in exclusive and imperative status categories, and second, an acceptance of the principle that standards applied to one such category can be different from that applied to another. Though this alone does not explain why cultural differences emerge, it does allow us to see how they persist. Each category can then be associated with a separate range of value standards. The greater the differences between these value orientations are, the more constraints on inter-ethnic interaction do they entail: the statuses and situations in the total social system involving behaviour which is discrepant with a person's value orientations must be avoided, since such behaviour on his part will be negatively sanctioned. Moreover, because identities are signalled as well as embraced, new forms of behaviour will tend to be dichotomized: one would expect the role constraints to operate in such a way that persons would be reluctant to act in new ways from a fear that such behaviour might be inappropriate for a person of their identity, and swift to classify forms of activity as associated with one or another cluster of ethnic characteristics. Just as dichotomizations of male versus female work seem to proliferate in some societies, so also the existence of basic ethnic categories would seem to be a factor encouraging the proliferation of cultural differentiae.

In such systems, the sanctions producing adherence to group-specific values are not only exercised by those who share the identity. Again, other imperative statuses afford a parallel: just as both sexes ridicule the male who is feminine, and all classes punish the proletarian who puts on airs, so also can members of all ethnic groups in a poly-ethnic society act to maintain dichotomies and differences. Where social identities are organized and allocated by such principles, there will thus be a tendency towards canalization and standardization of interaction and the emergence of boundaries which maintain and generate ethnic diversity within larger, encompassing social systems.

Interdependence of ethnic groups

The positive bond that connects several ethnic groups in an encompassing social system depends on the complementarity of the groups with respect to some of their characteristic cultural features. Such complementarity can give rise to interdependence or symbiosis, and constitutes the areas of articulation referred to above; while in the fields where there is no complementarity there can be no basis for organization on ethnic lines – there will either be no interaction, or interaction without reference to ethnic identity.

Social systems differ greatly in the extent to which ethnic identity, as an imperative status, constrains the person in the variety of statuses and roles he may assume. Where the distinguishing values connected with ethnic identity are relevant only to a few kinds of activities, the social organization based on it will be similarly limited. Complex poly-ethnic systems, on the other hand, clearly entail the existence of extensively relevant value differences and multiple constraints on status combinations and social participation. In such systems, the boundary maintaining mechanisms must be highly effective, for the following reasons: (i) the complexity is based on the existence of important, complementary cultural differences; (ii) these differences must be generally standardized within the ethnic group – i.e. the status cluster, or social person, of every member of a group must be highly stereotyped – so that inter-ethnic interaction can be based on ethnic identities; and (iii) the cultural characteristics of each ethnic group must be stable, so that the complementary differences on which the systems rest can persist in the face of close inter-ethnic contact. Where these conditions obtain, ethnic groups can make stable and symbiotic adaptations to each other: other ethnic groups in the region become a part of the natural environment; the sectors of articulation provide areas that can be exploited, while the other sectors of activity of other groups are largely irrelevant from the point of view of members of any one group.

Ecologic perspective

Such interdependences can partly be analysed from the point of view of cultural ecology, and the sectors of activity where other populations with other cultures articulate may be thought of as niches to which the group is adapted. This ecologic interdependence may take several different forms, for which one may construct a rough typology. Where two or more ethnic groups are in contact, their adaptations may entail the following forms:

1 They may occupy clearly distinct niches in the natural environment and be in minimal competition for resources. In this case their interdependence will be limited despite co-residence in the area, and the articulation will tend to be mainly through trade, and perhaps in a ceremonial-ritual sector.

2 They may monopolize separate territories, in which case they are in competition for resources and their articulation will involve politics along the border, and possibly other sectors.

3 They may provide important goods and services for each other, i.e. occupy reciprocal and therefore different niches but in close interdependence. If they do not articulate very closely in the political sector, this entails a classical symbiotic situation and a variety of possible fields of articulation. If they also compete and accommodate through differential monopolization of the means of production, this entails a close political and economic articulation, with open possibilities for other forms of interdependence as well.

These alternatives refer to stable situations. But very commonly, one will also find a fourth main form: where two or more interspersed groups are in fact in at least partial competition within the same niche. With time one would expect one such group to displace the other, or an accommodation involving an increasing complementarity and interdependence to develop.

From the anthropological literature one can doubtless think of type cases for most of these situations. However, if one looks carefully at most empirical cases, one will find fairly mixed situations obtaining, and only quite gross simplifications can reduce them to simple types. I have tried elsewhere (chapter 10, this volume) to illustrate this for an area of Baluchistan, and expect that it is generally true than an ethnic group, on the different boundaries of its distribution and in its different accommodations, exhibits several of these forms in its relations to other groups.

Demographic perspective

These variables, however, only go part of the way in describing the adaptation of a group. While showing the qualitative (and ideally quantitative) structure of the niches occupied by a group, one cannot ignore the problems of number and balance in its adaptation. Whenever a population is dependent on its exploitation of a niche in nature, this implies an upper limit on the size it may attain corresponding to the carrying capacity of that niche; and any stable adaptation entails a control on population size. If, on the other hand, two populations are ecologically interdependent, as two ethnic groups in a symbiotic relationship, this means that any variation in the size of one must have important effects on the other. In the analysis of any poly-ethnic system for which we assert any degree of time depth, we must therefore be able to explain the processes whereby the sizes of the interdependent ethnic groups are balanced. The demographic balances involved are thus quite complex, since a group's adaptation to a niche in nature is affected by its *absolute* size, while a group's adaptation to a niche constituted by another ethnic group is affected by its *relative* size.

The demographic problems in an analysis of ethnic inter-relations in a region thus centre on the forms of recruitment to ethnic groups and the question of how, if at all, their rates are sensitive to pressures on the different niches which each group exploits. These factors are highly critical for the stability of any poly-ethnic system, and it might look as if any population change would prove destructive. This does not necessarily seem to follow, as documented by Siverts, but in most situations the poly-ethnic systems we observe do entail quite complex processes of population movement and adjustment. It becomes clear that a number of factors other than human fertility and mortality affect the balance of numbers. From the point of view of any one territory, there are the factors of individual and group movements: emigration that relieves pressure, immigration that maintains one or several co-resident groups as outpost settlements of larger population reservoirs elsewhere. Migration and conquest play an intermittent role in redistributing populations and changing their relations. But the most interesting and often critical role is played by another set of processes that effect changes of the identity of individuals and groups. After all, the human material that is organized in an ethnic group is not immutable, and though the social mechanisms discussed so far tend to maintain dichotomies and boundaries, they do not imply 'stasis' for the human material they organize: boundaries may persist despite what may figuratively be called the 'osmosis' of personnel through them.

This perspective leads to an important clarification of the conditions for complex poly-ethnic systems. Though the emergence and persistence of such systems would seem to depend on a relatively high stability in the cultural features associated with ethnic groups – i.e. a high degree of rigidity in the interactional boundaries – they do *not* imply a similar rigidity in the patterns of recruitment or ascription to ethnic groups: on the contrary, the ethnic inter-relations that we observe frequently entail a variety of processes which effect changes in individual and group identity and modify the other demographic factors that obtain in the situation. Examples of stable and persisting ethnic boundaries that are crossed by a flow of personnel are clearly far more common than the ethnographic literature would lead us to believe. Different processes of such crossing are exemplified in these essays, and the conditions which cause them are shown to be various. We may look briefly at some of them.

Factors in identity change

The Yao described by Kandre (1967b) are one of the many hill peoples on the southern fringe of the Chinese area. The Yao are organized for productive purposes in extended family households, aligned in clans and in villages. Household leadership is very clear, while community and region are autochthonously acephalous, and variously tied to poly-ethnic political domains. Identity and distinctions are expressed in complex ritual idioms, prominently involving ancestor worship. Yet this group shows the drastic incorporation rate of 10 per cent non-Yao becoming Yao in each generation (Kandre, 1967a: 594). Change of membership takes place individually, mostly with children, where it involves purchase of the person by a Yao houseleader, adoption to kinship status, and full ritual assimilation. Occasionally, change of ethnic membership is also achieved by men through uxorilocal marriage; Chinese men are the acceptable parties to such arrangements.

The conditions for this form of assimilation are clearly twofold: first, the presence of cultural mechanisms to implement the incorporation, including ideas of obligations to ancestors, compensation by payment, etc., and secondly, the incentive of obvious advantages to the assimilating household and leader. These have to do with the role of households as productive units and agro-managerial techniques that imply an optimal size of six to eight working persons, and the pattern of intra-community competition between household leaders in the field of wealth and influence.

Movements across the southern and northern boundaries of the Pathan area illustrate quite other forms and conditions. Southern Pathans become Baluch and not vice versa; this transformation can take place with individuals but more readily with whole households or small groups of households; it involves loss of position in the rigid genealogical and territorial segmentary system of Pathans and incorporation through clientage contract into the hierarchical, centralized system of the Baluch. Acceptance in the receiving group is conditional on the ambition and opportunism of Baluch political leaders. On the other hand, Pathans in the north have, after an analogous loss of position in their native system, settled in and often conquered new territories in Kohistan. The effect in due course has been a reclassification of the settling communities among the congeries of locally diverse Kohistani tribes and groups.

Perhaps the most striking case is that from Darfur provided by Haaland, which shows members of the hoe-agricultural Fur of the Sudan changing their identity to that of nomadic cattle Arabs. This process is conditional on a very specific economic circumstance: the absence of investment opportunities for capital in the village economy of the Fur in contrast to the possibilities among the nomads. Accumulated capital, and the opportunities for its management and increase, provide the incentive for Fur households to abandon their fields and villages and change to the life of the neighbouring Baggara, incidentally also joining one of the loose but nominally centralized Baggara political units if the change has been economically completely successful.

These processes that induce a flow of personnel across ethnic boundaries will of necessity affect the demographic balance between different ethnic groups. Whether they are such that they contribute to stability in this balance is an entirely different question. To do so, they would have to be sensitive to changes in the pressure on ecologic niches in a feedback pattern. This does not regularly seem to be the case. The assimilation of non-Yao seems further to increase the rate of Yao growth and expansion at the expense of other groups, and can be recognized as one, albeit minor, factor furthering the progressive Sinization process whereby cultural and ethnic diversity has steadily been reduced over vast areas. The rate of assimilation of Pathans by Baluch tribes is no doubt sensitive to population pressure in Pathan areas, but simultaneously sustains an imbalance whereby Baluch tribes spread northward despite higher population pressures in the northern areas. Kohistani assimilation relieves population pressure in Pathan area while maintaining a geographically stable boundary. Nomadization of the Fur replenishes the Baggara, who are elsewhere becoming sedentarized. The rate, however, does *not* correlate with pressure on Fur lands – since nomadization is conditional on accumulated wealth, its rate probably decreases as Fur population pressure increases. The Fur case also demonstrates the inherent instability of some of these processes, and how limited changes can have drastic results: with the agricultural innovation of orchards over the last ten years, new investment opportunities are provided which will probably greatly reduce, or perhaps for a while even reverse, the nomadization process.

Thus, though the processes that induce change of identity are important to the understanding of most cases of ethnic interdependence, they need not be conducive to population stability. In general, however, one can argue that whenever ethnic relations are stable over long periods, and particularly where the interdependence is close, one can expect to find an approximate demographic balance. The analysis of the different factors involved in this balance is an important part of the analysis of the ethnic inter-relations in the area.

The persistence of cultural boundaries

In the preceding discussion of ethnic boundary maintenance and interchange of personnel there is one very important problem that I have left aside. We have seen various examples of how individuals and small groups, because of specific economic and political circumstances in their former position and among the assimilating group, may change their locality, their subsistence pattern, their political allegiance and form, or their household membership. This still does not fully explain why such changes lead to categorical changes of ethnic identity, leaving the dichotomized ethnic groups unaffected (other than in numbers) by the interchange of personnel. In the case of adoption and incorporation of mostly immature and in any case isolated single individuals into pre-established households, as among the Yao, such complete cultural assimilation is understandable: here every new person becomes totally immersed in a Yao pattern of relationships and expectations. In the other examples, it is less clear why this total change of identity takes place. One cannot argue that it follows from a universally imputable rule of cultural integration, so that the practice of the politics of one group or the assumption of its pattern of ecologic adaptation in subsistence and economy, entails the adoption also of its other parts and forms. Indeed, the Pathan case (Ferdinand, 1967) directly falsifies this argument, in that the boundaries of the Pathan ethnic group cross-cuts ecologic and political units. Using self-identification as the critical criterion of ethnic identity, it should thus be perfectly possible for a small group of Pathans to assume the political obligations of membership in a Baluch tribe, or the agricultural and husbandry practices of Kohistanis, and yet continue to call themselves Pathans. By the same token one might expect nomadization among the Fur to lead to the emergence of a nomadic section of the Fur, similar in subsistence to the Baggara but different from them in other cultural features, and in ethnic label.

Quite clearly, this is precisely what has happened in many historical situations. In cases where it does *not* happen we see the organizing and canalizing effects of ethnic distinctions. To explore the factors responsible for the difference, let us first look at the specific explanations for the changes of identity that have been advanced in the examples discussed above.

In the case of Pathan borderlands, influence and security in the segmentary and anarchic societies of this region derive from a man's previous actions, or rather from the respect that he obtains from these acts as judged by accepted standards of evaluation. The main fora for exhibiting Pathan virtues are the tribal council, and stages for the display of hospitality. But the villager in Kohistan has a standard of living where the hospitality he can provide can hardly compete with that of the conquered serfs of neighbouring Pathans, while the client of a Baluch leader cannot speak in any tribal council. To maintain Pathan identity in these situations, to declare oneself in the running as a competitor by Pathan value standards, is to condemn oneself in advance to utter failure in performance. By assuming Kohistani or Baluch identity, however, a man may, by the same performance, score quite high on the scales that then become relevant. The incentives to a change in identity are thus inherent in the change in circumstances.

Different circumstances obviously favour different performances. Since ethnic identity is associated with a culturally specific set of value standards, it follows that there are circumstances where such an identity can be moderately successfully realized, and limits beyond which such success is precluded. I will argue that ethnic identities will not be retained beyond these limits, because allegiance to basic value standards will not be sustained where one's own comparative performance is utterly inadequate.[3] The two components in this relative measure of success are, first, the performance of others and, secondly, the alternatives open to oneself. I am not making an appeal to ecologic adaptation. Ecologic feasibility, and fitness in relation to the natural environment, matter only in so far as they set a limit in terms of sheer physical survival, which is very rarely approached by ethnic groups. What matters is how well the others, with whom one interacts and to whom one is compared, manage to perform, and what alternative identities and sets of standards are available to the individual.

Ethnic identity and tangible assets

The boundary-maintaining factors in the Fur are not immediately illuminated by this argument. Haaland discusses the evaluation of the nomad's life by Fur standards and finds the balance between advantages and disadvantages inconclusive. To ascertain the comparability of this case, we need to look more generally at all the factors that affect the behaviour in question. The materials derive from grossly different ethnographic contexts and so a number of factors are varied simultaneously.

The individual's relation to productive resources stands out as the significant contrast between the two regions. In the Middle East, the means of production are conventionally held as private or corporate, defined and transferable property. A man can obtain them through a specific and restricted transaction, such as purchase or lease; even in conquest the rights that are obtained are standard, delimited rights. In Darfur, on the other hand, as in much of the Sudanic belt, the prevailing conventions are different. Land for cultivation is allocated, as needed, to members of a local community. The distinction between owner and cultivator, so important in the social structure of most Middle Eastern communities, cannot be made because ownership does not involve separable, absolute, and transferable rights. Access to the means of production in a Fur village is therefore conditional only on inclusion in the village community – i.e. on Fur ethnic identity. Similarly, grazing rights are not allocated and monopolized, even as between Baggara tribes. Though groups and tribes tend to use the same routes and areas every year, and may at times try in an *ad hoc* way to keep out others from an area they wish to use, they normally intermix and have no defined and absolute prerogatives. Access to grazing is thus an automatic aspect of practising husbandry, and entails being a Baggara.

The gross mechanisms of boundary maintenance in Darfur are thus quite simple: a man has access to the critical means of production by virtue of practising a certain subsistence; this entails a whole style of life, and all these characteristics are subsumed under the ethnic labels Fur and Baggara. In the Middle East, on the other hand, men can obtain control over means of production through a transaction that does not involve their other activities; ethnic identity is then not necessarily affected and this opens the way for diversification. Thus nomad, peasant, and city dweller can belong to the same ethnic group in the Middle East; where ethnic boundaries persist they depend on more subtle and specific mechanisms, mainly connected with the unfeasibility of certain status and role combinations.

Ethnic groups and stratification

Where one ethnic group has control of the means of production utilized by another group, a relationship of inequality and stratification
obtains. Thus Fur and Baggara do not make up a stratified system,
since they utilize different niches and have access to them independently of each other, whereas in some parts of the Pathan area one
finds stratification based on the control of land, Pathans being landowners, and other groups cultivating as serfs. In more general terms,
one may say that stratified poly-ethnic systems exist where groups are
characterized by differential control of assets that are valued by all
groups in the system. The cultures of the component ethnic groups in
such systems are thus integrated in a special way: they share certain
general value orientations and scales, on the basis of which they can
arrive at judgements of hierarchy.

Obversely, a system of stratification does not entail the existence
of ethnic groups. Leach (1967) argues convincingly that social classes
are distinguished by different sub-cultures, indeed, that this is a more
basic characteristic than their hierarchical ordering. However, in many
systems of stratification we are not dealing with bounded strata at all:
the stratification is based simply on the notion of scales and the recognition of an ego-centered level of 'people who are just like us'
versus those more select and those more vulgar. In such systems,
cultural differences, whatever they are, grade into each other, and
nothing like a social organization of ethnic groups emerges. Secondly,
most systems of stratification allow, or indeed entail, mobility based
on evaluation by the scales that define the hierarchy. Thus a moderate
failure in the 'B' sector of the hierarchy makes you a 'C', etc. Ethnic
groups are not open to this kind of penetration: the ascription of ethnic
identity is based on other and more restrictive criteria. This is most
clearly illustrated by Knutsson's analysis of the Galla in the context of
Ethiopian society – a social system where whole ethnic groups are
stratified with respect to their positions of privilege and disability
within the state. Yet the attainment of a governorship does not make
an Amhara of a Galla, nor does estrangement as an outlaw entail loss
of Galla identity.

From this perspective, the Indian caste system would appear to
be a special case of a stratified poly-ethnic system. The boundaries
of castes are defined by ethnic criteria: thus individual failures in

performance lead to out-casting and not to down-casting. The process whereby the hierarchical system incorporates new ethnic groups is demonstrated in the sanscriticization of tribals: their acceptance of the critical value scales defining their position in the hierarchy of ritual purity and pollution is the only change of values that is necessary for a people to become an Indian caste.

An analysis of the different processes of boundary maintenance involved in different inter-caste relations and in different regional variants of the caste system would, I believe, illuminate many features of this system.

The preceding discussion has brought out a somewhat anomalous general feature of ethnic identity as a status: ascription[4] is not conditional on the control of any specific assets, but rests on criteria of origin and commitment; whereas *performance* in the status, the adequate acting out of the roles required to realize the identity, in many systems does require such assets. By contrast in a bureaucratic office the incumbent is provided with those assets that are required for the performance of the role; while kinship positions, which are ascribed without reference to a person's assets, likewise are not conditional on performance – you remain a father even if you fail to feed your child.

Thus where ethnic groups are interrelated in a stratified system, this requires the presence of special processes that maintain differential control of assets. To schematize: a basic premise of ethnic group organization is that every A can act roles, 1, 2 and 3. If actors agree on this, the premise is self-fulfilling, unless acting in these roles requires assets that are distributed in a discrepant pattern. If these assets are obtained or lost in ways independent of being an A, and sought and avoided without reference to one's identity as an A, the premise will be falsified: some A's become unable to act in the expected roles. Most systems of stratification are maintained by the solution that in such cases, the person is no longer an A. In the case of ethnic identity, the solution on the contrary is the recognition that every A no longer can or will act in roles 1 and 2. The persistence of stratified poly-ethnic systems thus entails the presence of factors that generate and maintain a categorically different distribution of assets: state controls, as in some modern plural and racist systems; marked differences in evaluation that canalize the efforts of actors in different directions, as in systems with polluting occupations; or differences in culture that generate marked differences in political organization, economic organization, or individual skills.

Ethnic groups and boundaries

The problem of variation

Despite such processes, however, the ethnic label subsumes a number of simultaneous characteristics which no doubt cluster statistically, but which are not absolutely interdependent and connected. Thus there will be variations between members, some showing many and some showing few characteristics. Particularly where people change their identity, this creates ambiguity since ethnic membership is at once a question of source of origin as well as of current identity. Indeed, Haaland was taken out to see 'Fur who live in nomad camps', and I have heard members of Baluch tribal sections explain that they are 'really Pathan'. What is then left of the boundary maintenance and the categorical dichotomy, when the actual distinctions are blurred in this way? Rather than despair at the failure of typological schematism, one can legitimately note that people *do* employ ethnic labels and that there are in many parts of the world most spectacular differences whereby forms of behaviour cluster so that whole actors tend to fall into such categories in terms of their objective behaviour. What is surprising is not the existence of some actors that fall between these categories, and of some regions in the world where whole persons do not tend to sort themselves out in this way, but the fact that variations tend to cluster at all. We can then be concerned not to perfect a typology, but to discover the processes that bring about such clustering.

An alternative mode of approach in anthropology has been to dichotomize the ethnographic material in terms of ideal versus actual or conceptual versus empirical, and then concentrate on the consistencies (the 'structure') of the ideal, conceptual part of the data, employing some vague notion of norms and individual deviance to account for the actual, statistical patterns. It is of course perfectly feasible to distinguish between a people's model of their social system and their aggregate pattern of pragmatic behaviour, and indeed quite necessary not to confuse the two. But the fertile problems in social anthropology are concerned with how the two are interconnected, and it does not follow that this is best elucidated by dichotomizing and confronting them as total systems. In these essays we have tried to build the analysis on a lower level of interconnection between status and behaviour. I would argue that people's categories are for acting, and are significantly affected by interaction rather than contemplation. In showing the connection between ethnic labels and the maintenance of cultural diversity, I am therefore concerned primarily to show how, under varying circumstances, certain constellations of categorization and value orientation have a self-fulfilling character, how others will tend to be falsified by experience, while others again are incapable of consummation in interaction. Ethnic boundaries can emerge and persist only in the former situation, whereas they should dissolve or be absent in the latter situations. With such a feedback from people's experiences to the categories they employ, simple ethnic dichotomies can be retained, and their stereotyped behavioural differential reinforced, despite a considerable objective variation. This is so because actors struggle to maintain conventional definitions of the situation in social encounters through selective perception, tact, and sanctions, and because of difficulties in finding other, more adequate codifications of experience. Revision only takes place where the categorization is grossly inadequate – not merely because it is untrue in any objective sense, but because it is consistently unrewarding to act upon, within the domain where the actor makes it relevant. So the dichotomy of Fur villagers and Baggara nomads is maintained despite the patent presence of a nomadic camp of Fur in the neighbourhood: the fact that those nomads speak Fur and have kinship connections with villagers somewhere does not change the social situation in which the villager interacts with them – it simply makes the standard transactions of buying milk, allocating camp sites, or obtaining manure, which one would have with other Baggara, flow a bit more smoothly. But a dichotomy between Pathan landowners and non-Pathan labourers can no longer be maintained where non-Pathans obtain land and embarrass Pathans by refusing to respond with the respect which their imputed position as menials would have sanctioned.

Minorities, pariahs, and organizational characteristics of the periphery

In some social systems, ethnic groups co-reside though no major aspect of structure is based on ethnic inter-relations. These are generally referred to as societies with minorities, and the analysis of the minority situation involves a special variant of inter-ethnic relations. I think in most cases, such situations have come about as a result of external historical events; the cultural differentiae have not sprung from the local organizational context – rather, a pre-established cultural contrast is brought into conjunction with a pre-established social system, and is made relevant to life there in a diversity of ways.

An extreme form of minority position, illustrating some but not all

features of minorities, is that of pariah groups. These are groups
actively rejected by the host population because of behaviour or
characteristics positively condemned, though often useful in some
specific, practical way. European pariah groups of recent centuries
(executioners, dealers in horseflesh and -leather, collectors of night-
soil, gypsies, etc.) exemplify most features: as breakers of basic taboos
they were rejected by the larger society. Their identity imposed a
definition on social situations which gave very little scope for interaction with persons in the majority population, and simultaneously
as an imperative status represented an inescapable disability that
prevented them from assuming the normal statuses involved in other
definitions of the situation of interaction. Despite these formidable
barriers, such groups do not seem to have developed the internal
complexity that would lead us to regard them as fully fledged ethnic
groups; only the culturally foreign gypsies[5] clearly constitute such a
group.

The boundaries of pariah groups are most strongly maintained by
the excluding host population, and they are often forced to make use
of easily noticeable diacritica to advertise their identity (though since
this identity is often the basis for a highly insecure livelihood, such
over-communication may sometimes also serve the pariah individual's
competitive interests). Where pariahs attempt to pass into the larger
society, the culture of the host population is generally well known;
thus the problem is reduced to a question of escaping the stigmata of
disability by dissociating with the pariah community and faking another origin.

Many minority situations have a trace of this active rejection by the
host population. But the general feature of all minority situations lies
in the organization of activities and interaction: in the total social
system, all sectors of activity are organized by statuses open to members of the majority group, while the status system of the minority has
only relevance to relations within the minority and only to some sectors of activity, and does not provide a basis for action in other sectors, equally valued in the minority culture. There is thus a disparity
between values and organizational facilities: prized goals are outside
the field organized by the minority's culture and categories. Though
such systems contain several ethnic groups, interaction between members of the different groups of this kind does not spring from the
complementarity of ethnic identities; it takes place entirely within the
framework of the dominant, majority group's statuses and institutions,

where identity as a minority member gives no basis for action, though it may in varying degrees represent a disability in assuming the operative statuses. Eidheim's paper gives a very clear analysis of this situation, as it obtains among Coast Lapps.

But in a different way, one may say that in such a poly-ethnic system, the contrastive cultural characteristics of the component groups are located in the non-articulating sectors of life. For the minority, these sectors constitute a 'backstage' where the characteristics that are stigmatic in terms of the dominant majority culture can covertly be made the objects of transaction.

The present-day minority situation of Lapps has been brought about by recent external circumstances. Formerly, the important context of interaction was the local situation, where two ethnic groups with sufficient knowledge of each other's culture maintained a relatively limited, partly symbiotic relationship based in their respective identities. With the fuller integration of Norwegian society, bringing the northern periphery into the nation-wide system, the rate of cultural change increased drastically. The population of Northern Norway became increasingly dependent on the institutional system of the larger society, and social life among Norwegians in Northern Norway was increasingly organized to pursue activities and obtain benefits within the wider system. This system has not, until very recently, taken ethnic identity into account in its structure, and until a decade ago there was practically no place in it where one could participate *as a Lapp*. Lapps as Norwegian citizens, on the other hand, are perfectly free to participate, though under the dual disability of peripheral location and inadequate command of Norwegian language and culture. This situation has elsewhere, in the inland regions of Finnmark, given scope for Lappish innovators with a political program based on the ideal of ethnic pluralism (cf. Eidheim, 1969), but they have gained no following in the Coast Lapp area here discussed by Eidheim. For these Lapps, rather, the relevance of Lappish statuses and conventions decreases in sector after sector (cf. Eidheim, 1966), while the relative inadequacy of performance in the widest system brings about frustrations and a crisis of identity.

Culture contact and change

This is a very widespread process under present conditions as dependence on the products and institutions of industrial societies spreads in all parts of the world. The important thing to recognize is that a drastic reduction of cultural differences between ethnic groups does not correlate in any simple way with a reduction in the organizational relevance of ethnic identities, or a breakdown in boundary-maintaining processes. This is demonstrated in much of the case material.

We can best analyse the interconnection by looking at the agents of change: what strategies are open and attractive to them, and what are the organizational implications of different choices on their part? The agents in this case are the persons normally referred to somewhat ethno-centrically as the new elites: the persons in the less industrialized groups with greater contact and more dependence on the goods and organizations of industrialized societies. In their pursuit of participation in wider social systems to obtain new forms of value they can choose between the following basic strategies: (i) they may attempt to pass and become incorporated in the pre-established industrial society and cultural group; (ii) they may accept a 'minority' status, accommodate to and seek to reduce their minority disabilities by encapsulating all cultural differentiae in sectors of non-articulation, while participating in the larger system of the industrialized group in the other sectors of activity; (iii) they may choose to emphasize ethnic identity, using it to develop new positions and patterns to organize activities in those sectors formerly not found in their society, or inadequately developed for the new purposes. If the cultural innovators are successful in the first strategy, their ethnic group will be denuded of its source of internal diversification and will probably remain as a culturally conservative, low-articulating ethnic group with low rank in the larger social system. A general acceptance of the second strategy will prevent the emergence of a clearly dichotomizing poly-ethnic organization, and – in view of the diversity of industrial society and consequent variation and multiplicity of fields of articulation – probably lead to an eventual assimilation of the minority. The third strategy generates many of the interesting movements that can be observed today, from nativism to new states.

I am unable to review the variables that affect which basic strategy will be adopted, which concrete form it may take, and what its degree of success and cumulative implications may be. Such factors range from the number of ethnic groups in the system to features of the ecologic regime and details of the constituent cultures, and are illustrated in most of the concrete analyses of the following essays. It may be of interest to note some of the forms in which ethnic identity is made organizationally relevant to new sectors in the current situation.

Firstly, the innovators may choose to emphasize one level of identity among the several provided by the traditional social organization. Tribe, caste, language group, region or state all have features that make them a potentially adequate primary ethnic identity for group reference, and the outcome will depend on the readiness with which others can be led to embrace these identities, and the cold tactical facts. Thus, though tribalism may rally the broadest support in many African areas, the resultant groups seem unable to stand up against the sanctioning apparatus even of a relatively rudimentary state organization.

Secondly, the mode of organization of the ethnic group varies, as does the inter-ethnic articulation that is sought. The fact that contemporary forms are prominently political does not make them any less ethnic in character. Such political movements constitute new ways of making cultural differences organizationally relevant (Kleivan, 1967), and new ways of articulating the dichotomized ethnic groups. The proliferation of ethnically based pressure groups, political parties, and visions of independent statehood, as well as the multitude of sub-political advancement associations (Sommerfelt, 1967) show the importance of these new forms. In other areas, cult-movements or mission-introduced sects are used to dichotomize and articulate groups in new ways. It is striking that these new patterns are so rarely concerned with the economic sector of activities, which is so major a factor in the culture contact situation, apart from the forms of state socialism adopted by some of the new nations. By contrast, the traditional complex poly-ethnic systems have been prominently based on articulation in this sector, through occupational differentiation and articulation at the market place in many regions of Asia and Middle America, or most elaborately, through agrarian production in South Asia. Today, contending ethnic groups not infrequently become differentiated with respect to educational level and attempt to control or monopolize educational facilities for this purpose (Sommerfelt, 1967), but this is not so much with a view to occupational differentiation as because of the obvious connection between bureaucratic competence and opportunities for political advancement. One may speculate that an articulation entailing complex differentiation of skills, and sanctioned by the constant dependence on livelihood, will have far greater strength and stability than one based on revocable political affiliation and sanctioned by the exercise of force and political fiat, and that these new forms of poly-ethnic systems are probably inherently more turbulent and unstable than the older forms.

When political groups articulate their opposition in terms of ethnic criteria, the direction of cultural change is also affected. A political confrontation can only be implemented by making the groups similar and thereby comparable, and this will have effect on every new sector of activity which is made politically relevant. Opposed parties thus tend to become structurally similar, and differentiated only by a few clear diacritica. Where ethnic groups are organized in political confrontation in this way, the process of opposition will therefore lead to a reduction of the cultural differences between them.

For this reason, much of the activity of political innovators is concerned with the codification of idioms: the selection of signals for identity and the assertion of value for these cultural diacritica, and the suppression or denial of relevance for other differentiae. The issue as to which new cultural forms are compatible with the native ethnic identity is often hotly contended, but is generally settled in favour of syncretism for the reasons noted above. But a great amount of attention may be paid to the revival of select traditional culture traits, and to the establishment of historical traditions to justify and glorify the idioms and the identity.

The interconnection between the diacritica that are chosen for emphasis, the boundaries that are defined, and the differentiating values that are espoused, constitute a fascinating field for study.[6] Clearly, a number of factors are relevant. Idioms vary in their appropriateness for different kinds of units. They are unequally adequate for the innovator's purposes, both as means to mobilize support and as supports in the strategy of confrontation with other groups. Their stratificational implications both within and between groups are important: they entail different sources and distributions of influence within the group, and different claims to recognition from other groups through suppression or glorification of different forms of social stigmata. Clearly, there is no simple connection between the ideological basis of a movement and the idioms chosen; yet both have implications for subsequent boundary maintenance, and the course of further change.

Variations in the setting for ethnic relations

These modern variants for poly-ethnic organization emerge in a world of bureaucratic administration, developed communications, and progressive urbanization. Clearly, under radically different circumstances, the critical factors in the definition and maintenance of ethnic boundaries would be different. In basing ourselves on limited and contemporary data, we are faced with difficulties in generalizing about ethnic processes, since major variables may be ignored because they are not exhibited in the cases at our disposal. There can be little doubt that social anthropologists have tended to regard the rather special situation of colonial peace and external administration, which has formed the backdrop of most of the influential monographs, as if this were representative of conditions at most times and places. This may have biased the interpretation both of pre-colonial systems and of contemporary, emergent forms. The attempt in these essays to cover regionally very diverse cases is not alone an adequate defence against such bias, and the issue needs to be faced directly.

Colonial regimes are quite extreme in the extent to which the administration and its rules are divorced from locally based social life. Under such a regime, individuals hold certain rights to protection uniformly through large population aggregates and regions, far beyond the reach of their own social relationships and institutions. This allows physical proximity and opportunities for contact between persons of different ethnic groups regardless of the absence of shared understandings between them, and thus clearly removes one of the constraints that normally operate on inter-ethnic relations. In such situations, interaction can develop and proliferate – indeed, only those forms of interaction that are directly inhibited by other factors will be absent and remain as sectors of non-articulation. Thus ethnic boundaries in such situations represent a positive organization of social relations around differentiated and complementary values, and cultural differences will tend to be reduced with time and approach the required minimum.

In most political regimes, however, where there is less security and people live under a greater threat of arbitrariness and violence outside their primary community, the insecurity itself acts as a constraint on inter-ethnic contacts. In this situation, many forms of interaction between members of different ethnic groups may fail to develop, even though a potential complementarity of interests obtains. Forms of interaction may be blocked because of a lack of trust or a lack of opportunities to consummate transactions. What is more, there are also internal sanctions in such communities which tend to enhance overt conformity within and cultural differences between communities.

If a person is dependent for his security on the voluntary and spontaneous support of his own community, self-identification as a member of this community needs to be explicitly expressed and confirmed; and any behaviour which is deviant from the standard may be interpreted as a weakening of the identity, and thereby of the bases of security. In such situations, fortuitous historical differences in culture between different communities will tend to perpetuate themselves without any positive organizational basis; many of the observable cultural differentiae may thus be of very limited relevance to the ethnic organization.

The processes whereby ethnic units maintain themselves are thus clearly affected, but not fundamentally changed, by the variable of regional security. This can also be shown by an inspection of the cases analysed in these essays, which represent a fair range from the colonial to the poly-centric, up to relatively anarchic situations. It is important, however, to recognize that this background variable may change very rapidly with time, and in the projection of long-range processes this is a serious difficulty. Thus in the Fur case, we observe a situation of externally maintained peace and very small-scale local political activity, and can form a picture of inter-ethnic processes and even rates in this setting. But we know that over the last few generations, the situation has varied from one of Baggara-Fur confrontation under an expansive Fur sultanate to a nearly total anarchy in Turkish and Mahdi times; and it is very difficult to estimate the effects of these variations on the processes of nomadization and assimilation, and arrive at any long-range projection of rates and trends.

Ethnic groups and cultural evolution

The perspective and analysis presented here have relevance to the theme of cultural evolution. No doubt human history is a story of the development of emergent forms, both of cultures and societies. The issue in anthropology has been how this history can best be depicted, and what kinds of analyses are adequate to discover general principles in the courses of change. Evolutionary analysis in the rigorous sense of the biological fields has based its method on the construction of phyletic lines. This method presumes the existence of units where the boundaries and the boundary-maintaining processes can be described, and thus where the continuity can be specified. Concretely, phyletic lines are meaningful because specific boundaries prevent the interchange of genetic material, and so one can insist that the reproductive *isolate* is the unit, and that it has maintained an identity undisturbed by the changes in the morphological characteristics of the species.

I have argued that boundaries are also maintained between ethnic units, and that consequently it is possible to specify the nature of continuity and persistence of such units. These essays try to show that ethnic boundaries are maintained in each case by a limited set of cultural features. The persistence of the unit then depends on the persistence of these cultural differentiae, while continuity can also be specified through the changes of the unit brought about by changes in the boundary-defining cultural differentiae.

However, most of the cultural matter that at any time is associated with a human population is *not* constrained by this boundary; it can vary, be learnt, and change without any critical relation to the boundary maintenance of the ethnic group. So when one traces the history of a ethnic group through time, one is *not* simultaneously, in the same sense, tracing the history of 'a culture': the elements of the present culture of that ethnic group have not sprung from the particular set that constituted the group's culture at a previous time, whereas the group has a continual organizational existence with boundaries (criteria of membership) that despite modifications have marked off a continuing unit.

Without being able to specify the boundaries of cultures, it is not possible to construct phyletic lines in the more rigorous evolutionary sense. But from the analysis that has been argued here, it should be possible to do so for ethnic groups, and thus in a sense for those aspects of culture which have this organizational anchoring.

Notes

1 Anthropological models and social reality

1 Differences in behaviour between persons thus need not entail differences between persons in their evaluation of goods – indeed, it is a convenient and general assumption in anthropology that being a member of a culture consists precisely in sharing the major values of that culture. Nor need we dismiss variation as mere deviance, caused by stupidity or immorality, though admittedly both intelligence and integrity seem to be unequally distributed in every population. The factors of inequality of assets and opportunities provide far the most interesting explanatory models and are the ones that have been most fruitfully developed.

2 Models of social organization I

1 I reserve the term status set for clusters of reciprocal or complementary statuses, analogous to role set; for the sum of statuses occupied by a single incumbent I retain Radcliffe-Brown's term 'person'.

2 This example is meant to be illustrative and not documentary. Independent documentation and analysis will be forthcoming (Hansen, MS) and may modify the picture. The following pertains specifically to skipper-owned vessels from the Møre district; there are suggestions that both ownership patterns and regional differences modify some of the factors depicted here.

4 Models of social organization III

1 There are many further permutations to these ecologic circumstances, mainly arising from the dual nature of assets, in land and in herds, and the fact that the latter are also movable property. The most obvious one is the possibility of obtaining shepherding contracts on a transactional basis. However, these features are not particularly important to the empirical example, and cannot be pursued here.

5 'Models' reconsidered

1 This is particularly evident in Evens (1977), whose weak concept of 'group' (for everything from 'society' to 'corporate group') derives from this dichotomy. It leads him to do less than justice to the structural-functionalists, whose cause he partly champions, in their theory of groups. They were speaking of 'groups' in a narrower and more rigorous sense of *corporate* groups. It also occasions the misinterpretation of my own intentions which provides the basis for his groundless charge of physicalism on my part.

2 Paine's further polarization of 'ought' vs. 'want' (1974, p. 11) and 'ought' vs. 'need' within this single concept of value may indicate one reason for its infertility, if one applies the perspective provided in 'Models'. There is no doubt that people frequently assert ideals of 'ought' which may also be different from what they want. These, often upright and moral ideals, however, cannot provide guidelines for choice in transactions precisely because the 'ought' of their affirmation entails a denial of their realization in behaviour, and even perhaps a fear of their 'prostitution' if consummated as social fact through exchange. They can consequently, like Melanesian cargo, only be given factitious value (above pp. 52-3). Thus Paine can only affirm them to be 'inherently' rewarding, and essentially annihilated. For this reason they offer 'at best, but a severely limited basis for comparison with other values' (ibid., p. 12). Surely, little can be gained by insisting that such phenomena should be classified in the same specific rubric as the standards of comparison which lie behind concrete norms of equivalence in exchange?

3 So the paradox (cf. Kapferer, 1976:3 for a tentative formulation of this widely prevalent misunderstanding) of ubiquitous factors (maximizing) explaining variable forms (local societies and cultures) disappears: 'Models' presents no argument entailing universally valid decision rules and rationality, but seeks to explain (variously patterned) behaviour in terms of (contextually adapted) strategies adopted in the pursuit of (culturally diverse) values.

6 On the study of social change

1 This material derives from Gunnar Håland (1967) as well as my own field material.

7 Analytical dimensions in the comparison of social organizations

1 I have elsewhere (Barth, 1966) pleaded the utility of retaining the distinction between status and role and will here apply Nadel's arguments to the status level of analysis.

2 Merton speaks also of 'role sectors' for these different faces and introduced the concept of 'role set' for the whole interlocking system seen from the point of view of one ego. For the purpose of comparing whole systems it is better to avoid the egocentric perspective and focus on the total set of interrelated roles. Merton further uses 'status set' for the array of statuses occupied by one individual, i.e., what Radcliffe-Brown had already given the more useful name (social) 'person'. It seems to me that the term 'status set' can much more usefully be reserved for the whole interlocking system of positions, as I do here, and 'role set' be used to refer to the interlocking system of behavior or activities (cf. Barth, 1966).

8 Descent and marriage reconsidered

1 It might be noted that this form of reasoning is reminiscent in some respects of marginalism in economics or selection in evolutionary theory, though based on different mechanisms in each case. The force of such reasoning in explaining also the gross features of form in a system should not be underestimated.

2 See Peters (1967) who, while he emphasizes the distinction between

agnates and MoBr gives material consistent with the view expressed here: a MoBr gives access (on request) to the same resources of water and land as do agnates; he contributes voluntarily to bridewealth where agnates are obliged to; he gives support in revenge for homicide; the killing of a MoBr is as sinful an act as killing a close agnate; a case is even cited where revenge is wrought against a MoBr rather than an agnate.

3 This is clearly not a question of mere 'filiation', as it is visualized by informants as a *line*, reaching back to the creation of Adam, and forward into the future.

9 Economic spheres in Darfur

1 In this, I disregard the members of the craftsman caste, whose numbers are very small and whose style of life differs considerably from that of Village Fur.

2 In some cases of inheritance, when none of the heirs wishes to use the house, empty houses are indeed offered on the market and bring anywhere from 6 shillings to £2. The difficulty then is to find a buyer, since those in need of a house can call on friends and relatives to contribute towards the construction of an entirely new house, at a chosen site, through expending less than about 5 shillings-worth of their own millet on beer.

10 Competition and symbiosis in North East Baluchistan

1 I wish to thank the Wenner-Gren Foundation for a grant-in-aid that enabled me to visit the areas in which Pehrson had worked. The whole of his field material is currently being analysed and prepared for publication.

2 The Baluchistan District Gazetteers are the best sources of population data, but are not particularly reliable for Marri tribal area. However, all circumstantial evidence corroborates the picture of a marked population increase.

3 A recent policy of permanent allotment and division of land, as well as a traditional privileged right of the nobility to own land individually, will have the long-term effect of changing these basic conditions.

11 A general perspective on nomad-sedentary relations in the Middle East

1 It might be argued that the differences are not especially great, since both productive regimes require the same basic kinds of production factors: (i) land (= pastures) + capital(= herds) + labor; or (ii) land (= fields) + capital (= seed) + labor, and the capital factor is equally perishable and replaceable in both. Two immutable differences between the two regimes must, however, be remembered: the rate of return on seed is high (ten- to fifty-fold in Middle East cereal crops), so its value is low and attainability simple, while the rate of return on flocks rarely reaches one-fold, so the capital value is high and availability by loan, etc. problematical. In its foundations, agriculture is therefore labor-intensive, while pastoralism is capital-intensive. On the other hand, the time required to extract value from land is great in agriculture, so control of land is essential, while the time required by grazing is minimal, so control may well be precarious and *ad hoc*.

2 I use this expression in what I take to be the usual sense – i.e. an economic regime plus its associated context of social organization.

12 Ethnic groups and boundaries

1 The emphatic ideological denial of the primacy of ethnic identity (and rank) which characterizes the universal religions that have arisen in the Middle East is understandable in this perspective, since practically any movement for social or ethical reform in the poly-ethnic societies of that region would clash with conventions and standards of ethnic character.

2 The difference between ethnic groups and social strata, which seems problematical at this stage of the argument, will be taken up below.

3 I am here concerned only with individual failure to maintain identity, where most members do so successfully, and not with the broader questions of cultural vitality and anomie.

4 As opposed to presumptive classification in passing social encounters – I am thinking of the person in his normal social context where others have a considerable amount of previous information about him, not of the possibilities afforded occasionally for misrepresenting one's identity towards strangers.

5 The condemned behaviour which gives pariah position to the gypsies is compound, but rests prominently on their wandering life, originally in contrast to the serf bondage of Europe, later in their flagrant violation of puritan ethics of responsibility, toil and morality.

6 To my knowledge, Mitchell's essay on the Kalela dance (Mitchell, 1956) is the first and still the most penetrating study on this topic.

Bibliography

ARENSBERG, C. M. (1957), Anthropology as History, in *Trade and Market in the Early Empires*, Polanyi, K., Arensberg, C. M. and Pearson, H. W. (eds), Chicago: Free Press.

ARENSBERG, C. M. (1965), A Comparative Analysis of Culture and Community: Peoples of the Old World, in C. M. Arensberg and S. T. Kimball (eds), *Culture and Community*, New York: Harcourt Brace Jovanovich.

ASAD, TALAL (1972), Market model, class structure and consent: a reconsideration of Swat political organization. *Man* (NS), vol. 7, no. 1.

ASWAD, B. (1971), *Property Control and Social Strategies: Settlers in a Middle East Plain*, University Museum, Michigan, Anthropological Papers No. 44.

AYUB, M. (1959), Parallel cousin marriage reconsidered. *Man*, vol. 5, 5.

BAILEY, F. G. (1957), *Caste and the Economic Frontier*, Manchester: Manchester University Press.

BAILEY, F. G. (1960), *Tribe, Caste and Nation*, Manchester, Manchester University Press.

BAILEY, F. G. (1969), *Stratagems and Spoils*, Oxford: Blackwell.

Baluchistan District Gazetteer Series (1907), vol. II, Allahabad: The Pioneer Press; vol. III, Bombay: The Times Press.

BARNES, J. A. (1962), African models in the New Guinea highlands. *Man*, vol. 62, pp. 5-9.

BARTH, FREDRIK (1953), *Principles of Social Organization in Southern Kurdistan*, Oslo: Universitetets Etnografiske Museum Bulletin, no. 7.

BARTH, FREDRIK (1954), Father's brother's daughter marriage in Kurdistan. *Southwestern Journal of Anthropology*, vol. 10.

BARTH, FREDRIK (1959a), *Political Leadership among Swat Pathans*, London School of Economics, Monographs on Social Anthropology, no. 19.

BARTH, FREDRIK (1959b), Segmentary Opposition and the Theory of Games: a study of Pathan organization. *Journal of the Royal Anthropological Institute*, vol. 89, pt 1, pp. 5-22.

BARTH, FREDRIK (1960), Nomadism in the Mountain and Plateau Areas of Southwest Asia in *The Problems of the Arid Zone*, Paris: UNESCO, 1960.

BARTH, FREDRIK (1961), *Nomads of South Persia*, Oslo: Norwegian Universities Press, and Boston, Mass.: Little, Brown, 1968.

BARTH, FREDRIK (1963a), Ethnic processes on the Pathan-Baluch boundary, in G. Redard (ed.), *Indo-Iranica*, Wiesbaden.

BARTH, FREDRIK (1963|b), *The Role of the Entrepreneur in Social Change in Northern Norway*, Bergen/Oslo: Norwegian Universities Press.

BARTH, FREDRIK (1964), Capital, Investment and the Social Structure of a Pastoral Nomad Group in South Persia, in R. Firth and Bae S. Yamey (eds), *Capital, Saving and Credit in Peasant Societies*, London: Allen & Unwin.

BARTH, FREDRIK (1966), *Models of Social Organization*, London: Royal

Anthropological Institute, Occasional papers no. 23.
BARTH, FREDRIK (1967), Economic spheres in Darfur, in R. Firth (ed.), *Themes in Economic Anthropology*, London: Tavistock.
BARTH, FREDRIK (ed.) (1969), *Ethnic Groups and Boundaries*, Oslo: Universitetsforlaget, and Boston, Mass.: Little, Brown.
BARTH, FREDRIK (1975), *Ritual and Knowledge among the Baktaman of New Guinea*, Oslo: Norwegian Universities Press, and Cambridge, Mass.: Yale University Press.
BATESON, G. (1958), *Naven* (2nd edn), Stanford, Ca.: Stanford University Press.
BATESON, G. (1972), *Steps to an Ecology of the Mind*, New York: Chandler.
BELSHAW, C. (1955), The cultural milieu of the entrepreneur. *Explorations in Entrepreneurial History*, vol. 7, no. 3.
BIRDWHISTLE, R. (1970), *Kinesics and Context*, University of Philadelphia Press.
BLOCH, M. (1977), The past and the present in the present. *Man* (N. S.) Vol. 12 No. 2, pp. 278-292.
BLOM, J.-P. (1969), Ethnic and cultural differentiation in F. Barth (ed.), *Ethnic Groups and Boundaries*.
BOAS, F. (1940), *Race, Language and Culture*, New York and London: Macmillan.
BOGORAZ, V. (1904-9), *The Chuckchee*, New York: American Museum of Natural History, Anthropological Memoirs, vol. II.
BOHANNAN, L. and BOHANNAN, P. (1953), *The Tiv of Central Nigeria*, London.
BOHANNAN, P. and DALTON, G. (1962), *Markets in Africa*, New York: Doubleday.
BOURDIEU, P. (1977), *Outline of a Theory of Practice*, Cambridge University Press, Cambridge Studies in Social Anthropology, no. 16.
BRUCE, R. I. (1900), *The Forward Policy and its Results*, London: Longmans.
CHAPPLE, E. D. and COON, C. S. (1942), *Principles of Anthropology*, New York: Holt.
COON, C.S. (1952), *Caravan: The Story of the Middle East*, London: Cape.
DAMES, M. L. (1904), *The Baloch Race*, Asiatic Society Monographs vol. IV.
DOUGLAS, MARY (1970), *Natural Symbols*, London: Barrie & Jenkins.
DOUGLAS, MARY (1975), *Implicit Meanings*, London: Routledge & Kegan Paul.
EGGAN, F. (1950), *Social Organization of the Western Pueblos*, University of Chicago Press.
EGGAN, F. (1954), Social anthropology and the method of controlled comparison. *American Anthropologist*, vol. 56.
EIDHEIM, H. (1966), Lappish guest relationships under conditions of cultural change. *American Anthropologist*, vol. 68.
EIDHEIM, H. (1968), The Lappish Movement – an innovative political process, in M. Swartz (ed.), *Local-level Politics*, Chicago: Aldine.
EIDHEIM, H. (1969), When ethnic identity is a social stigma, in F. Barth (ed.), *Ethnic Groups and Boundaries*.
EIDHEIM, H. (1971), *Aspects of the Lappish Minority Situation*, Oslo: Universitetsforlaget.
EVANS-PRITCHARD, E. E. (1940), *The Nuer*, London: Oxford University Press.
EVANS-PRITCHARD, E. E. (1951), *Kinship and Marriage among the Nuer*, Oxford: Clarendon Press.
EVENS, T. M. S. (1977), The predication of the individual in anthropological interactionism. *American Anthropologist*, vol. 79.

FERDINAND, K. (1959), Les Nomades afghans, in J. Humlum (ed.), *La Géographie de l'Afghanistan*, Copenhagen.
FERDINAND, K. (1969), Ættelinjestabilitet blant nomader i Øst-Afghanistan (ms).
FIRTH, R. (1939), *Primitive Polynesian Economy*, London: Routledge & Kegan Paul.
FIRTH, R. (1954), Social organization and social change. *Journal of the Royal Anthropological Institute*, vol. 84.
FORTES, M. (1945), *The Dynamics of Clanship among the Tallensi*, London: Oxford University Press.
FORTES, M. (1953), The Structure of Unilineal Descent Groups. *American Anthropologist*, vol. 55, pp. 17–40.
FORTES, M. (1959), Descent, filiation and affinity. *Man*, nos 309 and 331.
FORTES, M. (1969), *Kinship and the Social Order*, London: Routledge & Kegan Paul.
FORTES, M. (1970), *Time and Social Structure and other essays*, London: Athlone Press.
FRAKE, C. O. (1962), The ethnographic study of cognitive systems, in *Anthropology and Human Behaviour*, Washington: The Anthropological Society of Washington.
FURNIVALL, J. S. (1944), *Netherlands India: A Study of Plural Economy*, Cambridge University Press.
GEERTZ, C. (1963), *Agricultural Involution*, Berkeley: University of California Press.
GEERTZ, C. (1973), *The Interpretation of Culture*, New York: Basic Books.
GELLNER, E. (1958), Time and theory in social anthropology. *Mind*, vol. 67, no. 266.
GILBERT, J. P. and HAMMEL, E. A. (1966), Computer simulation and analysis of problems in kinship and social structure. *American Anthropologist*, vol. 68.
GJESSING, G. (1954), *Changing Lapps: A Study in Culture Relations in Northernmost Norway*. London School of Economics, Monographs on Social Anthropology, no. 13.
GLUCKMAN, M. (1955), *The Judicial Process Among the Barotse*, Manchester University Press.
GLUCKMAN, M. (1956), *Custom and Conflict in Africa*, Oxford: Blackwell.
GLUCKMAN, M. (1958), *Analysis of a Social Situation in Modern Zululand*, Manchester University Press, Rhodes-Livingstone Papers no. 28. (Papers originally published in *Bantu Studies* 1940, and in *African Studies* 1942).
GLUCKMAN, M. (1962), *Essays in the Ritual of Social Relations*, Manchester University Press.
GOFFMAN, E. (1959), *The Presentation of Self in Everyday Life*. New York: Doubleday.
GOFFMAN, E. (1961), Role Distance, in *Encounters, Two Studies in the Sociology of Interaction*, Minneapolis and New York: Bobbs-Merrill.
GOLDBERG, H. (1967), FBD marriage and demography among Tripolitanian Jews in Israel. *Southwestern Journal of Anthropology*, vol. 23.
GOODENOUGH, W. H. (1956), Componential analysis and the study of meaning. *Language*, vol. 32, no. 1.
GOODENOUGH, W. H. (1965), Rethinking 'Status' and 'Role': Toward a General Model of the Cultural Organization of Social Relationships, in M. Banton (ed.), *The Relevance of Models for Social Anthropology*, ASA Monograph No. 1, London: Tavistock.

Bibliography 235

GOODY, J. (ed.) (1958), *The Developmental Cycle in Domestic Groups*, Cambridge University Press, Cambridge Papers in Social Anthropology, no. 1.

HÅLAND, G. (1967), Ervervsform og etnisk tilhørighet. En studie av nomadiseringsprosesser blant fastboende hakkebrukere i det vestlige Darfur. University of Bergen, unpublished thesis.

HÅLAND, G. (1969), Economic determinants in ethnic processes, in F. Barth (ed.), *Ethnic groups and Boundaries*.

HAMMEL, E. A. and GOLDBERG, H. (1971), Parallel cousin marriage, *Man 6*.

HEATH, A. F. (1976), Decision making and transactional theory in B. Kapferer (ed.) *Transaction and Meaning*. Philadelphia: Institute for the Study of Human Issues.

HOMANS, G. C. (1958), Social behaviour as exchange. *American Journal of Sociology*, vol. 63.

ITZIKOWITZ, K. G. (1969), Neighbours in Laos, in F. Barth (ed.), *Ethnic Groups and Boundaries*.

KANDRE, P. (1967a), Autonomy and integration in social systems: the Iu Mien (Yao) mountain population and their neighbours, in P. Kunstadter (ed.), *Southeast Asian Tribes, Minorities and Nations*, Princeton Unviersity Press.

KANDRE, P. (1967b), Om etnisitet hos Iu Mien-Yao (ms.).

KAPFERER, BRUCE (ed.) (1976), *Transaction and Meaning*, Philadelphia: Institute for the Study of Human Issues, ASA Essays in Social Anthropology, vol. 1.

KHURI, F. (1970), Parallel cousin marriage reconsidered: a Middle Eastern practice that nullifies the effects of marriage on the intensity of family relationships. *Man* vol. 5.

KLEIVAN, H. (1967), Grønlendere of andre dansker (ms.).

KNUTSSON, K. E. (1969), Dichotomization and integration, in F. Barth (ed.), *Ethnic Groups and Boundaries*.

KNUTSSON, K. E. (1970), Ploughland and Swidden: A Dual System of Agriculture in Western Ethiopia, mimeo.

LAMPEN, G. D. (1950), History of Darfur. *Sudan Notes and Records*, vol. 31, no. 2.

LEACH, E. R. (1951), The structural implications of matrilateral cross-cousin marriage. *Journal of the Royal Anthropological Institute*, vol. 81.

LEACH, E. R. (1957), Aspects of bridewealth and marriage stability among the Kachin and Lakher. *Man*, vol. 59.

LEACH, E. R. (ed.) (1960), *Aspects of Caste in South India, Ceylon, and North-West Pakistan*, Cambridge University Press, Cambridge Papers in Social Anthropology, No. 2.

LEACH, E. R. (1961), *Rethinking Anthropology*, London School of Economics, Monographs on Social Anthropology, no. 22.

LEACH, E. R. (1967), Caste, class and slavery – the taxonomic problem, in A. de Reuck and J. Knight (eds): *Caste and Race: Comparative Approaches*. London: Churchill.

LEACH, E. R. (1968), Social structure: The history of the concept, in David L. Sills (ed.) *International Encyclopedia of the Social Sciences*, New York: Macmillan and Free Press, vol. 14, pp. 482–88.

LEBON, J. H. G. and ROBERTSON, V. C. (1961), The Jebel Marra, Darfur, and its Region. *Geographical Journal*, vol. 127, no. 1.

LEVI-STRAUSS, C. (1963), The Bear and the Barber. The Henry Myers Memorial Lecture, 1962. *Journal of the Royal Anthropological Institute*, vol. 93, pp. 1–11.

LEVI-STRAUSS, C. (1966), The future of kinship studies. *Proceedings of the*

236   *Bibliography*

Royal Anthropological Institute for 1965.
LEWIS, I. M. (1961), *A Pastoral Democracy*, London: Oxford University Press.
MALINOWSKI, B. (1929), *The Sexual Life of Savages*, London: Routledge.
MAQUET, JACQUES (1968), African Society: Sub-Saharan Africa, in David L. Sills (ed.), *International Encyclopedia of the Social Sciences* New York: Macmillan and Free Press.
MARRIOTT, MCKIM (1959), *Changing Channels of Cultural Transmission in Indian Civilization*, Chicago: University of Chicago Committee on South Asian Studies Reprint Series no. 7.
MARRIOTT, MCKIM (1976), Hindu transactions: Diversity without dualism, in B. Kapferer (ed.): *Transaction and meaning*.
MARRIOTT, MCKIM and INDEN, R. (1974), Caste systems. *Encyclopaedia Britannica*.
MATHIESON, THOMAS (1965), *The Defences of the Weak*, London: Tavistosk.
MAYER, A. C. (1966), The Significance of Quasi-Groups in the Study of Complex Societies, in Michael Banton (ed.), *The Social Anthropology of Complex Societies*, ASA Monograph, no. 4, London: Tavistock.
MEEKER, B. F. (1971), Decisions and exchange. *American Sociological Review*, vol. 36.
MERTON, R. K. (1957), *Social Theory and Social Structure*, Revised and Enlarged Edition, Chicago: Free Press.
MITCHELL, J. C. (1956), *The Kalela Dance: Aspects of Social Relations among Urban Africans in N. Rhodesia*, The Rhodes-Livingstone Papers No. 27, Manchester University Press.
MORGENSTERN, O. (1968), Game theory: Theoretical aspects in David L. Sills (ed.), *International Encyclopedia of the Social Sciences* vol. 6, New York: Macmillan and Free Press.
MORGENSTIERNE, G. (1932), *Report on a Linguistic Mission to North-Western India*, Oslo: Norwegian Universities Press.
MURDOCK, G. P. (1949), *Social Structure*, New York: Macmillan.
MURPHY, R. F. and KASDAN, L. (1959), The structure of parallel cousin marriage. *American Anthropologist*, vol. 61.
MURPHY, F. R. and KASDAN, L. (1967), Agnation and monogamy. Some further considerations. *Southwestern Journal of Anthropology*, vol. 23.
MYRDAL, G. (1958), *Value in Social Theory*, London: Routledge & Kegan Paul.
NADEL, S. F. (1951), *The Foundations of Social Anthropology*, London: Routledge & Kegan Paul.
NADEL, S. F. (1952), Witchcraft in four African societies. *American Anthropologist*, vol. 54.
NADEL, S. F. (1957), *The Theory of Social Structure*, London: Cohen & West.
NARROLL, R. (1964), Ethnic unit classification. *Current Anthropology*, vol. 4, no. 4.
NEUMANN, J. VON and MORGENSTERN, O. (1944), *Theory of Games and Economic Behavior*, Princeton University Press.
NEUMANN, J. VON and MORGENSTERN, O. (1947), *Theory of games and economic behaviour* (2nd ed.), Princeton University Press.
PAINE, R. (1957), *Coast Lapp Society, I*. A Study of Neighbourhood in Revsbotn Fjord, Tromsö: Tromsö Museums Skrifter, vol. IV.
PAINE, R. (1965), *Coast Lapp Society, II*, Oslo: Universitetsforlaget.
PAINE, R. (1974), *Second Thoughts about Barth's Models*. Royal Anthropological Institute, Occasional Papers no. 32.
PAINE, R. (1976), Two modes of exchange and mediation, in B. Kapferer (ed.). *Transaction and Meaning*.

PARSONS, T. (1952), *The Social System*, London: Routledge & Kegan Paul.
PATAI, R. (1965), The structure of endogamous unilineal descent groups. *Southwestern Journal of Anthropology*, vol. 21.
PEHRSON, R. N. (1966), *The Social Organization of the Marri Baluch*, Viking Fund Publications in Anthropology No. 43, Chicago: Aldine.
PETERS, E. (1960), The proliferation of segments in the lineage of the Bedouin of Cyrenaica. *Journal of the Royal Anthropological Institute*, vol. 90.
PETERS, E. (1967), Some structural aspects of the feud among the camelherding Bedouin of Cyrenaica. *Africa*, vol. 37.
PITTENGER, R. E., HOCKETT, C. F. and DANEHY, J. J. (1960), *The First Five Minutes*, Ithaca: Cornell University Press.
RADCLIFFE-BROWN, A. R. (1913), Three Tribes of Western Australia. *Journal of the Royal Anthropological Institute*, vol. 43, pp. 143–94.
RADCLIFFE-BROWN, A. R. (1935), Patrilineal and matrilineal succession. *The Iowa Law Review*, vol. 20, no. 2. Reprinted in Radcliffe-Brown, (1952).
RADCLIFFE-BROWN, A. R. (1952), *Structure and Function in Primitive Society*. London: Cohen & West.
RADCLIFFE-BROWN, A. R. (1958), Method in social anthropology, in M. M. Srinivas (ed.), University of Chicago Press.
REUCK, A. DE and KNIGHT, J. (eds) (1967), *Caste and Race*, London: Churchill.
RUESCH, J. and BATESON, G. (1951), *Communication*, New York: Norton.
SAHLINS, MARSHALL (1972), *Stone Age Economics*, Chicago: Aldine.
SALISBURY, RICHARD F. (1976), Transactions or Transactors?An Economic Anthropologist's View in B. Kapferer (ed.): *Transaction and Meaning.*
SCHAPERA, I. (1953), Some comments on the comparative method in social anthropology. *American Anthropologist*, vol. 55.
SCHEFFLER, H. W. (1965), *Choiseul Island Social Structure*, Berkeley: University of California Press.
SCHEFFLER, H. W. (1966), Ancestor worship in anthropology: or, observations on descent and descent groups. *Current Anthropology*, pp. 541–52.
SCHNEIDER, D. M. (1965a), Some muddles in the models in *The Relevance of Models for Social Anthropology*, ASA Monographs No. 1, London:
SCHNEIDER, D. M. (1965b), Kinship and biology, in Coale, A. J. *et al., Aspects of the Analysis of Family Structure*, Princeton University Press.
SHARP, LAURISTON (1952), Steel axes for stone-age Australians in E. H. Spicer (ed.), *Human problems in technological change*, New York: Russell Sage Foundation.
SIVERTS, H. (1969), Ethnic stability and boundary dynamics in Southern Mexico, in F. Barth (ed.), *Ethnic Groups and Boundaries.*
SKJERVHEIM, H. (1959), *Objectivism and the Study of Man*, Oslo: Norwegian Universities Press.
SKVORETZ, J. V. and CONVISER, R. H. (1974), Interests and alliances: a reformulation of Barth's Models of social organization. *Man* (NS), vol. 9, no. 1.
SLAGSTAD, R. (ed.) (1976), *Positivisme, dialektikk, materialisme*, Oslo: Norwegian Universities Press.
SOLOW, R. M. (1965), Economic behaviour under uncertainty. *Proceedings of the Royal Society*, B, vol. 162, pp. 444–57.
SOMMERFELT, A. (1967), Inter-etniske relasjoner i Toro *(ms.).*
STANNER, W. H. E. (1958), On the interpretation of cargo cults. *Oceania*, vol. 29, no. 1.
STANNER, W. H. E. (1959), On aboriginal religion, Part I. *Oceania*, vol. 30, no. 2.

STRATHERN, A. J. (1969), Descent and alliance in the New Guinea Highlands: some problems of comparison. *Proceedings of the Royal Anthropological Institute for 1968*, pp. 37–52.

TINBERGEN, N. (1951), *The Study of Instinct*, Oxford: Clarendon Press.

VIDYARTHI (1961), *The Sacred Complex in Hindu Gaya*, Bombay: Asia Press.

WEBER, M. (1922), *Gesammelte Aufsätze zur Wissenschaftslehre*, Tübingen: J. C. B. Mohr.

WOLF, E. (1966), *Peasants*, Englewood Cliffs, New Jersey: Prentice-Hall.

Index

acculturation, 114f, 199, 201
adaptation, 179, 188, 200, 208f
agriculture, as opposed to pastoralism, 70f, 179ff, 189ff, 230n
allocation, 64, 67, 107ff, 111, 164ff, 174ff
altruism, 38
archeology, 112
arena, 104, 121
Arensberg, Conrad, 52, 194
Asad, Talal, 88
asset, 84, 86ff, 122, 136, 171, 214ff, 228n
Aswad, Barbara, 149f
Australian aborigines, 126, 134
authority, 27, 41, 88ff
awareness, 15, 79, 82, 90, 122
Ayoub, M., 148

Baggara Arabs, 113, 166, 212ff, 226
Bailey, F., 121, 133
Baluch, 142f, 150, 179ff, 196, 209, 211, 213f, 218, 230n
bands, 125f
bargaining, 57, 162f
Barnes, John A., 139
barrier, to conversion, 56, 110, 170ff, 177ff
Basseri, 70, 72, 187, 196
Bateson, Gregory, 3, 28, 45, 48
beer, beer brewing, 159ff, 170ff
beer party, 109, 161ff
Belshaw, Cyril, 56
Birdwhistle, Ray, 8
Bloch, Maurice, 80, 82
Blom, Jan-Petter, 202
blood feud, 66, 229n
Boas, Franz, 61
Bogoraz, Vladimir G., 202
Bohannan, Laura, 66
Bohannan, Paul, 55, 163

boundary, boundary maintenance, 133, 180, 198ff
Bourdieu, P., 5
brideprice, bridewealth, 142, 159, 167, 229n
bridge, of fishing vessel, 42ff, 89
bridging transaction, 56; see also conversion
broker, see entrepreneur
bureaucracy, 131, 217, 223
Bushman, 125f

capital, 167, 189, 192, 212, 230n
career, 86f, 120
cargo cult, 53, 228n
carrying capacity, of resources, 181ff, 209f
cash sphere, among Fur, 164ff
caste, caste identity, 134, 206, 229n; see also sub-caste
cattle, 165, 166f
change, 6, 60, 77, 81, 82, 84, 94, 103, 105ff, 141, 178, 186, 199, 203, 211ff, 221ff, 226
Chapple, E. D., 27
choice, 21, 34, 39, 88ff, 122, 191, 222, 228n
circle of conversion, 53f, 169ff, 177
civilizations, traditional, 135
client, 21, 54, 68, 80, 214, 216
coalition, 22
code, 3, 25, 81, 83, 205
codification, 3, 48, 219
collective representations, 103
colonialism, 132, 206, 225
communication, communicative, 25, 81f, 137, 219
comparison, comparative analysis, 61ff, 119ff, 137, 143, 187f
competition, 179, 184, 208f
complementarity, 37, 42, 207, 209

239

Routledge Social Science Series

Routledge & Kegan Paul   London, Henley and Boston

39 Store Street,
London WC1E 7DD
Broadway House,
Newtown Road,
Henley-on-Thames,
Oxon RG9 1EN
9 Park Street,
Boston, Mass. 02108

Contents

*Authors wishing to submit manuscripts for any series
in this catalogue should send them to the Social Science Editor,
Routledge & Kegan Paul Ltd, 39 Store Street,
London WC1E 7DD.*
● *Books so marked are available in paperback.*
○ *Books so marked are available in paperback only.*
*All books are in metric Demy 8vo format (216 × 138mm approx.)
unless otherwise stated.*

International Library of Sociology
General Editor John Rex

GENERAL SOCIOLOGY

Barnsley, J. H. The Social Reality of Ethics. *464 pp.*
Brown, Robert. Explanation in Social Science. *208 pp.*
● Rules and Laws in Sociology. *192 pp.*
Bruford, W. H. Chekhov and His Russia. *A Sociological Study. 244 pp.*
Burton, F. and **Carlen, P.** Official Discourse. *On Discourse Analysis, Government Publications, Ideology. About 140 pp.*
Cain, Maureen E. Society and the Policeman's Role. *326 pp.*
● **Fletcher, Colin.** Beneath the Surface. *An Account of Three Styles of Sociological Research. 221 pp.*
Gibson, Quentin. The Logic of Social Enquiry. *240 pp.*
Glassner, B. Essential Interactionism. *208 pp.*
Glucksmann, M. Structuralist Analysis in Contemporary Social Thought. *212 pp.*
Gurvitch, Georges. Sociology of Law. *Foreword by Roscoe Pound. 264 pp.*
Hinkle, R. Founding Theory of American Sociology 1881–1913. *About 350 pp.*
Homans, George C. Sentiments and Activities. *336 pp.*
Johnson, Harry M. Sociology: *A Systematic Introduction. Foreword by Robert K. Merton. 710 pp.*
● **Keat, Russell** and **Urry, John.** Social Theory as Science. *278 pp.*
Mannheim, Karl. Essays on Sociology and Social Psychology. *Edited by Paul Keckskemeti. With Editorial Note by Adolph Lowe. 344 pp.*
Martindale, Don. The Nature and Types of Sociological Theory. *292 pp.*
● **Maus, Heinz.** A Short History of Sociology. *234 pp.*
Myrdal, Gunnar. Value in Social Theory: *A Collection of Essays on Methodology. Edited by Paul Streeten. 332 pp.*
Ogburn, William F. and **Nimkoff, Meyer F.** A Handbook of Sociology. *Preface by Karl Mannheim. 656 pp. 46 figures. 35 tables.*
Parsons, Talcott and **Smelser, Neil J.** Economy and Society: *A Study in the Integration of Economic and Social Theory. 362 pp.*
Payne, G., Dingwall, R., Payne, J. and **Carter, M.** Sociology and Social Research. *About 250 pp.*
Podgórecki, A. Practical Social Sciences. *About 200 pp.*
Podgórecki, A. and **Łos, M.** Multidimensional Sociology. *268 pp.*
Raffel, S. Matters of Fact. *A Sociological Inquiry. 152 pp.*
● **Rex, John.** Key Problems of Sociological Theory. *220 pp.*
  Sociology and the Demystification of the Modern World. *282 pp.*
● **Rex, John.** (Ed.) Approaches to Sociology. *Contributions by Peter Abell, Frank Bechhofer, Basil Bernstein, Ronald Fletcher, David Frisby, Miriam Glucksmann Peter Lassman, Herminio Martins, John Rex, Roland Robertson, John Westergaard and Jock Young. 302 pp.*
Rigby, A. Alternative Realities. *352 pp.*
Roche, M. Phenomenology, Language and the Social Sciences. *374 pp.*
Sahay, A. Sociological Analysis. *220 pp.*
Strasser, Hermann. The Normative Structure of Sociology. *Conservative and Emancipatory Themes in Social Thought. About 340 pp.*
Strong, P. Ceremonial Order of the Clinic. *267 pp.*
Urry, John. Reference Groups and the Theory of Revolution. *244 pp.*
Weinberg, E. Development of Sociology in the Soviet Union. *173 pp.*

FOREIGN CLASSICS OF SOCIOLOGY

● **Gerth, H. H.** and **Mills, C. Wright.** From Max Weber: *Essays in Sociology. 502 pp.*

3

● **Tönnies, Ferdinand.** Community and Association *(Gemeinschaft und Gesell-schaft).\Translated and Supplemented by Charles P. Loomis. Foreword by Pitirim A. Sorokin. 334 pp.*

SOCIAL STRUCTURE

Andreski, Stanislav. Military Organization and Society. *Foreword by Professor A. R. Radcliffe-Brown. 226 pp. 1 folder.*
Broom, L., Lancaster Jones, F., McDonnell, P. and Williams, T. The Inheritance of Inequality. *About 180 pp.*
Carlton, Eric. Ideology and Social Order. *Foreword by Professor Philip Abrahams. About 320 pp.*
Clegg, S. and Dunkerley, D. Organization, Class and Control. *614 pp.*
Coontz, Sydney H. Population Theories and the Economic Interpretation. *202 pp.*
Coser, Lewis. The Functions of Social Conflict. *204 pp.*
Crook, I. and D. The First Years of the Yangyi Commune. *304 pp., illustrated.*
Dickie-Clark, H. F. Marginal Situation: *A Sociological Study of a Coloured Group. 240 pp. 11 tables.*
Giner, S. and Archer, M. S. (Eds) Contemporary Europe: *Social Structures and Cultural Patterns, 336 pp.*
● **Glaser, Barney and Strauss, Anselm L.** Status Passage: *A Formal Theory. 212 pp.*
Glass, D. V. (Ed.) Social Mobility in Britain. *Contributions by J. Berent, T. Bottomore, R. C. Chambers, J. Floud, D. V. Glass, J. R. Hall, H. T. Himmelweit, R. K. Kelsall, F. M. Martin, C. A. Moser, R. Mukherjee and W. Ziegel. 420 pp.*
Kelsall, R. K. Higher Civil Servants in Britain: *From 1870 to the Present Day. 268 pp. 31 tables.*
● **Lawton, Denis.** Social Class, Language and Education. *192 pp.*
McLeish, John. The Theory of Social Change: *Four Views Considered. 128 pp.*
● **Marsh, David C.** The Changing Social Structure of England and Wales, 1871–1961. *Revised edition. 288 pp.*
Menzies, Ken. Talcott Parsons and the Social Image of Man. *About 208 pp.*
● **Mouzelis, Nicos.** Organization and Bureaucracy. *An Analysis of Modern Theories. 240 pp.*
● **Ossowski, Stanislaw.** Class Structure in the Social Consciousness. *210 pp.*
● **Podgórecki, Adam.** Law and Society. *302 pp.*
Renner, Karl. Institutions of Private Law and Their Social Functions. *Edited, with an Introduction and Notes, by O. Kahn-Freud. Translated by Agnes Schwarzschild. 316 pp.*
Rex, J. and Tomlinson, S. Colonial Immigrants in a British City. *A Class Analysis. 368 pp.*
Smooha, S. Israel: Pluralism and Conflict. *472 pp.*
Wesolowski, W. Class, Strata and Power. *Trans. and with Introduction by G. Kolankiewicz. 160 pp.*
Zureik, E. Palestinians in Israel. *A Study in Internal Colonialism. 264 pp.*

SOCIOLOGY AND POLITICS

Acton, T. A. Gypsy Politics and Social Change. *316 pp.*
Burton, F. Politics of Legitimacy. *Struggles in a Belfast Community. 250 pp.*
Crook, I. and D. Revolution in a Chinese Village. *Ten Mile Inn. 216 pp., illustrated.*
Etzioni-Halevy, E. Political Manipulation and Administrative Power. *A Comparative Study. About 200 pp.*
Fielding, N. The National Front. *About 250 pp.*
● **Hechter, Michael.** Internal Colonialism. *The Celtic Fringe in British National Development, 1536–1966. 380 pp.*
Kornhauser, William. The Politics of Mass Society. *272 pp. 20 tables.*

Korpi, W. The Working Class in Welfare Capitalism. *Work, Unions and Politics in Sweden. 472 pp.*
Kroes, R. Soldiers and Students. *A Study of Right- and Left-wing Students. 174 pp.*
Martin, Roderick. Sociology of Power. *About 272 pp.*
Merquior, J. G. Rousseau and Weber. *A Study in the Theory of Legitimacy. About 288 pp.*
Myrdal, Gunnar. The Political Element in the Development of Economic Theory. *Translated from the German by Paul Streeten. 282 pp.*
Varma, B. N. The Sociology and Politics of Development. *A Theoretical Study. 236 pp.*
Wong, S.-L. Sociology and Socialism in Contemporary China. *160 pp.*
Wootton, Graham. Workers, Unions and the State. *188 pp.*

CRIMINOLOGY

Ancel, Marc. Social Defence: *A Modern Approach to Criminal Problems. Foreword by Leon Radzinowicz. 240 pp.*
Athens, L. Violent Criminal Acts and Actors. *104 pp.*
Cain, Maureen E. Society and the Policeman's Role. *326 pp.*
Cloward, Richard A. and Ohlin, Lloyd E. Delinquency and Opportunity: *A Theory of Delinquent Gangs. 248 pp.*
Downes, David M. The Delinquent Solution. *A Study in Subcultural Theory. 296 pp.*
Friedlander, Kate. The Psycho-Analytical Approach to Juvenile Delinquency: *Theory, Case Studies, Treatment. 320 pp.*
Gleuck, Sheldon and Eleanor. Family Environment and Delinquency. *With the statistical assistance of Rose W. Kneznek. 340 pp.*
Lopez-Rey, Manuel. Crime. *An Analytical Appraisal. 288 pp.*
Mannheim, Hermann. Comparative Criminology: *A Text Book. Two volumes. 442 pp. and 380 pp.*
Morris, Terence. The Criminal Area: *A Study in Social Ecology. Foreword by Hermann Mannheim. 232 pp. 25 tables. 4 maps.*
Rock, Paul. Making People Pay. *338 pp.*
● Taylor, Ian, Walton, Paul and Young, Jock. The New Criminology. *For a Social Theory of Deviance. 325 pp.*
● Taylor, Ian, Walton, Paul and Young, Jock. (Eds) Critical Criminology. *268 pp.*

SOCIAL PSYCHOLOGY

Bagley, Christopher. The Social Psychology of the Epileptic Child. *320 pp.*
Brittan, Arthur. Meanings and Situations. *224 pp.*
Carroll, J. Break-Out from the Crystal Palace. *200 pp.*
● Fleming, C. M. Adolescence: Its Social Psychology. *With an Introduction to recent findings from the fields of Anthropology, Physiology, Medicine, Psychometrics and Sociometry. 288 pp.*
● The Social Psychology of Education: *An Introduction and Guide to Its Study. 136 pp.*
Linton, Ralph. The Cultural Background of Personality. *132 pp.*
● Mayo, Elton. The Social Problems of an Industrial Civilization. *With an Appendix on the Political Problem. 180 pp.*
Ottaway, A. K. C. Learning Through Group Experience. *176 pp.*
Plummer, Ken. Sexual Stigma. *An Interactionist Account. 254 pp.*
● Rose, Arnold M. (Ed.) Human Behaviour and Social Processes: *an Interactionist Approach. Contributions by Arnold M. Rose, Ralph H. Turner, Anselm Strauss, Everett C. Hughes, E. Franklin Frazier, Howard S. Becker et al. 696 pp.*
Smelser, Neil J. Theory of Collective Behaviour. *448 pp.*
Stephenson, Geoffrey M. The Development of Conscience. *128 pp.*
Young, Kimball. Handbook of Social Psychology. *658 pp. 16 figures. 10 tables.*

SOCIOLOGY OF THE FAMILY

Bell, Colin R. Middle Class Families: *Social and Geographical Mobility. 224 pp.*
Burton, Lindy. Vulnerable Children. *272 pp.*
Gavron, Hannah. The Captive Wife: *Conflicts of Household Mothers. 190 pp.*
George, Victor and **Wilding, Paul.** Motherless Families. *248 pp.*
Klein, Josephine. Samples from English Cultures.
  1. Three Preliminary Studies and Aspects of Adult Life in England. *447 pp.*
  2. Child-Rearing Practices and Index. *247 pp.*
Klein, Viola. The Feminine Character. *History of an Ideology. 244 pp.*
McWhinnie, Alexina M. Adopted Children. *How They Grow Up. 304 pp.*
● **Morgan, D. H. J.** Social Theory and the Family. *About 320 pp.*
● **Myrdal, Alva** and **Klein, Viola.** Women's Two Roles: *Home and Work. 238 pp.*
  27 tables.
Parsons, Talcott and **Bales, Robert F.** Family: Socialization and Interaction Process.
  In collaboration with James Olds, Morris Zelditch and Philip E. Slater. 456 pp.
  50 figures and tables.

SOCIAL SERVICES

Bastide, Roger. The Sociology of Mental Disorder. *Translated from the French by Jean McNeil. 260 pp.*
Carlebach, Julius. Caring For Children in Trouble. *266 pp.*
George, Victor. Foster Care. *Theory and Practice. 234 pp.*
  Social Security: *Beveridge and After. 258 pp.*
George, V. and **Wilding, P.** Motherless Families. *248 pp.*
● **Goetschius, George W.** Working with Community Groups. *256 pp.*
Goetschius, George W. and **Tash, Joan.** Working with Unattached Youth. *416 pp.*
Heywood, Jean S. Children in Care. *The Development of the Service for the Deprived Child. Third revised edition. 284 pp.*
King, Roy D., Ranes, Norma V. and **Tizard, Jack.** Patterns of Residential Care. *356 pp.*
Leigh, John. Young People and Leisure. *256 pp.*
● **Mays, John.** (Ed.) Penelope Hall's Social Services of England and Wales. *368 pp.*
Morris, Mary. Voluntary Work and the Welfare State. *300 pp.*
Nokes, P. L. The Professional Task in Welfare Practice. *152 pp.*
Timms, Noel. Psychiatric Social Work in Great Britain (1939–1962). *280 pp.*
●   Social Casework: *Principles and Practice. 256 pp.*

SOCIOLOGY OF EDUCATION

Banks, Olive. Parity and Prestige in English Secondary Education: a Study in Educational Sociology. *272 pp.*
● **Blyth, W. A. L.** English Primary Education. *A Sociological Description.*
  2. Background. *168 pp.*
Collier, K. G. The Social Purposes of Education: *Personal and Social Values in Education. 268 pp.*
Evans, K. M. Sociometry and Education. *158 pp.*
● **Ford, Julienne.** Social Class and the Comprehensive School. *192 pp.*
Foster, P. J. Education and Social Change in Ghana. *336 pp. 3 maps.*
Fraser, W. R. Education and Society in Modern France. *150 pp.*
Grace, Gerald R. Role Conflict and the Teacher. *150 pp.*
Hans, Nicholas. New Trends in Education in the Eighteenth Century. *278 pp.*
  19 tables.
●   Comparative Education: *A Study of Educational Factors and Traditions. 360 pp.*
● **Hargreaves, David.** Interpersonal Relations and Education. *432 pp.*
●   Social Relations in a Secondary School. *240 pp.*
  School Organization and Pupil Involvement. *A Study of Secondary Schools.*

6

● **Mannheim, Karl** and **Stewart, W. A. C.** An Introduction to the Sociology of Education. *206 pp.*
● **Musgrove, F.** Youth and the Social Order. *176 pp.*
● **Ottaway, A. K. C.** Education and Society: An Introduction to the Sociology of Education. *With an Introduction by W. O. Lester Smith. 212 pp.*
Peers, Robert. Adult Education: *A Comparative Study. Revised edition. 398 pp.*
Stratta, Erica. The Education of Borstal Boys. *A Study of their Educational Experiences prior to, and during, Borstal Training. 256 pp.*
● **Taylor, P. H., Reid, W. A.** and **Holley, B. J.** The English Sixth Form. *A Case Study in Curriculum Research. 198 pp.*

SOCIOLOGY OF CULTURE

Eppel, E. M. and **M.** Adolescents and Morality: *A Study of some Moral Values and Dilemmas of Working Adolescents in the Context of a changing Climate of Opinion. Foreword by W. J. H. Sprott. 268 pp. 39 tables.*
● **Fromm, Erich.** The Fear of Freedom. *286 pp.*
● The Sane Society. *400 pp.*
Johnson, L. The Cultural Critics. *From Matthew Arnold to Raymond Williams. 233 pp.*
Mannheim, Karl. Essays on the Sociology of Culture. *Edited by Ernst Mannheim in co-operation with Paul Kecskemeti. Editorial Note by Adolph Lowe. 280 pp.*
Merquior, J. G. The Veil and the Mask. *Essays on Culture and Ideology. Foreword by Ernest Gellner. 140 pp.*
Zijderfeld, A. C. On Clichés. *The Supersedure of Meaning by Function in Modernity. 150 pp.*

SOCIOLOGY OF RELIGION

Argyle, Michael and **Beit-Hallahmi, Benjamin.** The Social Psychology of Religion. *256 pp.*
Glasner, Peter E. The Sociology of Secularisation. *A Critique of a Concept. 146 pp.*
Hall, J. R. The Ways Out. *Utopian Communal Groups in an Age of Babylon. 280 pp.*
Ranson, S., Hinings, B. and **Bryman, A.** Clergy, Ministers and Priests. *216 pp.*
Stark, Werner. The Sociology of Religion. *A Study of Christendom.*
Volume II. *Sectarian Religion. 368 pp.*
Volume III. *The Universal Church. 464 pp.*
Volume IV. *Types of Religious Man. 352 pp.*
Volume V. *Types of Religious Culture. 464 pp.*
Turner, B. S. Weber and Islam. *216 pp.*
Watt, W. Montgomery. Islam and the Integration of Society. *320 pp.*

SOCIOLOGY OF ART AND LITERATURE

Jarvie, Ian C. Towards a Sociology of the Cinema. *A Comparative Essay on the Structure and Functioning of a Major Entertainment Industry. 405 pp.*
Rust, Frances S. Dance in Society. *An Analysis of the Relationships between the Social Dance and Society in England from the Middle Ages to the Present Day. 256 pp. 8 pp. of plates.*
Schücking, L. L. The Sociology of Literary Taste. *112 pp.*
Wolff, Janet. Hermeneutic Philosophy and the Sociology of Art. *150 pp.*

SOCIOLOGY OF KNOWLEDGE

Diesing, P. Patterns of Discovery in the Social Sciences. *262 pp.*

● **Douglas, J. D.** (Ed.) Understanding Everyday Life. *370 pp.*
● **Hamilton, P.** Knowledge and Social Structure. *174 pp.*
  Jarvie, I. C. Concepts and Society. *232 pp.*
  Mannheim, Karl. Essays on the Sociology of Knowledge. *Edited by Paul Kecskemeti. Editorial Note by Adolph Lowe. 353 pp.*
  Remmling, Gunter W. The Sociology of Karl Mannheim. *With a Bibliographical Guide to the Sociology of Knowledge, Ideological Analysis, and Social Planning. 255 pp.*
  Remmling, Gunter W. (Ed.) Towards the Sociology of Knowledge. *Origin and Development of a Sociological Thought Style. 463 pp.*
  Scheler, M. Problems of a Sociology of Knowledge. *Trans. by M. S. Frings. Edited and with an Introduction by K. Stikkers. 232 pp.*

URBAN SOCIOLOGY

  Aldridge, M. The British New Towns. *A Programme Without a Policy. 232 pp.*
  Ashworth, William. The Genesis of Modern British Town Planning: *A Study in Economic and Social History of the Nineteenth and Twentieth Centuries. 288 pp.*
  Brittan, A. The Privatised World. *196 pp.*
  Cullingworth, J. B. Housing Needs and Planning Policy: *A Restatement of the Problems of Housing Need and 'Overspill' in England and Wales. 232 pp. 44 tables. 8 maps.*
  Dickinson, Robert E. City and Region: *A Geographical Interpretation. 608 pp. 125 figures.*
  The West European City: *A Geographical Interpretation. 600 pp. 129 maps. 29 plates.*
  Humphreys, Alexander J. New Dubliners: *Urbanization and the Irish Family. Foreword by George C. Homans. 304 pp.*
  Jackson, Brian. Working Class Community: *Some General Notions raised by a Series of Studies in Northern England. 192 pp.*
● **Mann, P. H.** An Approach to Urban Sociology. *240 pp.*
  Mellor, J. R. Urban Sociology in an Urbanized Society. *326 pp.*
  Morris, R. N. and **Mogey, J.** The Sociology of Housing. *Studies at Berinsfield. 232 pp. 4 pp. plates.*
  Mullan, R. Stevenage Ltd. *About 250 pp.*
  Rex, J. and **Tomlinson, S.** Colonial Immigrants in a British City. *A Class Analysis. 368 pp.*
  Rosser, C. and **Harris, C.** The Family and Social Change. *A Study of Family and Kinship in a South Wales Town. 352 pp. 8 maps.*
● **Stacey, Margaret, Batsone, Eric, Bell, Colin** and **Thurcott, Anne.** Power, Persistence and Change. *A Second Study of Banbury. 196 pp.*

RURAL SOCIOLOGY

  Mayer, Adrian C. Peasants in the Pacific. *A Study of Fiji Indian Rural Society. 248 pp. 20 plates.*
  Williams, W. M. The Sociology of an English Village: *Gosforth. 272 pp. 12 figures. 13 tables.*

SOCIOLOGY OF INDUSTRY AND DISTRIBUTION

  Dunkerley, David. The Foreman. *Aspects of Task and Structure. 192 pp.*
  Eldridge, J. E. T. Industrial Disputes. *Essays in the Sociology of Industrial Relations. 288 pp.*
  Hollowell, Peter G. The Lorry Driver. *272 pp.*
● **Oxaal, I., Barnett, T.** and **Booth, D.** (Eds) Beyond the Sociology of Development.

Economy and Society in Latin America and Africa. 295 pp.
Smelser, Neil J. Social Change in the Industrial Revolution: *An Application of Theory to the Lancashire Cotton Industry, 1770–1840. 468 pp. 12 figures. 14 tables.*
Watson, T. J. The Personnel Managers. *A Study in the Sociology of Work and Employment, 262 pp.*

ANTHROPOLOGY

Brandel-Syrier, Mia. Reeftown Elite. *A Study of Social Mobility in a Modern African Community on the Reef. 376 pp.*
Dickie-Clark, H. F. The Marginal Situation. *A Sociological Study of a Coloured Group. 236 pp.*
Dube, S. C. Indian Village. *Foreword by Morris Edward Opler. 276 pp. 4 plates.*
India's Changing Villages: *Human Factors in Community Development. 260 pp. 8 plates. 1 map.*
Fei, H.-T. Peasant Life in China. *A Field Study of Country Life in the Yangtze Valley. With a foreword by Bronislaw Malinowski. 328 pp. 16 pp. plates.*
Firth, Raymond. Malay Fishermen. *Their Peasant Economy. 420 pp. 17 pp. plates.*
Gulliver, P. H. Social Control in an African Society: a Study of the Arusha, Agricultural Masai of Northern Tanganyika. *320 pp. 8 plates. 10 figures.*
Family Herds. *288 pp.*
Jarvie, Ian C. The Revolution in Anthropology. *268 pp.*
Little, Kenneth L. Mende of Sierra Leone. *308 pp. and folder.*
Negroes in Britain. *With a New Introduction and Contemporary Study by Leonard Bloom. 320 pp.*
Tambs-Lyche, H. London Patidars. *About 180 pp.*
Madan, G. R. Western Sociologists on Indian Society. *Marx, Spencer, Weber, Durkheim, Pareto. 384 pp.*
Mayer, A. C. Peasants in the Pacific. *A Study of Fiji Indian Rural Society. 248 pp.*
Meer, Fatima. Race and Suicide in South Africa. *325 pp.*
Smith, Raymond T. The Negro Family in British Guiana: *Family Structure and Social Status in the Villages. With a Foreword by Meyer Fortes. 314 pp. 8 plates. 1 figure. 4 maps.*

SOCIOLOGY AND PHILOSOPHY

Adriaansens, H. Talcott Parsons and the Conceptual Dilemma. *About 224 pp.*
Barnsley, John H. The Social Reality of Ethics. *A Comparative Analysis of Moral Codes. 448 pp.*
Diesing, Paul. Patterns of Discovery in the Social Sciences. *362 pp.*
● **Douglas, Jack D.** (Ed.) Understanding Everyday Life. *Toward the Reconstruction of Sociological Knowledge. Contributions by Alan F. Blum, Aaron W. Cicourel, Norman K. Denzin, Jack D. Douglas, John Heeren, Peter McHugh, Peter K. Manning, Melvin Power, Matthew Speier, Roy Turner, D. Lawrence Wieder, Thomas P. Wilson and Don H. Zimmerman. 370 pp.*
Gorman, Robert A. The Dual Vision. *Alfred Schutz and the Myth of Phenomenological Social Science. 240 pp.*
Jarvie, Ian C. Concepts and Society. *216 pp.*
Kilminster, R. Praxis and Method. *A Sociological Dialogue with Lukács, Gramsci and the Early Frankfurt School. 334 pp.*
● **Pelz, Werner.** The Scope of Understanding in Sociology. *Towards a More Radical Reorientation in the Social Humanistic Sciences. 283 pp.*
Roche, Maurice. Phenomenology, Language and the Social Sciences. *371 pp.*
Sahay, Arun. Sociological Analysis. *212 pp.*
● **Slater, P.** Origin and Significance of the Frankfurt School. *A Marxist Perspective. 185 pp.*

Spurling, L. Phenomenology and the Social World. *The Philosophy of Merleau-Ponty and its Relation to the Social Sciences. 222 pp.*

Wilson, H. T. The American Ideology. *Science, Technology and Organization as Modes of Rationality. 368 pp.*

International Library of Anthropology
General Editor Adam Kuper

● Ahmed, A. S. Millennium and Charisma Among Pathans. *A Critical Essay in Social Anthropology. 192 pp.*
  Pukhtun Economy and Society. *Traditional Structure and Economic Development. About 360 pp.*

Barth, F. Selected Essays. *Volume I. About 250 pp.* Selected Essays. *Volume II. About 250 pp.*

Brown, Paula. The Chimbu. *A Study of Change in the New Guinea Highlands. 151 pp.*

Foner, N. Jamaica Farewell. *200 pp.*

Gudeman, Stephen. Relationships, Residence and the Individual. *A Rural Panamanian Community. 288 pp. 11 plates, 5 figures, 2 maps, 10 tables.*
  The Demise of a Rural Economy. *From Subsistence to Capitalism in a Latin American Village. 160 pp.*

Hamnett, Ian. Chieftainship and Legitimacy. *An Anthropological Study of Executive Law in Lesotho. 163 pp.*

Hanson, F. Allan. Meaning in Culture. *127 pp.*

Hazan, H. The Limbo People. *A Study of the Constitution of the Time Universe Among the Aged. About 192 pp.*

Humphreys, S. C. Anthropology and the Greeks. *288 pp.*

Karp, I. Fields of Change Among the Iteso of Kenya. *140 pp.*

Lloyd, P. C. Power and Independence. *Urban Africans' Perception of Social Inequality. 264 pp.*

Parry, J. P. Caste and Kinship in Kangra. *352 pp. Illustrated.*

Pettigrew, Joyce. Robber Noblemen. *A Study of the Political System of the Sikh Jats. 284 pp.*

Street, Brian V. The Savage in Literature. *Representations of 'Primitive' Society in English Fiction, 1858–1920. 207 pp.*

Van Den Berghe, Pierre L. Power and Privilege at an African University. *278 pp.*

International Library of Phenomenology and Moral Sciences
General Editor John O'Neill

Apel, K.-O. Towards a Transformation of Philosophy. *308 pp.*

Bologh, R. W. Dialectical Phenomenology. *Marx's Method. 287 pp.*

Fekete, J. The Critical Twilight. *Explorations in the Ideology of Anglo-American Literary Theory from Eliot to McLuhan. 300 pp.*

Medina, A. Reflection, Time and the Novel. *Towards a Communicative Theory of Literature. 143 pp.*

International Library of Social Policy
General Editor Kathleen Jones

Bayley, M. Mental Handicap and Community Care. *426 pp.*

Bottoms, A. E. and McClean, J. D. Defendants in the Criminal Process. *284 pp.*

Bradshaw, J. The Family Fund. *An Initiative in Social Policy. About 224 pp.*

Butler, J. R. Family Doctors and Public Policy. *208 pp.*
Davies, Martin. Prisoners of Society. *Attitudes and Aftercare. 204 pp.*
Gittus, Elizabeth. Flats, Families and the Under-Fives. *285 pp.*
Holman, Robert. Trading in Children. *A Study of Private Fostering. 355 pp.*
Jeffs, A. Young People and the Youth Service. *160 pp.*
Jones, Howard and Cornes, Paul. Open Prisons. *288 pp.*
Jones, Kathleen. History of the Mental Health Service. *428 pp.*
Jones, Kathleen with Brown, John, Cunningham, W. J., Roberts, Julian and Williams, Peter. Opening the Door. *A Study of New Policies for the Mentally Handicapped. 278 pp.*
Karn, Valerie. Retiring to the Seaside. *400 pp. 2 maps. Numerous tables.*
King, R. D. and Elliot, K. W. Albany: Birth of a Prison—End of an Era. *394 pp.*
Thomas, J. E. The English Prison Officer since 1850: *A Study in Conflict. 258 pp.*
Walton, R. G. Women in Social Work. *303 pp.*
● Woodward, J. To Do the Sick No Harm. *A Study of the British Voluntary Hospital System to 1875. 234 pp.*

International Library of Welfare and Philosophy
General Editors Noel Timms and David Watson

● McDermott, F. E. (Ed.) Self-Determination in Social Work. *A Collection of Essays on Self-determination and Related Concepts by Philosophers and Social Work Theorists. Contributors: F. P. Biestek, S. Bernstein, A. Keith-Lucas, D. Sayer, H. H. Perelman, C. Whittington, R. F. Stalley, F. E. McDermott, I. Berlin, H. J. McCloskey, H. L. A. Hart, J. Wilson, A. I. Melden, S. I. Benn. 254 pp.*
● Plant, Raymond. Community and Ideology. *104 pp.*
Ragg, Nicholas M. People Not Cases. *A Philosophical Approach to Social Work. 168 pp.*
● Timms, Noel and Watson, David. (Eds) Talking About Welfare. *Readings in Philosophy and Social Policy. Contributors: T. H. Marshall, R. B. Brandt, G. H. von Wright, K. Nielsen, M. Cranston, R. M. Titmuss, R. S. Downie, E. Telfer, D. Donnison, J. Benson, P. Leonard, A. Keith-Lucas, D. Walsh, I. T. Ramsey. 320 pp.*
● Philosophy in Social Work. *250 pp.*
● Weale, A. Equality and Social Policy. *164 pp.*

Library of Social Work
General Editor Noel Timms

● Baldock, Peter. Community Work and Social Work. *140 pp.*
○ Beedell, Christopher. Residential Life with Children. *210 pp. Crown 8vo.*
● Berry, Juliet. Daily Experience in Residential Life. *A Study of Children and their Care-givers. 202 pp.*
○ Social Work with Children. *190 pp. Crown 8vo.*
● Brearley, C. Paul. Residential Work with the Elderly. *116 pp.*
● Social Work, Ageing and Society. *126 pp.*
● Cheetham, Juliet. Social Work with Immigrants. *240 pp. Crown 8vo.*
● Cross, Crispin P. (Ed.) Interviewing and Communication in Social Work. *Contributions by C. P. Cross, D. Laurenson, B. Strutt, S. Raven. 192 pp. Crown 8vo.*

- **Curnock, Kathleen** and **Hardiker, Pauline**. Towards Practice Theory. *Skills and Methods in Social Assessments. 208 pp.*
- **Davies, Bernard.** The Use of Groups in Social Work Practice. *158 pp.*
- **Davies, Martin.** Support Systems in Social Work. *144 pp.*
- **Ellis, June.** (Ed.) West African Families in Britain. *A Meeting of Two Cultures. Contributions by Pat Stapleton, Vivien Biggs. 150 pp. 1 Map.*
- **Hart, John.** Social Work and Sexual Conduct. *230 pp.*
- **Hutten, Joan M.** Short-Term Contracts in Social Work. *Contributions by Stella M. Hall, Elsie Osborne, Mannie Sher, Eva Sternberg, Elizabeth Tuters. 134 pp.*
- **Jackson, Michael P.** and **Valencia, B. Michael.** Financial Aid Through Social Work. *140 pp.*
- **Jones, Howard.** The Residential Community. *A Setting for Social Work. 150 pp.*
- (Ed.) Towards a New Social Work. *Contributions by Howard Jones, D. A. Fowler, J. R. Cypher, R. G. Walton, Geoffrey Mungham, Philip Priestley, Ian Shaw, M. Bartley, R. Deacon, Irwin Epstein, Geoffrey Pearson. 184 pp.*
- **Jones, Ray** and **Pritchard, Colin.** (Eds) Social Work With Adolescents. *Contributions by Ray Jones, Colin Pritchard, Jack Dunham, Florence Rossetti, Andrew Kerslake, John Burns, William Gregory, Graham Templeman, Kenneth E. Reid, Audrey Taylor. About 170 pp.*
- ○ **Jordon, William.** The Social Worker in Family Situations. *160 pp. Crown 8vo.*
- **Laycock, A. L.** Adolescents and Social Work. *128 pp. Crown 8vo.*
- **Lees, Ray.** Politics and Social Work. *128 pp. Crown 8vo.*
- Research Strategies for Social Welfare. *112 pp. Tables.*
- ○ **McCullough, M. K.** and **Ely, Peter J.** Social Work with Groups. *127 pp. Crown 8vo.*
- **Moffett, Jonathan.** Concepts in Casework Treatment. *128 pp. Crown 8vo.*
- **Parsloe, Phyllida.** Juvenile Justice in Britain and the United States. *The Balance of Needs and Rights. 336 pp.*
- **Plant, Raymond.** Social and Moral Theory in Casework. *112 pp. Crown 8vo.*
- **Priestley, Philip, Fears, Denise** and **Fuller, Roger.** Justice for Juveniles. *The 1969 Children and Young Persons Act: A Case for Reform? 128 pp.*
- **Pritchard, Colin** and **Taylor, Richard.** Social Work: Reform or Revolution? *170 pp.*
- ○ **Pugh, Elisabeth.** Social Work in Child Care. *128 pp. Crown 8vo.*
- **Robinson, Margaret.** Schools and Social Work. *282 pp.*
- ○ **Ruddock, Ralph.** Roles and Relationships. *128 pp. Crown 8vo.*
- **Sainsbury, Eric.** Social Diagnosis in Casework. *118 pp. Crown 8vo.*
- Social Work with Families. *Perceptions of Social Casework among Clients of a Family Service. 188 pp.*
- **Seed, Philip.** The Expansion of Social Work in Britain. *128 pp. Crown 8vo.*
- **Shaw, John.** The Self in Social Work. *124 pp.*
- **Smale, Gerald G.** Prophecy, Behaviour and Change. *An Examination of Self-fulfilling Prophecies in Helping Relationships. 116 pp. Crown 8vo.*
- **Smith, Gilbert.** Social Need. *Policy, Practice and Research. 155 pp.*
- Social Work and the Sociology of Organisations. *124 pp. Revised edition.*
- **Sutton, Carole.** Psychology for Social Workers and Counsellors. *An Introduction. 248 pp.*
- **Timms, Noel.** Language of Social Casework. *122 pp. Crown 8vo.*
- Recording in Social Work. *124 pp. Crown 8vo.*
- **Todd, F. Joan.** Social Work with the Mentally Subnormal. *96 pp. Crown 8vo.*
- **Walrond-Skinner, Sue.** Family Therapy. *The Treatment of Natural Systems. 172 pp.*
- **Warham, Joyce.** An Introduction to Administration for Social Workers. *Revised edition. 112 pp.*
- An Open Case. *The Organisational Context of Social Work. 172 pp.*
- ○ **Wittenberg, Isca Salzberger.** Psycho-Analytic Insight and Relationships. *A Kleinian Approach. 196 pp. Crown 8vo.*

Primary Socialization, Language and Education
General Editor Basil Bernstein

Adlam, Diana S., *with the assistance of Geoffrey Turner and Lesley Lineker.* Code in Context. *272 pp.*
Bernstein, Basil. Class, Codes and Control. *3 volumes.*
● 1. Theoretical Studies Towards a Sociology of Language. *254 pp.*
2. Applied Studies Towards a Sociology of Language. *377 pp.*
● 3. Towards a Theory of Educational Transmission. *167 pp.*
Brandis, W. and **Bernstein, B.** Selection and Control. *176 pp.*
Brandis, Walter and **Henderson, Dorothy.** Social Class, Language and Communication. *288 pp.*
Cook-Gumperz, Jenny. Social Control and Socialization. *A Study of Class Differences in the Language of Maternal Control. 290 pp.*
● **Gahagan, D. M.** and **G. A.** Talk Reform. *Exploration in Language for Infant School Children. 160 pp.*
Hawkins, P. R. Social Class, the Nominal Group and Verbal Strategies. *About 220 pp.*
Robinson, W. P. and **Rackstraw, Susan D. A.** A Question of Answers. *2 volumes. 192 pp. and 180 pp.*
Turner, Geoffrey J. and **Mohan, Bernard A.** A Linguistic Description and Computer Programme for Children's Speech. *208 pp.*

Reports of the Institute of Community Studies

Baker, J. The Neighbourhood Advice Centre. *A Community Project in Camden. 320 pp.*
● **Cartwright, Ann.** Patients and their Doctors. *A Study of General Practice. 304 pp.*
Dench, Geoff. Maltese in London. *A Case-study in the Erosion of Ethnic Consciousness. 302 pp.*
Jackson, Brian and **Marsden, Dennis.** Education and the Working Class: *Some General Themes Raised by a Study of 88 Working-class Children in a Northern Industrial City. 268 pp. 2 folders.*
Marris, Peter. The Experience of Higher Education. *232 pp. 27 tables.*
● Loss and Change. *192 pp.*
Marris, Peter and **Rein, Martin.** Dilemmas of Social Reform. *Poverty and Community Action in the United States. 256 pp.*
Marris, Peter and **Somerset, Anthony.** African Businessmen. *A Study of Entrepreneurship and Development in Kenya. 256 pp.*
Mills, Richard. Young Outsiders: *a Study in Alternative Communities. 216 pp.*
Runciman, W. G. Relative Deprivation and Social Justice. *A Study of Attitudes to Social Inequality in Twentieth-Century England. 352 pp.*
Willmott, Peter. Adolescent Boys in East London. *230 pp.*
Willmott, Peter and **Young, Michael.** Family and Class in a London Suburb. *202 pp. 47 tables.*
Young, Michael and **McGeeney, Patrick.** Learning Begins at Home. *A Study of a Junior School and its Parents. 128 pp.*
Young, Michael and **Willmott, Peter.** Family and Kinship in East London. *Foreword by Richard M. Titmuss. 252 pp. 39 tables.*
The Symmetrical Family. *410 pp.*

Reports of the Institute for Social Studies in Medical Care

Cartwright, Ann, Hockey, Lisbeth and **Anderson, John J.** Life Before Death. *310 pp.*
Dunnell, Karen and **Cartwright, Ann.** Medicine Takers, Prescribers and Hoarders. *190 pp.*
Farrell, C. My Mother Said. . . *A Study of the Way Young People Learned About Sex and Birth Control. 288 pp.*

Medicine, Illness and Society
General Editor   W. M. Williams

Hall, David J. Social Relations & Innovation. *Changing the State of Play in Hospitals. 232 pp.*
Hall, David J. and **Stacey, M.** (Eds) Beyond Separation. *234 pp.*
Robinson, David. The Process of Becoming Ill. *142 pp.*
Stacey, Margaret *et al.* Hospitals, Children and Their Families. *The Report of a Pilot Study. 202 pp.*
Stimson, G. V. and **Webb, B.** Going to See the Doctor. *The Consultation Process in General Practice. 155 pp.*

Monographs in Social Theory
General Editor   Arthur Brittan

● **Barnes, B.** Scientific Knowledge and Sociological Theory. *192 pp.*
   Bauman, Zygmunt. Culture as Praxis. *204 pp.*
● **Dixon, Keith.** Sociological Theory. *Pretence and Possibility. 142 pp.*
   The Sociology of Belief. *Fallacy and Foundation. About 160 pp.*
   Goff, T. W. Marx and Mead. *Contributions to a Sociology of Knowledge. 176 pp.*
   Meltzer, B. N., Petras, J. W. and **Reynolds, L. T.** Symbolic Interactionism. *Genesis, Varieties and Criticisms. 144 pp.*
● **Smith, Anthony D.** The Concept of Social Change. *A Critique of the Functionalist Theory of Social Change. 208 pp.*

Routledge Social Science Journals

The British Journal of Sociology. *Editor – Angus Stewart; Associate Editor – Leslie Sklair. Vol. 1, No. 1 – March 1950 and Quarterly. Roy. 8vo. All back issues available. An international journal publishing original papers in the field of sociology and related areas.*
Community Work. *Edited by David Jones and Marjorie Mayo. 1973. Published annually.*
Economy and Society. *Vol. 1, No. 1. February 1972 and Quarterly. Metric Roy. 8vo. A journal for all social scientists covering sociology, philosophy, anthropology, economics and history. All back numbers available.*

Ethnic and Racial Studies. *Editor – John Stone. Vol. 1 – 1978. Published quarterly.*
Religion. Journal of Religion and Religions. *Chairman of Editorial Board, Ninian Smart. Vol. 1, No. 1, Spring 1971. A journal with an inter-disciplinary approach to the study of the phenomena of religion. All back numbers available.*
Sociology of Health and Illness. *A Journal of Medical Sociology. Editor – Alan Davies; Associate Editor – Ray Jobling. Vol. 1, Spring 1979. Published 3 times per annum.*
Year Book of Social Policy in Britain. *Edited by Kathleen Jones. 1971. Published annually.*

Social and Psychological Aspects of Medical Practice
Editor   Trevor Silverstone

Lader, Malcolm. Psychophysiology of Mental Illness. *280 pp.*
● **Silverstone, Trevor** and **Turner, Paul.** Drug Treatment in Psychiatry. *Revised edition. 256 pp.*
Whiteley, J. S. and **Gordon, J.** Group Approaches in Psychiatry. *240 pp.*